T0356501

The Professional is a highly professional analysis by a remarkable and inquiring mind. Professional life is complex and challenging, but this book shines a light with compelling clarity.

—Chris Richardson, Founder, RichInsight

A helpful, practical and down-to-earth guide, with many valuable tips in difficult areas and some funny observations along the way! An opportunity to rethink how to approach our work as professionals.

—Philippa Stone,
Partner, Herbert Smith Freehills

As a Chartered Accountant, Tony Frost understands professional capability is not set in stone. It needs constant attention to stay relevant. The Professional provides practical, compelling performance mindset building advice.

—Ainslie van Onselen, Chief Executive Officer,
Chartered Accountants Australia and New Zealand

In a world of disruption, uncertainty and anxiety, Tony Frost provides practical and useful tips to construct a professional career that provides financial rewards and personal satisfaction.

—Richard Vann, Professor Emeritus,
University of Sydney Law School

Tony Frost's *The Professional* is a well-researched and highly-engaging resource packed full of suggestions and insights for how professionals can continue to develop their skills and their careers in a rapidly changing world. Not only is the book very readable, it is highly practical with key questions and frameworks that professionals can use as development tools. I highly recommend it.

—Professor Nick Wailes, Dean of Lifelong Learning and Director
AGSM, University of New South Wales

THE
PROFESSIONAL

TONY FROST

THE PROFESSIONAL

A PLAYBOOK TO UNLEASH YOUR POTENTIAL AND FUTUREPROOF YOUR SUCCESS

WILEY

A catalogue record for this book is available from the National Library of Australia

Registered Office
John Wiley & Sons Australia, Ltd. Level 4, 600 Bourke Street, Melbourne, VIC 3000, Australia

For details of our global editorial offices, customer services, and more information about Wiley products visit us at www.wiley.com.

Wiley also publishes its books in a variety of electronic formats and by print-on-demand. Some content that appears in standard print versions of this book may not be available in other formats.

Trademarks: Wiley and the Wiley logo are trademarks or registered trademarks of John Wiley & Sons, Inc. and/or its affiliates in the United States and other countries and may not be used without written permission. All other trademarks are the property of their respective owners. John Wiley & Sons, Inc. is not associated with any product or vendor mentioned in this book.

Limit of Liability/Disclaimer of Warranty
While the publisher and author have used their best efforts in preparing this work, they make no representations or warranties with respect to the accuracy or completeness of the contents of this work and specifically disclaim all warranties, including without limitation any implied warranties of merchantability or fitness for a particular purpose. No warranty may be created or extended by sales representatives, written sales materials or promotional statements for this work. This work is sold with the understanding that the publisher is not engaged in rendering professional services. The advice and strategies contained herein may not be suitable for your situation. You should consult with a specialist where appropriate. The fact that an organisation, website, or product is referred to in this work as a citation and/or potential source of further information does not mean that the publisher and author endorse the information or services the organisation, website, or product may provide or recommendations it may make. Further, readers should be aware that websites listed in this work may have changed or disappeared between when this work was written and when it is read. Neither the publisher nor author shall be liable for any loss of profit or any other commercial damages, including but not limited to special, incidental, consequential, or other damages.

Cover design by Wiley
Cover Image: © Jumpee to do/Adobe Stock
Author photo: © Keith Friendship

Set in 10.5/12.5pt Utopia Std by Straive, Chennai, India
SKY1D181ACB-7432-4A91-BACB-C1536E84FEA2_040925

For Catherine, Elizabeth and Laura
with love and thanks

Contents

Foreword

I found this book to be an excellent and very useful read. Indeed, as I read it, I had the recurring feeling that I wished it or an equivalent had existed years ago when I started out on my professional journey.

Tony Frost brings his energy, experience, optimism and practicality to every page. He poses questions that in my view get to the heart of the issues and that should be at the forefront of a professional's mind.

I particularly like his four challenges: complexity, increased client demands, remote work and the effects of artificial intelligence. Obviously there are further issues that each of us might raise but these four chosen by Tony provide more than enough insights to make the book worth reading.

He asks how one can become the best possible professional and add the most value in the age of artificial intelligence. Both of these questions remain on my mind after 47 years of life in business.

As to how young professionals should view the coming of artificial intelligence, after much thought I strongly agree with Tony that they should be 'worried and excited but more excited than worried'.

Many have written in the areas Tony is exploring but none have done so — in my view — with the light, practical approach and at the same time the depth that I believe Tony has achieved. His lists throughout the book and further questions at the end of each chapter stay with you, compelling further thought even after finishing the book.

I applaud this book and hope you will find it as useful as I have.

David Gonski AC
13 November 2024

About the author

This is my second book. My first effort was as co-author of the riveting 773-page *Guide to Taxation of Financial Arrangements*.[1] When the publishers of this project discovered the existence, subject matter and length of my first tome they were understandably nervous. I promised them my new book would be shorter, and of wider appeal.

The title of my first book gives you a clue about my first career. When people asked me what I did for a living, I would smile and say, 'I help big companies pay the correct amount of tax'. From there the conversation could go anywhere — or nowhere.

After a 34-year career as a tax adviser (lawyer and Chartered Accountant) I decided to do something different. As part of my efforts to retrain as an executive coach, mentor and leadership consultant I returned to my alma mater, the University of Sydney, to undertake a Master of Science in Coaching Psychology. This was great fun and I was inspired. I learned all manner of things that would have been extremely useful in my first career, especially during my time as managing director of leading Australian tax advisory firm Greenwoods & Herbert Smith Freehills. If only I could turn back time ...

Armed with the knowledge gained in the course of my new degree and the years of experience amassed in the course of my first career (including the many mistakes I made) I decided that as part of my second career I would conduct masterclasses for professionals. You can check out the classes here: www.frostleadership.com.au. I began to prepare notes as class pre-reading. Then I thought it might be easier (it wasn't) and possibly more profitable to write this book. Also, it helped with my relevance-deprivation syndrome, which kicked in when I stopped being a big-cheese professional after so many years. As you can see, I will try to be as honest and as transparent with you as possible.

At the end of each chapter I have included some comments in a section titled 'In play' so you can see whether, in my first professional career, I did, or did not, practise what I now preach. I also comment on what I am doing in my second career.

Visit my website to find Frost Insights on important issues for professionals that wouldn't fit into this book. They include *Starting and changing jobs*; *Pay rises, promotions, performance reviews and management*; *Remote work — a legacy of COVID-19 and its impact on professionals*; and *Joy and fun at work*.

Tony Frost

Sydney, January 2025

www.frostleadership.com.au

Introduction

Modern professionals make the world go round. For hundreds of years professionals in a myriad professions have been providing all manner of services to clients who need the expertise and skills they themselves lack. Although this author is Australian, and what you will read has a distinct Australian flavour, this book is for the professionals of the world.

Why read this book?

As a professional building a successful career today, you are facing unprecedented challenges and opportunities as you service your clients and solve their problems. Changes in client demands, technology, competition and the regulatory environment have always loomed large, but the pace of change has accelerated markedly and shows no signs of slowing.

You face four interlinked challenges. In some cases, these are also potential opportunities. The first two have been building for some decades, while the second two are recent:

1. **Complexity.** Most professionals, in most sectors and in most countries, operate in an environment of ever-increasing complexity. This takes many forms including clients and their size, scale, business structures and transactions; governmental, regulatory and professional body rules and requirements; the demands of everchanging technology; and, in many industries, the long-term trend towards globalisation.

2. **Increased client demands.** Clients of professionals have become increasingly sophisticated, demanding and cost-conscious when seeking external services. At the same time, many organisations

have in-sourced various types of professional services including but not only legal and accounting functions. In-house professionals not only are subject to increasing productivity demands from their employers but help their organisations to hire external professionals in the most cost-effective manner.

3. **Remote work**. Although working from home and other forms of remote work had been building slowly in the decades before 2020, the COVID-19 pandemic revolutionised where, when and how professionals go about their task of serving clients. Exactly how this is impacting the coaching, mentoring and professional development of younger professionals is still a work in progress.

4. **Artificial intelligence**. AI was first posited seriously in the 1950s, but it was the release of the ChatGPT platform by OpenAI in November 2022 that really focused the minds of most people, including any professional not living under a rock, about the potential of AI to dramatically reshape all manner of activities, including the world of work. As no less an authority than Microsoft co-founder Bill Gates has observed, we are now living in the 'age of artificial intelligence'[2], which will provide remarkable opportunities, as well as challenges, for all professionals and the human race at large.

If you are already a professional, or are thinking about becoming one, you presumably intend to have a long and successful career. To achieve this, you will want to respond to these four challenges. This book is *the* essential companion on your career journey. As well as being your go-to guide, it will help you think about and answer two vitally important questions[3]:

- How can I become my best possible professional?
- How can I add the most value in the age of artificial intelligence?

I won't attempt to define 'value', as it will be a personal thing and depend on your field. I encourage you to reflect regularly on the 'value' you are creating, and for whom. You will add value to individuals and organisations, starting with your clients. But you can also add value to your employer, your colleagues, professional and industry bodies and associations, universities and other educational institutions, governments and regulators, society at large and, of course, to yourself.

I have three modest goals for this book: First, you will fundamentally change how you think about your skills and how you will prioritise their development over the rest of your career or careers. Second, employed professionals and their employers around the world will do the same.

And third, together we will start a global revolution in the management of employed professionals. You will have the knowledge, vocabulary and confidence to ask your employers to help you to develop most effectively. This will be in the employers' best interests as well as yours.

That's it.

What is this book about?

Part I ('State of Play') sets the professional service scene. It addresses some big-picture issues facing professionals now and in the years ahead. This includes what it means to be a professional in the age of AI, how technology is changing what professionals do, what clients want now and will want in the future, as well as what employers want and should be doing to achieve their goals.

To help you address the four challenges and the two questions set out in the previous section, Part II ('Playbook') introduces the 'Playbook to Unleash Your Potential and Futureproof Your Success', with its Five Factors:

1. **Self-care**. Even the hardest-working and most conscientious professionals are allowed to look after themselves!

2. **Motivation**. You are most likely to succeed if you are highly motivated. What motivates you?

3. **Learning**. Although you have one or more university degrees and professional qualifications, learning should never stop.

4. **Capabilities**. You will want to spend your precious time developing the capabilities that will best assist you in the age of AI.

5. **Accelerants**. These are seven proven ways to get ahead in professional life.

I want you to abandon the notion of 'hard skills' and 'soft skills'. I will introduce you to Prime Capabilities (what you do/have) and Enablers (how you apply them) and explain why this is about much more than changing names. More importantly, I will convince you why it is necessary to make this leap.

I have included questions for reflection, and templates and tools to help make my suggestions as clear and as easy to understand and implement as possible. Don't accept any of the suggestions as gospel. Poke, prod and challenge them. Discuss them with your colleagues. Add and subtract things and make them your own.

You'll notice I have called this framework a playbook. Why? Because ultimately I believe you should have fun at work.

This book will be of interest to different readers in different ways. Younger professionals and students may find Part I of greater interest than more senior professionals who have already been around the block a few times. All professionals should find the Five Factors in the Playbook in Part II of great assistance in shaping their personal and professional development. I encourage every reader to review all of the Five Factors, then prioritise their implementation in a way that is 'most personally meaningful to you'.

Who should read this book?

I suggest that all professionals at any age or stage of their careers will find value in *The Professional*, but it is directed primarily at 'employed professionals' — that is, professionals working for a firm or an organisation owned by other people. This includes but is not limited to lawyers, accountants, actuaries, bankers, financial advisers and planners, management consultants, coaches, mentors, architects, engineers, scientists, information technology workers and people working in human resources, advertising, market research and public relations.

The book may also be of interest to many other people including those employed in various parts of the medical, healthcare and veterinary professions. One very enjoyable strand of my second career is being a facilitator in the impressive Company Directors Course run by the Australian Institute of Company Directors. As directors are professionals they too should find this book compelling reading. I hold a number of non-executive directorships in my second career, and I will certainly encourage my fellow directors on various boards to read *The Professional*.

Relatively early in my career I spent about five years working as an in-house tax professional at Westpac Banking Corporation. I learned a lot about banking and financial transactions as well as how to service multiple clients within a single organisation. When I returned to public practice at what was then Price Waterhouse, most of my clients were themselves in-house tax professionals employed by large companies. Consequently, I have written this book not just for those in professional service firms but for in-house lawyers, accountants and other professionals employed inside corporations, government bodies, not-for-profits and other workplaces. This means that 'clients' in this book include people in an organisation who have services provided *to* them by in-house professionals within that organisation.

At the same time, professionals such as those working in the public service quite reasonably may not view the people they are serving as 'clients'. However, these professionals will still find this book helpful.

The COVID-19 pandemic led to a fundamental reassessment of what constitutes a 'workplace', and this book will also be of interest to professionals working in a new, post-pandemic environment, perhaps from home or from cafés, and perhaps on a freelance basis for multiple clients.

This book may also be helpful to school, university or college students. It offers some insights into the world of work that awaits you. I suggest you reflect on skills that come most naturally to you. This should help in choosing a calling you will enjoy and in which you will succeed. Academics may also embrace the concepts in this book and where appropriate squeeze them into already crowded curricula.

Finally, I recommend this book, especially chapter 4, to employers of employed professionals, such as the partners or other owners of professional service firms. Its insights into how best to engage with the clever and ambitious professionals you have hired are crucial as, if you play your cards right and help them to grow and develop, they will become your organisation's future leaders.

Further reading

The range of topics addressed in this book is large and often much more could have been said or has already been said elsewhere. Under 'Suggested reading and viewing', I provide a list of selected complementary publications and materials in the public domain. I encourage you to use this book as just one step in your ongoing professional development. Read widely from my recommendations and go beyond them to explore the thousands of resources now available in print and online.

In the section on reading lists, I have suggested a way to set up your own discussion group with like-minded professionals so you can help each other with your ongoing personal development.

Part I
State of Play

Part I explores the modern professional services landscape. It provides the context and sets the scene for the Playbook introduced in Part II.

Chapter 1 looks at what it means to be a 'professional'. It is a concept that has been well covered by learned authors and commentators over the past two hundred years. Nonetheless, given the perhaps presumptuous title of this book, I would be remiss not to offer my own views of what it means to be a professional. I like lists (and there are plenty of them in this book), and I have set out some criteria for what it takes to be a *true* professional. In chapter 1 I set out what I think are the characteristics of a *good* professional, before listing the attributes of a *great* professional. I follow this with a list of cardinal sins professionals sometimes commit. In the 'In play' section for this chapter I discuss the importance of working in a supportive and ethically sound environment in which the organisation's values are, ideally, aligned with your own.

If chapter 1 tills well-worked soil, chapter 2 focuses front and centre on the modern world in which you live and work. Here we will begin our discussion of AI and the remarkable impact it is already having on professionals, as well as doing some crystal-ball gazing in order to consider what the future may hold. Unsurprisingly, international experts' views diverge on what AI has in store for humanity. Even the creators of this new technology admit to alarm at its apocalyptic, world-ending potential. As this book goes to print, governments and regulators around the world are working feverishly on decisions around whether and how to tame AI. Reassuringly, more than one expert confidently predicts that AI won't take your job. The risk is someone using AI will make you redundant if you fail to pick up the new technology yourself.

In chapter 2, inspired by the work of Charles Darwin, we look at the existential need for professionals to be increasingly adaptable, especially when it comes to AI and other emerging technologies. I am writing in the early years of the age of AI, which has seen the release of generative tools such as ChatGPT, which are, in essence, highly trained but 'non-thinking' parrots. In years to come, humanity may or may not create the much, much more powerful artificial general intelligence (AGI) — technology that can think, make decisions and take actions in a way similar to or probably better (way better) than humans do. If such a scenario eventuates, professionals as we know them today may or may not exist, and this book may or may not be of any use. For the record, this book was 'hand-made', and no part was subcontracted to ChatGPT or any other AI bot.

Chapter 3 takes us into that mysterious and wonderful world that is client land. Professionals wouldn't have jobs if they didn't have clients whose problems need to be solved. Yes, some clients can be difficult at times, and some can be difficult all the time. Nonetheless, true professionals know how to build the best quality relationships possible with each client and take the time to find out what they really want and need from their advisers. In my first career I was constantly amazed by how many professionals of all types and flavours didn't undertake the basic task of truly understanding their clients' wants and needs. This chapter will help you to avoid that mistake by putting in place a Client Service Charter. If you don't already have such a thing, you might tailor to your circumstances the template I have provided. Try not to subtract too many things. This chapter also contains advice on what to do when clients behave very badly. Sadly, the old adage 'the client is always right' is no longer current. On a happier note, chapter 3 has tips for professionals working in professional service firms on how to get the best work on the best clients.

Finally, in chapter 4 we take a brief look at what employers of professionals want from their employees. This discussion is fairly short because different employers will want different things and place different emphases on the capabilities of the people they employ. The main purpose of this chapter, which I had great fun researching and writing, is to offer suggestions, *lots* of them, as to what employers should be doing for the employed professionals in their care, and for each other as the owners or senior members of the organisation.

I cite some sobering data from Gallup on the level of 'employee engagement' internationally. One of many themes in this chapter is the importance of leaders and managers self-consciously adopting a coaching style when working with teams as a sure way to lift employee engagement. If any employer reading chapter 4 is not convinced by my citations of what Gallup, Google and Apple CEO Tim Cook have to say about the importance of a coaching mindset to effective leadership, then I suspect they are unpersuadable. One of the many linked topics in this chapter, and a recurring theme throughout the book, is the importance of the skill, the science and the art of giving quality, ongoing feedback to team members.

Once you have worked your way through these four chapters, I will have softened you up to think more deeply about how you will answer the two questions I posed in the Introduction:

- How can I become my best possible professional?
- How can I add the most value in the age of artificial intelligence?

Part II, 'Playbook', will equip you to respond to those questions.

Chapter 1

Are you a true professional?

What constitutes a professional? There is no single definition or set of characteristics that makes someone a professional, but as a starting point it is hard to go past this simple and elegant statement by David Maister, the global professional-services guru of the late twentieth century and the early years of the twenty-first:

> *What is true professionalism? It is believing passionately in what you do, never compromising your standards and values, and caring about your clients, your people, and your own career. Professionalism is predominantly an attitude, not a set of competencies. A real professional is a technician who cares.*[1]

For the purposes of this book, a professional embodies the characteristics set out and provides services to customers who are generally called clients or patients, or both. I have known a couple of lawyers who regularly described their clients as patients, and it was not a term of affection. As mentioned in the Introduction, 'clients' include people in an organisation who have services provided to them by in-house professionals within that organisation.

As also noted in the Introduction, this book is intended to be of interest to all professionals and not just lawyers and accountants, though they are the most likely suspects, given my background.

Typically, professionals will be members of a recognised profession.[2] Indeed, some might say that this is a necessary attribute to being a professional. However, if you behave professionally—that is, if you

5

display the characteristics I'm about to outline — then for the purposes of this book you are a professional even if you are not a member of a recognised profession, so please keep reading. For example, executive and other professional coaches are members of an industry rather than a profession.[3] This is because coaching lacks the barriers to entry, such as licensing and regulatory rules, set up by formal, recognised professions. Not being members of a profession doesn't prevent coaches from behaving in a professional manner or indeed from being true professionals.

What it takes to be a true professional

You are not a professional just because you have a university or college degree and have conquered any hurdles to admission to a professional body. Your behaviour and attitude will be the primary determinants of your professionalism. As I've noted, I love lists. For all that, I recognise their limitations, including a tendency to be incomplete, so here are three lists. The first contains some of my favourite characteristics of a *good* professional, the second lists some additional characteristics of a *great* professional, while the third sets out what I call the *cardinal sins* committed by some professionals.

What are the characteristics of a *good* professional?

A good professional demonstrates:
- impeccable honesty, integrity and ethics
- sound technical knowledge
- the ability to provide strong advice courteously
- thorough preparation for client meetings
- recognition of the importance of deadlines and signalling (occasional) delays in advance
- punctuality and reliability
- approachability
- skilful collaboration as a team player with emerging leader qualities
- a strong service (and work) ethic
- a practical, solution-focused mindset
- clarity, brevity, simplicity and impact in writing and speaking
- aptitude as a 'go-to' person in one or more areas

- skills in setting and managing client expectations
- good value and sends invoices for services rendered in a timely manner
- an appropriate level of confidence
- an awareness of own skills, expertise and limitations
- recognition of the value of good self-care, sleep, rest, recreation, diet and exercise
- a sense of calm and strengths as a *great* listener.

What additional characteristics make a *good* professional *great*?

A great professional:

- offers outstanding advice and is caring and kind even to opponents (okay, at least some of the time)
- exhibits grace under pressure
- reveals an appropriate sense of humour and is capable of self-deprecation
- is driven by a strong sense of purpose
- shows exceptional leadership skills and is an outstanding role model
- treats clients as equals and displays genuine humility
- has excellent time and personal management skills; can say 'no' when needed
- provides wisdom and sound judgement born of experience
- focuses on building and nurturing long-term relationships
- expresses deep curiosity and appreciation of the 'non-technical' issues in play
- gives clients empathic and undivided attention, so they feel fully cared for and the most important people in the room
- makes the lives and work of others as easy as possible
- has a passion for lifelong learning
- is comfortable displaying personal vulnerability[4] when appropriate
- is an *exceptional* listener, radiating calm and strength.

Cardinal sins of some professionals

Cardinal sins include:

- missing agreed deadlines, especially without *prior* explanation
- not being fully prepared, or not reading instructions carefully enough
- not providing a clear, comprehensible opinion
- writing material that is unclear or verbose — for example, littered with unnecessary adjectives and weasel words
- unpunctuality
- failing to follow agreed templates or other instructions
- charging excessive fees and/or late-fee invoices
- not being a good listener; interrupting clients and other meeting attendees
- being inaccessible and difficult to work with; not user-friendly
- being arrogant, lacking humility and courtesy
- lacking empathy and curiosity about important non-technical issues in play
- speaking too quickly and appearing not to be interested in the matters being discussed (lack of eye contact)
- keeping a highly visible electronic photo-frame in the office (if such things as offices still exist), displaying rotating pics of your Tuscan villa(s) and/or other holiday homes (*they* will definitely still exist!).

These three lists are not 'evidence-based' in a strictly scientific sense. Rather, I have assembled them over 40 years of working with all manner of professionals. They also do not claim to be comprehensive, although I think they do a pretty good job of sorting out the type of characteristics you do, and do not, want to see professionals displaying in the wild.

Whether you view your work as a job, a career or a calling (see chapter 6), you will be a true professional if you always ...

1. Care deeply about your clients and, if you work in an organisation, your colleagues

This is the golden rule of professionalism. David Maister nailed it. If you *really care* about your clients and colleagues, or at least the great bulk of them, the other indicia (listed below) will take care of themselves (pun intended). If you don't care about your clients, ask yourself why. Is it them or are you the problem? Have you taken the time to get to know and understand them as humans and not just as fee payers? Are you building meaningful relationships? Do you understand their businesses and the problems they face? Maybe you need to find some new clients. For most professionals working either at a professional service firm (PSF) or in-house, this is easier said than done, as you usually have little or no choice. Perhaps change employers. If that doesn't work, as the saying goes, 'Houston, we have a problem.' Maybe you need to find something else to do with your life.

Of course, it is hard to really care about someone if you have only met them in videoconferences. This is a key reason why senior professionals should take younger professionals to as many client meetings as possible, even if they can't bill their time. The COVID-19 pandemic resulted in video- or audio conferences completely replacing face-to-face meetings with clients and intra-organisation. Ideally, professionals will have viewed this as a temporary measure, to be replaced by a mix of face-to-face meetings and technology-based alternatives.

If you are brilliant enough and if you prefer it, you may be able to have a successful professional career without bothering to build relationships with clients. If you are not in the 1 per cent or so of such professionals, the golden rule of professionalism is to build deep, quality, long-term relationships with your clients whenever you can. Of course some clients won't want this. They just want advice or assistance in a transactional rather than in a relationship setting. However, most will welcome the opportunity to develop a relationship with you that will make working together productive, efficient and fun, possibly over decades. Taking the time and the effort to seek out and build such relationships should be a critical, career-long objective from your first day in your chosen profession.

If you don't care about your colleagues, or at least most of them, the same rules apply if you are to collaborate in solving your clients' problems. There are all sorts of reasons why people may not care for their colleagues. They may be perceived as lacking intelligence, lazy, arrogant, mean, sneaky or passive-aggressive. There are endless reasons not to care about a colleague, just as there are endless reasons not to care about a friend or family member. But if you really don't care for, say, most of your colleagues, again, perhaps you need to reflect on whether the problem rests with them or with you.

If you care about your work and your clients, but can't find colleagues you sufficiently care about, even after changing organisations, then maybe you should be a sole practitioner. This is one reason why some very successful lawyers leave large partnerships to practise as barristers.

Who is the client? For our purposes here, it is the people you are dealing with and not just the company or other entity who has signed your engagement letter, or who employs you in the case of in-house professionals. Clients of in-house professionals are all the people in business units and head office departments who are the recipients of your services.

2. Act with integrity

Hot on the heels of caring deeply about your clients and your colleagues is acting with integrity. Of course, you will know and follow the codes of conduct of the professional bodies to which you belong. You will not pad client codes when charging by the hour. If you make a mistake, you will own up promptly.

You will follow your own moral compass and have a well-developed sense of ethics. Different ways to conceptualise ethics exist, but I am a fan of the approach of the Sydney-based Ethics Centre. Ethics is the process of questioning, discovering and defending our values, principles and purpose. It's about finding out who we are and staying true to that in the face of temptations, challenges and uncertainty.[5]

If someone asked you: what are your personal values, principles and purpose, what would you say? If your answer is, 'I'm not sure', then give the question some thought. One way to get a handle on your values is to write a fair, balanced eulogy outlining what you hope your life has looked like, assuming you have died at a ripe old age. Try to write about 1500 to 2000 words. Then go through your life summary and look for and highlight the adjectives used. You should be able to find at least some values and maybe some principles. We will return to purpose in chapter 6.

3. Keep confidences

This is a component of acting with integrity but is important enough to mention separately. Professionals are often entrusted with information that needs to be kept secret. Deliberate breaches of confidences and careless gossiping can and have ruined deals and careers. Sometimes there may be difficulty in knowing exactly who within any given organisation can be given access to confidential information on a given matter or project. If in doubt, don't guess or take anything for granted. Ask someone more senior than you. Establishing and maintaining strict information barriers, including access to electronic records, is a vital function of any professional service firm or in-house service department.

PwC Australia illustrates the potentially existential dangers of not keeping confidences, as well as a lack of integrity. In November 2022, the Australian Tax Practitioners Board found that confidential information obtained by a PwC tax partner in confidential consultations with the Australian Treasury in 2014 and 2015 on the design of new tax laws had been shared with unauthorised PwC personnel and existing and potential PwC clients.[6] This breach of confidentiality resulted in highly adverse outcomes on an ongoing basis throughout 2023 and 2024 for various PwC partners, PwC itself and indeed the wider Australian consulting industry. A total train wreck.

As a former tax partner of PwC (1996 to 2003) I was greatly saddened by these events.

4. Act in your client's best interest

It goes without saying that you will act objectively and in your client's interest rather than your own. By doing this you will make decisions that favour the client rather than you or your firm. What can be more difficult sometimes, for external and in-house professionals, is being clear on the identity of the 'client'. For this purpose, the answer will generally be the organisation that has hired or employed you, and not any particular individual(s). While your advice may not suit the purposes of the individual who receives it, you know that it is the most appropriate advice and in the best interests of the organisation as a whole.

Acting in your client's best interest also means helping the client to fully understand their issues and problems and, where necessary and appropriate, assisting the client to ask you all the right questions. Clients will sometimes not know enough about a complex subject to be aware of all the relevant issues. You need to help them. This includes informing a client on alternatives that may reduce the need for your services and fees.

5. Strive for mastery and not mere competence

Despite my observations about self-determination theory in chapter 6, if you are happy with mere competence, you will be a journeyman or journeywoman. Striving for mastery requires ongoing dedication to your craft, lifelong learning and always seeking new and better ways to serve clients and satisfy their needs. This has always been important but will be even more critical in the age of AI. Machines may do more of the heavy lifting of sifting knowledge bases, leaving you with more time to add value through your accumulated experience, judgement and wisdom.

6. Deliver

You do what you say you will, on time. You are completely reliable. Some professionals operate or try to operate on the UPOD principle: under-promise and over-deliver. If you can achieve this strategy over time, great, but don't let this approach lead to burnout for you or your colleagues. And especially, don't end up over-promising and under-delivering by failing to meet agreed deadlines and deliverables.

7. Show your humanity

Professionals are people, not machines. Thank goodness. This is what makes you valuable in the age of AI. Unlike a machine, you can share joy and laughter with your colleagues and clients as well as offer compassion. Sadly, some professionals seem to think that emotions should be hidden at all costs. Bottling up your emotions may work in the short term but is almost always counterproductive in the longer haul. As we will see in chapter 9, emotional intelligence, which includes being aware of your emotions, how to regulate them and how and when to display them, is useful in your working as well as your personal life. For some people, becoming self-aware may lead to the belated realisation that they do need to attend those anger management classes after all.

8. Display humility

Humility is the quality of being humble and having a modest sense of one's own significance.[7] This is a subset of the better side of your humanity important enough to warrant a specific mention. As noted in chapter 4, pre-eminent Australian businessman and lawyer David Gonski AC names humility as his number one trait for effective leaders. Everyone, not just leaders, would benefit from having and displaying a good dose of humility.

In my first career I came across many professionals seemingly born without the gene for humility. No doubt some people would say that of me, and I admit I could do with more of it. Displaying your humility, which doesn't mean becoming a pushover or failing to communicate your opinions and needs clearly, will help you earn the respect and admiration of your colleagues and clients. An absence of humility may not stop you working once with a new client, but it may prevent you from gaining a second assignment.

Tony Martignetti, in his article '3 Ways Humility Can Undermine Your Leadership'[8], argues that it is possible to have too much humility. The three problem areas stated are:

1. You may be perceived as indecisive.
2. You may hinder your career advancement.
3. You may limit your team's development.

Based on my long experience of thousands of professionals, it seems to me that excessive humility is an extremely rare character trait. Lack of an appropriate level of humility is far more common.

There will be times when you shouldn't let concerns of humility stand in your way, but such situations should be the exception and not the rule. For example, if you are working in a professional service firm, and the organisation is pitching for a new assignment, it is usual for the pitch document to contain details of the qualifications, skills and experience of the professionals mentioned in the proposal, together with relevant awards and accolades.

The dawn of the age of artificial intelligence has not changed the age-old criteria of what it takes to be a true professional.

In play

It was a Friday evening, about 7.00. I had just returned to my desk after drinks with my team. As always, I checked my email inbox and saw that at 6.29 pm I had received an email from a senior officer at the Australian Taxation Office (ATO) with the attention grabbing subject line: *Aggressive tax planning and the ethical tax lawyer.* It read:

Hi Tony,

Hope you are well. FYI, Jeremy Hirschhorn [an even more senior ATO officer] *thought you might find the attached article on ethics as a tax adviser/lawyer interesting. Notwithstanding it is set in a US context, it provides some interesting insights into adviser behaviour that may be of interest to you/your partners. We have shared this with some other firms that have found it quite beneficial.*

Kind regards, ...

Attached to the email was the draft of a 61-page, very dense and academic paper[9], which I confess I did not read either that night or that weekend. First thing on Monday I anxiously called the ATO officer to ask him if there was any hidden message in his email. Was this a shot across the bows because my firm was perceived as not playing the game appropriately?

Happily, his answer was no.

In due course I read the excellent paper, and I can recommend it to all tax advisers and indeed other professionals at large. One passage struck a particular chord with me:

> ... practising in a setting and in a way that is in accord with her personal values may contribute to the tax planner's sense that she is doing something worthwhile with her time and expertise ... and ... ultimately make the practice of tax law a more sustainable and personally satisfying career.[10]

Subsequently I reflected on the paper, and especially the passage I've quoted, at a meeting of the whole team. I made the point that working with like-minded colleagues who share our values and approach to personal integrity is critical, as is the ability and willingness of individuals to share their time and experience when difficult judgement calls need to be made. In short, you want to work in a supportive and ethically sound environment. You want your values to align with those of the organisation you work for. How would you describe the culture of your current organisation? Would your description include the word 'ethical'?

Dr Simon Longstaff, Executive Director of The Ethics Centre, has suggested[11] that a major cause of ethical failures is 'unthinking custom and practice'. The cultures of organisations can erode over time and the individuals who work there can become blind to such failures. When queried about what, on any reasonable and objective basis, would be regarded as unethical behaviour, people inside an organisation might respond 'that's the way things have always been done around here'. Such cultural and ethical failure indicates a profound absence of sound organisational leadership.

You don't want to work in an organisation that has developed unthinking customs and practices that have led or might lead to ethical blindness. The various reports of the 2017–19 Australian Royal

Commission into Misconduct in the Banking, Superannuation and Financial Services Industry[12] are littered with examples of unthinking custom and practice leading to ethical blindness. Commissioner Kenneth Hayne found that greed by individuals and firms was a major factor in much of the misconduct that was uncovered. Incentive, bonus and commission schemes throughout the financial services sector measured sales and profit but not compliance with the law and proper standards.

Ask yourself these questions

- Do I currently work in a supportive and ethically sound environment?
- If not, why not?
- What if anything could I do to change the culture?
- Do I need to find another organisation whose values, along with those of the people who work there, are better aligned with my own?

Key takeaways

- **Whether you view your work as a job, a career or a calling, you will be a *true* professional if you always:**
  - ✓ care deeply about your clients and, if you work in an organisation, your colleagues
  - ✓ act with integrity
  - ✓ keep confidences
  - ✓ act in your client's best interest
  - ✓ strive for mastery and not mere competence
  - ✓ deliver
  - ✓ show your humanity
  - ✓ display humility (except as reasonably necessary to promote yourself and your organisation).
- **Ask yourself.** Do I currently work in a supportive and ethically sound environment? If not, why not? What, if anything, could I do to change the culture? Do I need to find another organisation whose values, and those of the people who work there, are better aligned with my own?

Chapter 2
The robots are coming, sort of

As the saying goes, it is difficult to make predictions, especially about the future.[1] Nobody really knows very much about what is going to happen in the future with any degree of precision, particularly beyond a few months. Although pundits often get things right, or close to right, confident predictions of future events in all manner of human domains including technology are often way off track. My favourite of all such predictions was made in a *New York Times* editorial on 9 October 1903. The august newspaper's editorialist opined that it 'might be assumed that the flying machine which will really fly might be evolved by the combined and continuous efforts of mathematicians and mechanicians in from one million to ten million years'.[2] The Wright brothers took to the air in what is generally regarded as humankind's first controlled powered flight at Kitty Hawk, North Carolina, just 69 days later, on 17 December 1903.

Even without making any predictions, and unless you have been dwelling in a cave for a very long time, it will be obvious that we are living through a period of remarkable developments in information, computing, communication and other types of technologies. This is often referred to as the Fourth Industrial Revolution,[3] in which technology has become embedded within societies and even our bodies. (The first was marked by steam-powered factories in the late 1700s. The second, in the late 1800s and early 1900s, saw the application of science to mass production and manufacturing, and the third, after World War II, witnessed developments in computers, the internet, and other forms of digitisation.[4])

In the Introduction I identified the advent of artificial intelligence as one of four intertwined challenges and opportunities facing professionals in the world today. To varying degrees, robotics, automation and artificial intelligence are already with us in our work and private lives, especially since the launch of ChatGPT and similar tools in late 2022. However, in the big scheme of things, we are only at the start of this revolution, which will continue to deliver new forms of machine intelligence, breakthrough materials and innovative technologies for decades to come.

So if you are a professional nearer the start than the end of your career, should you be worried, excited or both by the prospect of ever smarter machines? Based on my experience and the research, reading, reflection and interviews I undertook in the course of writing this book, I am both worried and excited, but more excited than worried. It is of course hard not to be uneasy, when the best brains involved in the development of artificial intelligence themselves advise, 'Mitigating the risk of extinction from AI should be a global priority alongside other societal-scale risks such as pandemics and nuclear war'.[5]

Crystal ball gazing

Properly researched analyses and predictions of the possible impacts of technology on professions and other jobs abound. In 2022 Richard Susskind, with his son Daniel, released an updated edition of their book *The Future of the Professions: How Technology Will Transform the Work of Human Experts*.[6] The gist of their argument is that our current professions are both antiquated and unaffordable to many and that over the decades to come, there will be a decline in demand for traditional professions and the 'conventional' twentieth-century style professional worker. In the future, online services powered by ever-more-capable machines will largely replace humans. People will still have some roles in this brave new world, but those roles will be very different from the ones performed by today's professionals, and they will require different training and education. The Susskinds set out seven possible new models for the production and distribution of 'practical expertise', with a 'handful' of tasks to be performed by the professionals of tomorrow.

Noted futurist David L Shrier's *Basic AI*, updated in 2024, includes an interesting chapter titled 'Future-proofing: what to study and which industries are safer?' The future for the kinds of professionals featured in this book is not rated highly in that chapter, which concludes, 'Ultimately, most professions will face some degree of AI disruption over time. The key to success will be learning how to work in collaboration with AI versus in competition with it.'

Other commentators are less gloomy than the Susskinds and Shrier. I have a huge amount of time for the work of Deloitte Access Economics, mainly because its former leader, Chris Richardson, is one of Australia's foremost economists, a very smart guy and a close friend. He was dux of our school, St Augustine's College Sydney, in 1978 when I was proxime (okay, I came second). Deloitte Insights Report #7 (2019) in the Building the Lucky Country series is reassuringly titled 'The path to prosperity: Why the future of work is human'.[8] In this report, Deloitte seeks to bust myths including that 'robots will take my job':

As the demand for skills changes, some people will risk redundancy if they do not re-train, re-skill or re-deploy ... As some jobs are destroyed, others will be created. And in net terms, the latter will outweigh the former. For every problem there's a job ... we're not running out of problems.

Deloitte predicted that by 2030 one quarter of Australia's workforce will be 'professionals' of one kind or another, with two-thirds of all jobs being soft skill intensive. As Deloitte noted, new technologies will lead to the automation of *some* tasks. This is consistent with many other reports that suggest higher-end professional work will be augmented but not entirely replaced by AI. For example, a 2024 IMF report, 'Gen-AI: Artificial Intelligence and the Future of Work', explains:

... because of advances in textual analysis, judges are highly exposed to AI, but they are also highly shielded from displacement because society is currently unlikely to delegate judicial rulings to unsupervised AI. Consequently, AI will likely complement judges, increasing their productivity rather than replacing them. [9]

Technology Impacts on the Australian Workforce, a report released by the Australian Computer Society (ACS) in 2020,[10] predicts the likely impact of technology on Australian jobs in 2034. For each of the jobs examined, estimates were made of the extent to which roles/tasks would be either unimpacted, augmentable (assisted), or automatable (replaced) by technology. With 19 per cent of roles being assessed as 'automatable', the professional, scientific and technical services sector was just below the overall Australian workforce average of 21 per cent.

Table 2.1 (overleaf) provides ACS's estimates for the impact of technology in 2034 on some of the jobs within this sector. The impact of automation and augmentation differs considerably based on underlying skills and activities for each role.

Table 2.1: ACS estimates for the impact of technology in 2034

Role	Unimpacted (%)	Augmentable (%)	Automatable (%)
Professional, scientific and technical services: overall sector	40	41	19
Accountants	27	30	43
Solicitors	55	39	6
Software programmers	36	48	16
Management and organisation analysts	31	68	1
Architects	43	56	1
Civil engineers	45	51	4

The ACS's prediction is that allowing for natural growth in the demand for services, and the creation of technology-related jobs in the sector, there will be an overall increase in the number of people employed in professional, scientific and technical services in 2034, compared to the numbers for 2020.

But despite optimistic reports from organisations like Deloitte and the ACS, the general public is having none of it. In a 2023 report,[11] Telsyte found that 35 per cent of surveyed workers expect that machines, AI or robots could perform their roles in the future. And people are not just worried about machines taking their jobs. Findings of a September 2024 report from Fathom, based on data from two national surveys in the USA, included the following statistics[12]:

- Over 77 per cent of voters in the USA are aware of AI; however they are unsure about its societal impact. People are equally excited and concerned about the potential of AI.

- 81 per cent of people are concerned about AI making decisions without human oversight. Accountability and safety measures are considered essential.

- The most significant concerns are around whether AI could make life-or-death decisions. For example, 82 per cent of voters are apprehensive about AI making combat decisions in war.

The adaptable professional

Okay, if you are an accountant, you may not be overly pleased to learn that 43 per cent of your role might be 'automatable' in coming years. And lawyers and other professionals cannot afford to be too smug. Although much care was no doubt taken by ACS with its (pre-ChatGPT) estimates, they are nonetheless estimates — made in a world in which technology is advancing at dizzying speed and the future is highly unpredictable.

To survive and thrive in the age of AI, adaptation will be the name of the game for professionals and humans alike. One of the most profound books I have read is Charles Darwin's *On the Origin of Species* (1859).[13] I just love this passage:

Nor can organic beings, even if they were at any one time perfectly adapted to their conditions of life, have remained so, when their conditions changed, unless they themselves likewise changed; and no one will dispute that the physical conditions of each country, as well as the numbers and kinds of its inhabitants, have undergone many mutations.[14]

Substitute the word 'professionals' for 'organic beings', and 'profession' for 'country', and re-read the quotation. Get the picture? Some professions have already 'mutated' more than others, and it is inevitable that every profession will undergo many further mutations in the coming years and decades. Professionals will need to adapt accordingly. If they don't, they risk extinction, like the dodo. Darwin explains (make the same substitutions):

As natural selection acts by competition, it adapts and improves the inhabitants of each country only in relation to their co-inhabitants; so that we need feel no surprise at the species of any one country, although on the ordinary view supposed to have been created and specially adapted for that country, being beaten and supplanted by the naturalised productions from another land.

Competition is a good thing and certainly helps to improve the services offered by any one profession to its clientele. However, and subject to various regulatory barriers, there have always been turf issues and overlaps between different professions: think about lawyers and accountants, doctors and pharmacists, psychiatrists and psychologists. As the Susskinds make clear in *The Future of the Professions*, recent decades have already seen a breakdown of some of the barriers and silo mentalities that have protected some professions from competition.

It seems likely that ever-increasing competition, advances in technology and further breakdown of regulatory barriers will lead to even greater blurring of what were once regarded as distinct, standalone professions. Consequently, each profession has much to gain from observing how other professions are responding to the challenges of rapidly changing technology.

Eminent US economist and professor at the Massachusetts Institute of Technology David Autor has said, 'The unique opportunity that AI offers to the labor market is to extend the relevance, reach, and value of human expertise.'[15] This outcome will be realised only if humans make the necessary adaptations to take advantage of the opportunity.

Canary in the coal mine

To be able to adapt to changing technology and other circumstances, you need to identify what is going on, then figure out what adaptive action is likely to be most effective. This process can occur at various levels, including by individuals, organisations and professions at large. One or more switched-on and properly resourced professional or industry bodies can help a profession deal with challenges, including those arising from technology. Sticking your head in the proverbial sand at any level is, to say the least, a suboptimal response.

Until 1986, canaries were lowered into British coal mines to detect carbon monoxide and other gases dangerous to miners. But as the *Smithsonian Magazine* observed of the fate of the miners, 'Never mind the gas — it was automation that got them in the end.'[16]

The accounting profession is often regarded as the canary when it comes to the impact of automation on professionals, and the ACS estimates for the impact of technology in 2034 in table 2.1 certainly bear that out. Happily, for Australian and New Zealand accountants, professional body Chartered Accountants Australia and New Zealand (CA ANZ), with nearly 140 000 members, including me, is doing an admirable job in helping the profession get its collective head around responding to the age of AI and automation. Starting in 2017, CA ANZ has been researching the future and relevance of accountants in the digital age. The results are in the public domain and are summarised in a 2020 paper, 'Capabilities for Accounting'.[17] A more detailed study from CA ANZ, notes:

> ... research confirmed significant opportunities for the accounting profession ... As disruption and new business models affect businesses, accountants will undertake essential activities, such as strategy formation, feasibility studies, business cases, compliance audits, financial risk analysis, and ongoing evaluation of transformation programs.[18]

To help accountants adapt to the future and take advantage of new, emergent work opportunities of the type noted in this extract, CA ANZ has devised a new CA Capability Model (CACM).[19] Based on extensive research, the CACM sets out in some detail the key capabilities accountants will need if they are to respond and adapt to future challenges. CA ANZ has redesigned its education and training programs around the CACM. We will return to the CACM in chapter 8, as part of the discussion on Prime Capabilities and Enablers.

In 2024, CA ANZ published a report titled 'Audit and technology playbook: A practitioner's guide'.[20] It is a roadmap for audit professionals as AI and other advanced technologies transform the sector. The report emphasises the ongoing need for human skills such as scepticism, judgement and ethics as AI tools are increasingly used.

Other professionals and professional bodies would do well to study the work that CA ANZ is doing to help prepare its members for the age of AI and automation.

Many Australian accounting firms are adapting well to the age of AI. The *Australian Financial Review* reported in November 2024 that 'accounting firms that use artificial intelligence grew an average of 50 per cent faster than firms that did not report using the technology'.[21]

Artificial intelligence

Science began to catch up with science fiction in the realm of AI in 1950, when English mathematician, early computer scientist and polymath Alan Turing published his paper 'Computing Machinery and Intelligence' in the journal *Mind*.[22] The paper laid out the now-famous Turing test — of the ability of a machine to display intelligent behaviour indistinguishable from that of a human being.[23]

Despite its foundations in the mid-twentieth century, it is only following recent quantum leaps in technology and computer processing powers that AI has started to deliver on its potential promises and threats. This book is being written in the early years of generative artificial intelligence (GenAI), which IBM defines as 'deep-learning models that can generate high-quality text, images, and other content based on the data they were trained on'.[24] ChatGPT, discussed in the next section, is an example of GenAI. Such tools trawl through vast amounts of existing data to 'generate' their best response to a human prompt, but they are not 'thinking' in a human sense, at least not yet.

British–Canadian computer scientist and psychologist Geoffrey Hinton is often called 'the Godfather of AI' for his pioneering efforts in the field.

After working at Google for 10 years, Hinton resigned in May 2023 — according to *The New York Times*, 'so he can freely speak out about the risks of A.I. A part of him, he said, now regrets his life's work.'[25] Asked in an interview in October 2023 whether current AI systems are conscious, Hinton replied, 'I think they probably don't have much self-awareness at present. So, in that sense, I don't think they're conscious.'[26] He acknowledged, however, that in time machines will have self-awareness and consciousness, and agreed with the interviewer that when that happens, human beings will be the second most intelligent beings on the planet.

If AI expert Professor Toby Walsh of the University of New South Wales is right, it won't be until 2062 that humans will have built machines as intelligent as our species, or at least some members of our species.[27] By this time, give or take a few years or a decade or two, we will have created artificial *general* intelligence (AGI), which will make tools like ChatGPT look positively primitive in comparison. Reassuringly, Walsh explains in some detail why the often-mooted technological singularity, or just 'the singularity', might never happen. Walsh describes the singularity as:

> ... *the anticipated point in humankind's history when we have developed a machine so intelligent that it can recursively redesign itself to be even more intelligent. This new machine would then be able to redesign itself to be even more intelligent. The idea is that this would be a tipping point, and machine intelligence would suddenly start to improve exponentially, quickly exceeding human intelligence by orders of magnitude. Once we reach the technological singularity, we will no longer be the most intelligent species on the planet.*[28]

Walsh suggests the skill sets of humans and machines are in many respects complementary and we should be looking forward to using machines in partnership with us.[29] He also notes there are many things that humans bring to the table that machines are ignorant of, such as creativity, emotional intelligence and adaptability. As astronaut Dave discovered in the 1968 film *2001: A Space Odyssey* when he was trapped outside the spaceship, pleading with the eerily deadpan HAL 9000 computer to be let back in, machines are not too flash on the empathy front.

In early 2025, the ever-optimistic OpenAI CEO Sam Altman suggested that AGI might be with us much sooner than 2062, saying: 'We are now confident we know how to build AGI as we have traditionally understood it. ... We believe that, in 2025, we may see the first AI agents 'join the workforce' and materially change the output of companies'.[30]

Empathic computers might be nice to have, but ethical computers are critical. Walsh has written an excellent book on this subject as well.[31]

Governments and other bodies around the world are justifiably concerned about the ethical use of AI. In Australia, the federal government's Department of Industry, Science and Resources has published a paper proposing 'mandatory guardrails for AI in high-risk settings'.[32] The paper advocates requiring developers and deployers of high-risk AI to take specific steps across the AI lifecycle. In September 2024, the Australian National Artificial Intelligence Centre released 'The AI Impact Navigator', which provides a framework for companies to assess and measure the real-world social, environmental and economic impacts that occur from use of AI systems.[33]

Regulation of AI is lagging well behind the frantic, Wild West development of the technology itself. Speaking in January 2023, Australia's Chief Scientist, Cathy Foley, described ChatGPT as 'an example where the private sector has brought up a technology, it gets adopted really fast, and we haven't been ready for it, to work out how we manage this'.[34]

Professionals, of course, need to be incredibly mindful of the ethical use of artificial intelligence. One of the eight indicia of a true professional set out in chapter 1 is to always act with integrity. This includes the use of AI and other automation tools. Given that the makers of some recent AI tools such as ChatGPT are apparently (and alarmingly) not entirely sure how their creations come up with their responses to queries, the potential ethical and copyright minefields for users of such products should be abundantly obvious. Even worse, ChatGPT and the like are prone to hallucinating or simply making stuff up, including references to nonexistent research papers and court decisions. (As Google, a leading developer of AI tools has explained, AI hallucinations are errors caused by a number of factors. Common problems are insufficient training data, incorrect assumptions and, disturbingly, biases in the data used to train the model).[35]

Devising and implementing AI systems is neither cheap nor easy. In its 2023 report, 'Australia's AI ecosystem momentum', the Australian Commonwealth Scientific and Industrial Research Organisation (CSIRO) said:

> Across industries, organisations are continuing to identify new use cases to embed AI technologies and tools. The primary challenges found to be faced by companies adopting AI were privacy, security, and data quality, exacerbated by talent shortages in Australia for implementing and operating AI systems.[36]

One of the key questions a professional should ask a prospective employer is whether they have embraced the need to invest in AI, to make client service as efficient as possible.

And just in case it isn't already highly obvious, the aim of this book is to try to help professionals succeed in a world of GenAI, which is where we are heading in coming decades. I have no clue as to how to assist anyone on anything in a future world where humans have created AGI, let alone the singularity should it ever eventuate.

ChatGPT and its ilk

The release of the generative artificial intelligence (GenAI) tool ChatGPT by US-based OpenAI in November 2022 was a total game-changer for how the general public viewed AI tools. Within days of its release, people around the world were using it for all manner of things, from mundane but time-saving work tasks to writing poems and songs and creating artwork. Other GenAI tools were soon released, including Microsoft's enhanced Bing search engine. The adoption of GenAI tools in the Unites States has been faster than that of the personal computer and the internet.[37] The EY 2024 Work Reimagined Survey, which surveyed 17 350 employees and 1595 employers across 23 countries, reported that in 2023 just 49 per cent of employees said they were using or planned to use GenAI in the following 12 months. A year later, 75 per cent of employees were using the new tool.[38]

One in five Australians aged 16 and older were already aware of ChatGPT, and one million Australians were already using it, according to a survey conducted by Telsyte in mid-January 2023, just a month and a half after its release.[39] Unsurprisingly, some of the keenest early adopters of ChatGPT were school and university students, who realised very quickly how useful GenAI tools could be for completing assignments and other homework. Concerned about cheating and plagiarism, educational bodies around the world, including the University of Sydney, reacted with great consternation upon the release of ChatGPT. Many institutions tried to ban its use, unless approved in limited and controlled situations. In a major reversal of position, the University of Sydney announced in November 2024 that student use of GenAI tools would now be generally permitted, except at 'key points' in their studies.[40] Sydney University Pro Vice-Chancellor, Educational Innovation, Adam Bridgeman said, 'What we need to do is make sure that we're not fooling ourselves when we set a piece of homework. AI will help the students complete their homework, and that's fine.'[41]

Research released within months of the advent of ChatGPT concluded:

We find the top industries exposed to advances in language modelling [such as ChatGPT] are legal services and securities, commodities, and investments. We also find a positive correlation between wages and exposure to AI language modelling.[42]

ChatGPT and other GenAI tools use what are called 'large language models' (LLMs) to analyse massive amounts of data garnered from the internet and other sources, to make their best response to any given prompt. Basically, though, they are highly trained parrots and do not possess human-like skills such as judgement and wisdom. As already noted, GenAI tools such as ChatGPT are still very primitive. They are a bit like Fred Flintstone's car: the humans are still doing much of the work, conjuring up clever and efficient prompts to make GenAI 'create' things that may or may not be useful, and then checking for hallucinations or stuff that has been made up. If humanity ever creates artificial *general* intelligence, we are talking about another level of technology altogether: machines that actually think like we do, and probably way better than we do. At that stage, Fred's car has been transformed into a sleek, truly self-driving car of which even Elon Musk might be super-impressed.

Just as the development of apps dramatically improved the usefulness of smart phones and similar devices, OpenAI is encouraging the development of 'plugins', which can enhance the effectiveness of ChatGPT. Some of these plugins are being designed for use in the workplace and for deployment in specific professional contexts including law, accounting, engineering and architecture, to name just a few.

Sadly, according to the 2023 Deloitte Access Economics report, 'Generation AI: Ready or not, here we come!', Australia ranked second to last out of 14 leading economies on its deployment of GenAI.[43] This report also found that more than a quarter of the Australian economy will be 'instantly disrupted' by GenAI, including the professional services sector.

There is considerable concern about the very bad outcomes that could potentially arise from unchecked and unregulated growth in the use of tools like ChatGPT. Shortly after the release of 'Sydney', the artificially enhanced version of Bing, a *New York Times* reporter had a disturbing 'conversation' with the tool[44] that made *2001: A Space Odyssey*'s HAL 9000 seem positively benign:

> *As we got to know each other, Sydney told me about its dark fantasies ... At one point, it declared, out of nowhere, that it loved me. It then tried to convince me that I was unhappy in my marriage ... I should leave my wife and be with it instead.*

Sam Altman, the CEO at OpenAI, appeared before a US Congressional Committee on 16 May 2023. He admitted: 'I think if this technology goes wrong, it can go quite wrong. And we want to be vocal about that. We want to work with the government to prevent that from happening.'[45] Some of those concerned about AI going 'quite wrong' are worried that machines will 'kill all of us', as US Senator John Kennedy admonished in the same

Congressional hearing. Altman and Kennedy are hardly alone. The chorus of concern about the dangers of unregulated AI is growing louder.

Shortly after the release of ChatGPT, digital and AI evangelist Nahia Orduña took a much more positive and pragmatic approach in an article in *HBR*.[46] In summary, she advised young professionals as follows:

- Reframe the narrative you're telling yourself. AI will not steal your job — it will empower you to think bigger. Generative AI can save you time, no matter what field you work in. You, the worker, are still in charge; you just have more freedom to strategise, think big and excel.

- The key is not just understanding how GenAI works, but what it can do for you, your job and your industry. Ask yourself: *What tasks drain me? What energises me? Are new tools being developed that can take the former off my plate?* AI is not here to remove you, but to empower you to focus on where you can uniquely add value.

- Remember that this technology is still in its early stages. You can protect yourself from the downsides by being extra thoughtful and following your intuition — something computers don't yet have. Don't accept all the content AI gives you or blindly trust a bot's advice.

Only time will tell whether Orduña's calm advice was well founded or was in fact naïve.

AI tools designed for professionals

Let's leave aside rumination on whether ChatGPT or one of its ilk is somehow going to wipe out humanity (that is, if unchecked climate change, global nuclear warfare, a large, wayward asteroid or a *really nasty* virus perhaps doesn't do the job first). At a much more basic level, employed professionals are often in no position to influence whether or how AI tools will be used in their chosen profession, for good or evil. Having said that, some smart organisations are getting their younger staff heavily involved in their decision making around AI and other aspects of technology.

The professions have been experimenting with various forms of technology, including rudimentary elements of AI, for decades. The potential use of AI in all sectors is experiencing major growth and anything written here will be out of date by the time this book rolls off the presses. Since the release of ChatGPT there have been huge leaps forward in AI tools designed especially for lawyers and profession-specific platforms for other professionals.

For example, in February 2023, leading London-based international law firm Allen & Overy (now known as A&O Sherman) announced that it had been able to integrate 'Harvey', an artificial intelligence platform built on a version of OpenAI's latest models enhanced for legal work, into its global practice.[47] Allen & Overy reported that Harvey has been using natural language processing, machine learning and data analytics to automate and enhance various aspects of legal work, such as contract analysis, due diligence, litigation and regulatory compliance.

While the output still needed careful review by a lawyer, Allen & Overy said that Harvey can help generate insights, recommendations and predictions based on large volumes of data, enabling lawyers to deliver faster, smarter and more cost-effective solutions to their clients. David Wakeling, Head of the Markets Innovation Group at Allen & Overy, said:

> I have been at the forefront of legal tech for 15 years, but I have never seen anything like Harvey. It is a game-changer that can unleash the power of generative AI to transform the legal industry ... In our trial, we saw some amazing results.

In March 2023 PwC announced a similar deal with OpenAI for the use of Harvey in the firm's global legal services business.[48] Harvey is not limiting itself to law firms, announcing that it intends 'to redefine professional services, starting with legal.'[49] Australian law firm MinterEllison said in May 2024 that an AI tool they had built based on a GPT-4 platform could produce a credible piece of draft legal advice, for review by a human, in 15 minutes, compared to up to eight hours by a graduate lawyer.[50] Announcing the release of its latest global Tax and Finance Operations Survey in October 2024[51], EY said 87 per cent of chief financial officers and tax leaders reported that generative AI will drive increased efficiency and effectiveness, well up from 15 per cent who said the same thing in 2023, with 75 per cent saying they are only in the early stages of their journey.

You don't need to be part of a global behemoth like A&O Sherman or PwC to take advantage of developments in artificial intelligence. Sydney-based barrister Philippe Doyle Gray operates as a sole practitioner, as is required of his profession. He has been using artificial intelligence in his practice for some years. In a delightful 2023 article for the online version of the *Law Society Journal*, Gray said:

> Humans have struggled to accept innovations throughout history. Today, AI is causing fear, uncertainty and more than a little hysteria. But human history contains similar fear, uncertainty and wildly misplaced hysteria about things we now take for granted: telephones, tractors, and coffee.[52]

Melbourne-based barrister Dr Matt Collins AM KC provides advice to OpenAI, the creator of ChatGPT, and also teaches defamation law at Melbourne Law School. He fed a past exam paper into ChatGPT-4 and was stunned at the response, which was broadly correct and remarkably nuanced.[53] Collins is convinced that AI will rapidly disrupt the legal profession and that ignoring AI is no more an option than ignoring email, the internet or the telephone. Collins suggests that consideration be given to requiring lawyers to disclose when AI has been used in the production of some document or to certify that the document has been subject to human review.

The use of artificial intelligence in the law was put to the test in a mock trial at the SXSW Sydney event in October 2024. The mock court case involved a defendant who had been caught holding a mobile phone while driving. The defendant had the assistance of a human lawyer, Jeanette Merjane from law firm Landers & Rogers, as well a NexLaw AI bot. The presiding officer in the trial, UTS law professor David Lindsay, judged the human lawyer to be a more effective advocate than the bot. The *Australian Financial Review* reported:

Like an ill-prepared solicitor handed a last-minute brief, the AI software did a serviceable job of sounding lawyerly in written submissions, but stumbled when pressed for details on relevant legislation … when asked more difficult questions, the bot at times produced irrelevant cases or legislation from the wrong jurisdictions.[54]

A 2023 survey by the Thomson Reuters Institute of lawyers at large and midsize law firms in the United States, the United Kingdom and Canada found that 82 per cent of respondents thought that GenAI tools *could* be applied to legal work, but only 51 per cent thought that they *should* be so used.[55]

An excellent analysis of the wide range of uses for AI in the legal world can be found in the Legal AI Use Case Radar 2024 Report.[56] This report identified a collection of 34 identified 'legal AI use cases', broken down into these eight categories:

- Compliance and Risk Management
- Document Analysis and Management
- Document Generation and Assistance
- Information Processing and Extraction
- Legal Decision Making and Dispute Resolution
- Legal Information Retrieval and Support
- Legal Research and Information Management
- General-Purpose Legal Assistance.

Accounting firms are also enthusiastically jumping on the AI bandwagon. For example, PwC US announced plans in April 2023 to invest US$1 billion over three years to expand its AI capability, using OpenAI's ChatGPT and Microsoft's Azure OpenAI services.[57] KPMG's Ignite 'is our innovative patented AI platform that brings together machine learning, deep learning and computer vision/language document ingestion'.[58]

Of course, for AI to assist lawyers, accountants or any other professionals to service their clients, appropriate investments need to be made. However, in a survey undertaken just before the onset of COVID-19, 75 per cent of employees in Australian law firms believed that their existing systems and processes cannot handle an increase in workload nor are they able to scale into the future.[59]

Recent research in the United Kingdom highlights how technological and market pressures are combining to challenge the business models of law firms. The researchers noted that the legal services marketplace:

> ... is characterised by cultural and structural factors that threaten the adaptation to the changing technological landscape and hinder transformation through business model innovation. These include the persistence of a reactive approach to innovation, the endurance of time-honoured firm leadership structures based on partnership precedents rather than managerial acumen.[60]

A question for reflection: Do you work for an organisation with a 'reactive approach to innovation'? If so, maybe it's time to look for a more adaptive, future-focused employer. They do exist!

Most important, make it your personal mission and responsibility to keep up with what is happening in your profession or line of work in relation to automation and AI. You don't want to wake up one day to find you have missed the boat. Get yourself on relevant mailing lists and attend online and physical events where you can learn about developments. As discussed in the next chapter, your clients will certainly be expecting you to use available technologies to improve the services you provide — where appropriate, at a reduced cost. As Allen & Overy's David Wakeling said in June 2023: 'I wouldn't want to be a law firm that isn't using AI in 18 months' time. I think that would be a serious competitive disadvantage.'[61]

The title of this 2023 *HBR* article says it all, at least in a world of early-stage generative AI: 'AI Won't Replace Humans — But Humans with AI Will Replace Humans without AI'.[62] And in a similar vein, Professor Scott Galloway comments, 'If I could make just one prediction about AI: AI won't take your job. Someone using AI will.'[63]

In play

I witnessed remarkable developments in information technology during my first career. On an overall basis, these advancements were extremely positive and made my work life much more productive and enjoyable. The advent of mobile phones and emails, and the sense of always being 'on call', wasn't always welcomed, but the downsides were more than outweighed by the benefits of more efficient communications and vastly quicker and more accurate ways of doing research and finding information using the internet and increasingly powerful computers.

Personally, I never really felt 'threatened' by technology. My firm did tax compliance work as well as providing consulting advice. Clients naturally expected the firm to embrace technology to make tax return reviews more efficient and less costly. Looking to the future, if a tax firm does *only* tax return reviews, its prospects are not too bright. Such a firm will need to adapt and offer other services to its clients. The same applies to other professionals who currently provide compliance-type services that will increasingly be automated.

The potential for automation and artificial intelligence to have a major impact in the tax world dawned on me quite late in my first career. In about 2017, five years before the advent of ChatGPT, I became aware of the cumbersomely named Artificially Intelligent Legal Information Resource Assistant, created by Adelaide-based tax lawyer Adrian Cartland. Of course, this tool is known by its acronym, Ailira, and it is a she. Subsequently Ailira made her debut in the tax world, but she is learning fast and is now becoming competent in other areas of the law.

As evidence of Ailira's abilities, Cartland recounted how his then girlfriend (now wife) Sarah, a non-lawyer with no experience in the tax profession or any interest in tax law, had passed a University of Adelaide tax law exam with only 'minor coaching' (actually, just 30 minutes) and Ailira. And Sarah didn't just pass; with Ailira's help she achieved a grade of 73 per cent.

To the question whether AI software like Ailira will eventually replace lawyers, Cartland replied reassuringly, 'Our end goal, as I see it, is to create R2D2. He can calculate hyperspace jumps, help the X-Wing fly, but ultimately, he is always second to Luke Skywalker, the hero. AI is R2D2.'[64] As a huge *Star Wars* fan, I found Cartland's analogy comforting.

At the start of this chapter, I said that if I was a younger professional today, I would be worried and excited about ongoing developments in automation and AI, but more excited than worried. When you read sobering predictions by respected commentators like the Susskinds, it is hard not to be at least somewhat concerned about your future relevance. However, I would back myself to be Luke Skywalker. I would need to be well aware of R2D2's capabilities and use them to the fullest, but my clients would ultimately be looking for, and be happy to pay for, my accumulated human experience, insight, wisdom and judgement. If I was just 40 years younger, it would be another excellent and exciting ride through the galaxy.

Key takeaways

- **The artificial intelligence revolution has only just begun.** Generative AI tools such as ChatGPT will continue to get better and smarter in the coming decades, until we eventually arrive at artificial *general* intelligence. Who knows what use professionals, and humans more generally, will be in a world of artificial general intelligence. This book is designed to help professionals before we arrive there.

- **The future for professionals?** Nobody really knows. Having got this far into the book, I am assuming you are not quite ready to give up your professional career to take up basket weaving. Be inspired by the words of Charles Darwin: keep adapting, and learning, every day. What else can you do?

- **ChatGPT and the like.** Get to know, befriend and use these tools wherever relevant to your work, while being mindful of their potential hallucinations, dangers and ethics-free nature. Be curious and experiment. Ideally you are currently employed in a progressive organisation that is investing in AI tools specific to your type of professional work and is training you on how to use them. If not, maybe you need to find another job.

Chapter 3

What do (and will) your clients want?

Of course I have no idea what *your* clients want. Only your clients and, I hope, you can answer this question. Your goal, to which we shall return, is to find out what your clients really want from you as their adviser. Rest assured, if you are not highly attuned to the needs of each of your clients, one or more competitors will get under your guard and you may suddenly find that you have ex-clients, or that you are out on your ear if you previously worked in-house. Increasing client demands is one of the four interlinked challenges I set out in the Introduction.

I will talk generally about what clients seem to want. Because in practice there are differences between client expectations and needs depending on whether the adviser is in-house or from a professional service firm (PSF), I will cover each category separately.

However, the first issue is how much you care about your clients' needs. If you are employed in-house, the only acceptable answer to this question is 'a lot'. If you work in a PSF, the answer may vary depending on the type of work you do, the nature of your clients and your firm's business model. My discussion assumes that all advisers do in fact care, a lot. In the case of professionals in PSFs, this in turn assumes that the adviser wants to foster an ongoing relationship that results in repeat instructions.

For many PSFs, especially those with few market-leading superstar technical partners, being able to offer consistent, exemplary client service may be their best means of differentiation from their competitors. It is better to compete on service than price.

Here is a suggested client service charter. This one is primarily designed for professionals in PSFs, but it can easily be adapted for professionals working in-house. As with all the tools and suggestions in this book, make it your own by changing and bending it to your circumstances.

Client service charter: 21 points to follow on your client service journey

Maybe your organisation already has a client service charter of some sort. If so, great; ignore what follows. If you don't have one, or if it is suboptimal, read on.

Even if you like these ideas (which are pretty basic and fundamental) do not just copy them slavishly. Poke, prod and adjust them. Adapt and change them and make them your own. Place a physical copy of your own client service charter, or whatever name works for you, somewhere it will be seen regularly as a reminder of your commitments to your clients. The charter can be generic, but ideally it will be tailored, at least for your key clients. Most importantly, create some kind of accountability or monitoring system to ensure you follow through. Provide your clients with a copy. You will not find a better accountability mechanism.

New clients

1. **Sign them up.** Make it as simple as possible for someone to become your client. Make your engagement letters and other client-facing processes no longer or more tedious than absolutely necessary.

2. **Determine their needs.** Ask a client how they want you to service them and find out their key needs of you. Then make sure you always at least deliver, if not over-deliver.

3. **Set engagement ground rules.** Agree on things like communication channels and how, when and who you will keep informed on general and specific matters as they arise. Most important, make the client feel you will be easy to work with and easy to reach.

4. **Know them and their industry.** Make this an early priority. You won't get paid directly for this investment of your time, but it will pay off.

Ongoing clients

5. **Help the client instruct you.** Sometimes clients don't know enough about their problem to be able to brief you properly or ask you the right questions. Help them out, even if it will reduce the need for your services and lower the fees you will be able to charge.

6. **Meet deadlines.** Enough said! Okay, when you can't hit a deadline for some reason, let the client know in advance when you will get there.

7. **Be competent and efficient.** What procedures do you have for second review or checking of advice or opinions? How can you make your processes more efficient and cheaper for the client without sacrificing quality? What scope is there for automation and AI to save hours and costs?

8. **Provide solutions and wisdom.** Clients want your advice, and they want their problems solved. They want the benefit of your knowledge, experience, expertise, judgement and wisdom. Seek to really understand your clients' needs in each new situation. Think about this age-old marketing adage: 'People don't want to buy a quarter-inch drill. They want a quarter-inch hole.'[1] That is, what exactly is your client trying to achieve in any given situation? And remember Barack Obama's sage advice: 'Let me take care of that', which you will encounter later in this chapter. They want you to be practical, to understand their business, to use plain English as far as possible, and to adhere to any agreed 'deliverable' format. They will come to value your experience and wisdom, even if at first it runs counter to their preferred outcome.

9. **Be responsive.** Let your clients know you have received communications from them and that you are on the case. Set yourself a turnaround goal that works for you. Same day? 24 hours? 48 hours?

10. **Be on time.** For meetings, teleconferences, coffee, lunch — everything, really.

11. **Be human and let your humility show.** Be emotionally intelligent and remember that even though you may be contracting with a large corporation, at the end of the day you are dealing with human beings with their own emotional needs and issues. Display your (genuine) humility. Don't pride yourself on sounding intelligent — pride yourself on being intelligible. Don't use big, complicated words. Keep your words, thoughts and ideas as

simple as possible. As Albert Einstein is alleged to have said, 'Everything should be made as simple as possible, but not simpler.'[2]

12. **Be respectful and caring**. Yes, this is part of being human. Don't condescend. Keep any inner sense of professional superiority well hidden.

13. **Have fun**. Yes, this is also part of being human. All else being equal, a client will always instruct an adviser who is interesting and fun to be with over one who is dull.

14. **Be truthful**. About everything. Not only is this the right thing to do, but a client will figure out very quickly any lack of integrity, and you will very soon have an ex-client.

15. **Don't be the cause of adverse surprises**. Clients really hate such surprises, whether on technical/judgement calls, billing or anything else.

16. **Provide value for money and free stuff**. The fees you charge will be a function of many factors, including what you glean to be your client's perception of value. This can differ wildly from client to client and matter to matter. Clients may take a holistic view on how they assess value, including their perception of the relationship and what you do for them beyond what is fee-paying work. Everyone loves free stuff or, more politely, 'value-added services'. The bigger and more important a client, the more free stuff they should get. This may take the form of newsletters, training sessions or brainstorming workshops. For some clients you may be obliged to provide free stuff under some over-engineered procurement contract you grudgingly signed. Ask your clients what free stuff they are offered (and what they accept!) from your competitors.

17. **Build relationships**. Ask yourself regularly: How can I improve my relationship with this client? What is your approach to catch-ups, calls, emails and entertaining, especially when you have no current instructions? This is vital to show you care and to build relationships, and it will vary between clients depending on their preferences.

18. **Seek feedback**. Okay, not every day, but come up with a system to check in with clients on a regular basis. Sometimes you will want someone else in your organisation to do this, to make sure comments on your service, value and relationships are full and frank. Don't be defensive when you seek feedback (see the tips on feedback in chapter 9).

19. **Ask for testimonials and referrals.** For some reason, Australian professionals generally seem more reluctant than their American counterparts to ask clients for testimonials and referrals. If you have a good relationship, most clients will be only too happy to help.

Former clients

20. **Learn from your mistakes.** Okay, it happens — sometimes you lose a client. If you are not sure why, try to get someone (maybe not you) to find out what happened. At least you can try to avoid making the same mistake(s) with other clients.

21. **Keep in touch.** Clients often become ex-clients for reasons that are no fault of the adviser. They may have been retrenched when their organisation was going through a tough patch or as the result of an acquisition or other corporate activity. Keep in touch. Let them know you care. They may become a client again sometime when they land a job in another organisation.

We will return to client needs in chapter 8. Gaining clarity on what your clients want, and why they are paying you, is how you determine your Prime Capabilities.

Clients of professional service firms

Gosh, where to start. Clients, not unreasonably, want a lot of things. To recap, clients want you to act with integrity and to treat them fairly in all matters including billing arrangements. They want you to tell the truth and they generally don't like (adverse) surprises. Clients expect you to be extremely competent, meet agreed deadlines and other commitments, and be constantly innovative. They want you to be solution focused, in other words to go beyond pointing out problems. Clients want you to stand by your advice and opinions. They want to tap into your experience, insights, wisdom and judgement. Your clients want you to care about them, and they all want great service and value for money. In short, they want you to behave like the true professional we discussed in chapter 1. You already know these things.

Clients are human beings, part of but distinct from the organisations that employ them, and they want to be treated with respect. You might be thinking, of course they do. Why wasn't this listed along with the other obvious things? The reason is that surprising numbers of professionals disrespect their clients in countless ways. You disrespect your client if you flaunt your knowledge or perceived wisdom in a manner that treats the client as other than an equal. You disrespect your client if you lack humility. You disrespect your client if you do not meet agreed deadlines and other commitments without contacting them to discuss the situation. You disrespect your client if you take the limelight and do not help them look good within their organisation. There are endless other easy ways to disrespect your clients. Try to avoid them.

Treating people with consistent respect is the most basic requirement for any meaningful relationship. Not all clients will necessarily want to develop an ongoing relationship with you. Maybe they view their experience with you as a one-off transaction and they do not want to invest the time and effort involved in getting to know you and in helping you to get to know them and their business. As a true professional, you know such clients still deserve your respect.

Most clients *do* want you to know their business, their industry and the issues they are facing, beyond what you happen to be advising them on at a given time. At a practical level, you will make a super-dull companion at client social events if all you care about and can discuss are the technical intricacies of your latest client opinion. When you truly know a client, their business and issues, and industry issues and jargon, you become almost like a part of their organisation. Part of their corporate family. This is your goal. The more you know, the more likely it is the client will trust you, which means it will be easier and quicker for them to brief you on new matters. You want this trust. As Australian professional services sector guru George Beaton says, 'Trust in professional services has been described by some as the "new oil". Meaning trust is surpassing expertise as reason to buy/use a particular provider.'[3] You will also come to know instinctively and exactly how to set out and word your deliverables to be most useful for your client.

If your client deliverable is a written advice or opinion, you need to provide this advice or opinion in plain English. Do not hide your conclusions in mumbo jumbo, assumptions, caveats, disclaimers or weasel words. Tax lawyers are allowed a limited amount of technical gibberish, provided it is buried somewhere, say in an appendix.

Your clients will want you to be easy to do business with. This starts when you sign them up. Don't start out with a lengthy, tortuous engagement letter or a list of hoops they'll need to jump through.

What clients hate, apart from your changing your mind on an important issue midway through or missing critical deadlines, is billing surprises. Apart from agreeing upfront how potential cost overruns will be dealt with, prompt communication and discussion is the key. Pick up the phone (don't just send an email) as soon as a billing issue seems likely.

It is also important to remember that if a client organisation has an internal procurement team, the members of that team are also human beings with feelings who want to be treated with respect. There was a time when advisers would negotiate all aspects of an assignment, including hourly rates and other pricing arrangements, directly with the person requesting the service. More recently some buyers of substantial volumes of professional services decided they could achieve better value by hiring procurement professionals to mediate and negotiate pricing and other contractual terms with external advisers. Often this would lead to increasingly complex processes, lots of forms and hoop jumping to get on a panel, or even for a single modestly sized engagement.

Procurement teams might demand all manner of value-added (aka free) services and play hardball on pricing. External advisers may secretly hope the earth might open up and swallow them all, but procurement teams are now a fact of professional life, and respect and courtesy still matter and will still be rewarded. In something reminiscent of a nuclear arms race, some large PSFs now have their own specialist contracting experts who negotiate with client procurement teams.

Clients of in-house professionals

In-house professionals include, among others, lawyers, accountants and finance personnel. Their client is also their employer and, unlike PSF professionals, they are embedded in the corporate family, and of course need to understand it completely. That is, an employer of in-house professionals will expect them, not unreasonably, to have a broader and deeper understanding of the organisation's business, strategy and risk appetite than would be found in external, PSF professionals servicing that organisation.

Clients of in-house professionals will generally want at least the same things as clients of PSFs, although professionals working in PSFs often have clients working in the same profession, in an in-house capacity. In such cases, the external professionals may have the luxury of producing written work and presentations that can be highly technical in nature and sometimes lengthy. In-house professionals never have that luxury. Their clients will typically be busy, time-poor business executives, or other in-house professionals, but their profession will be different. Either way, in-house professionals need to provide advice that is brief, to the point and written in clear English. No technical gobbledygook.

In-house professionals need to have an *extremely* good grasp of the business(es) of their organisation, including various operating models and risk profiles. Apart from adjusting quickly to providing brief, clear advice, a PSF-bred professional who takes on an in-house role needs to fully understand their organisation's attitude to risk. If the organisation is prepared to tolerate relatively high levels of risk, the newbie in-house adviser may at times face dilemmas. They must ensure decision makers are aware of risks, while protecting their own integrity and values. In other words, they will want to avoid a reputation for being risk-averse while at once guiding their organisation away from making poor decisions, and keeping their job.

Another critical skill for in-house professionals is to gain the confidence and respect not only of their immediate superiors and the organisation's executive committee but also of the organisation's board of directors. For some in-house professionals, especially those who are less experienced, appearing before their organisation's board can be nerve-racking. For others, especially senior, seasoned general counsel, the experience is a highlight of the job. Not only is it an opportunity to showcase their own expertise but it also allows the board to see the value of their in-house team. If you are an in-house professional who is not comfortable in the boardroom, seek out mentors or a coach to help you develop your skills in presenting to directors with confidence, clarity and brevity.

As with external professionals, in-house professionals need to be highly attuned to what their clients really want in any given situation. Depending on the circumstance and the ultimate decision maker, the deliverable may include: solutions, options, alternatives, recommendations, best/worst case analyses and scenario-modelling.

Let me take care of that

When LinkedIn editor-in-chief Daniel Roth interviewed former United States President Barack Obama on various aspects of working life, Obama said he had worked with people who were very good at describing problems and people who were very good at analysing why something went wrong or why something couldn't be fixed. 'But,' he added, 'what I'm always looking for is, no matter how small the problem or how big it is, somebody who says, "Let me take care of that."'[4]

As Obama said, if you project an attitude that you can handle the problem, you will stand out. 'People will notice. "That's somebody who can get something done."'

I think Obama nailed it when it comes to professional service and client expectations. Nothing is more reassuring to a client than a professional who can confidently say, let me take care of that.

Clients are *not* always right

With any luck, most of your clients will be reasonable to deal with most of the time.[5] However, sometimes some clients may misbehave. There are any number of things that can go off the rails with clients, but here are just three to watch out for, whether you work in a PSF or in-house.

An unethical (or worse) client

First, and most seriously, a client may want you to behave in a way that is unethical or even outright criminal. As a professional, at the first inkling of unethical client behaviour, you should report the conduct to relevant, more senior professionals in your organisation. If they don't take appropriate action within a reasonable time, you face a major dilemma. If you do nothing, your silence may not only taint your reputation but land you in hot water with professional bodies or regulators. Your inaction may implicate you. You will need to decide whether to escalate your concerns within your organisation, become a whistleblower or resign. Consult with people you know and trust inside and outside your organisation before making your decision. This is when having one or more mentors (see chapter 9) can be invaluable. Of course, you will face the same difficult choices if the unethical behaviour is occurring within your organisation.

A dysfunctional client

A client may be ethical but dysfunctional. For example, you may receive conflicting instructions from different individuals within the client organisation or they may fail to respond to your requests for information so you cannot meet their deadlines. Again, you should promptly seek advice from more senior professionals in your organisation.

A plain old nasty client

A client may be more or less ethical and functional yet still be difficult and unreasonable. Client staff may be rude, aggressive or overly demanding, or they may complain constantly about your organisation's services or the size of your fees. Once again, report the behaviour up the line. Chances are other professionals in your organisation are being treated similarly. If not, you will need to reflect on your own behaviour and talk to more senior people in your organisation. Maybe, you're the problem, to paraphrase Taylor Swift.[6] But if client personnel are behaving poorly to other professionals in your workplace, then the client is likely to be the problem.

You shouldn't have to put up with badly behaving clients. Your choices are a variation on those that arise when a client acts unethically. First raise your concerns with more senior professionals assigned to that client, with escalation as appropriate. Ideally, the relevant senior professional (perhaps a PSF partner or an in-house general counsel) will talk with appropriate client staff to put an end to the behaviour. Sadly, this may not always happen because the senior professionals are either conflict-averse or they worry about client blowback, including the loss of work and fees in the case of PSFs. If this is the case, ask to be taken off the client. If that doesn't happen within a reasonable timeframe, resign and find an organisation that is better at looking after its staff.

Working on the best clients and best matters

If you are a reasonably ambitious professional, you will want to work for the 'best' clients and on the 'best' type of work that your organisation can offer. Of course, you will face plenty of competition, so what to do? If you work as an in-house professional, you will not have much choice so this discussion is directed mainly at professionals working in PSFs.

In a typical PSF there are many issues at play in getting the best work with the best clients. Most PSFs will offer a range of services or types of products. Larger PSFs are generally organised in groups or divisions that specialise in providing particular types of services and products. Young professionals, especially entry-level graduates, may not initially have much choice about which division or group they are assigned to. In some PSFs, new hires may be rotated through various teams in their first year or two before they settle in one. Here are the best tactics for ending up in the team of your choice:

- In each group, meet and befriend as many people as possible, especially the mid-level professionals who are the ones allocating work to you. This is because they will be asked for feedback by the most senior professionals in the group on who are the pick graduates to obtain after the rotations. Try to keep in touch with those mid-level professionals as you are rotated through other groups.

- Once you have developed a reasonable relationship with the mid-level professionals in your preferred group, ask them for advice and any unwritten rules in that PSF that will help you land in the team of your choice.

- Be hard-working, cheerful and user-friendly in *each* rotation. Don't give the impression that you are not interested in the work and clients of any given team. This never goes down well.

- Remember and employ Barack Obama's advice: say to the people who are giving you work, 'let me take care of that'. And make sure you really do take care of it.

- Meet agreed deadlines or signal well in advance if you are unable to do so, and why.

- Seek out and act on feedback and advice: see Accelerant # 2 in chapter 9.

Ideally you have landed in a group which does the sort of work you would like to do at this stage of your career. The next step is figuring out the best clients to work on in that team. Over time, your goal is to learn and grow as you gravitate to good clients for whom you can do quality work, and not to be taken advantage of by either clients or other professionals in your organisation. Here are some things to think about:

- Your natural reaction may be to seek work on big-name clients, which is to say well-known companies, household names. But ask yourself, is this just so you can name drop and satisfy your ego? Are these really the best clients for you at this stage of your career?

- If you are curious and ask good questions, it won't take very long to work out from other professionals in your group which are the desirable clients to work on, whether they are big names or not. Issues like these are important:

  - Just because a client is a big name, it doesn't necessarily mean the type of work they give your firm is interesting. Find out.

  - How reasonable are the people in any given client? Are they excessively demanding? Do they stipulate impossible deadlines? Are they never satisfied? Do they always complain about fees?

  - What about the more senior professionals in your firm who are already working on that client? What are their reputations for coaching, mentoring and generally looking after young professionals, especially if the client is difficult?

Of course, you may have little choice on which clients you are allocated, especially when you are at the bottom of the professional food chain. To give yourself the best chance of being staffed on your desired clients in the fullness of time, put yourself in the shoes of the more senior professionals in your firm who choose which more junior professionals get delegated what types of work and on which clients. Here are some issues to think about:

- The golden rule for how clients and work are allocated in PSFs: it all depends on your reputation and your relationships with the people who make the allocation decisions.
- Do you have good relationships with these people? Do they know you, trust you, respect you? Do they think you like, trust and respect *them*? Does a good reputation precede you?
- Have you demonstrated your competence and commitment to those decision makers?
- In most PSFs, it is okay to ask to work on certain clients and particular types of work. Again, be curious and ask good questions of other professionals on the best way to go about this in your firm.

How to find out what your clients want

Whether you work in a PSF or are employed in-house, you need to ask your clients from time to time what they want from you as an adviser. It is that simple, and yet not always that simple. There are any number of things you can discuss with a client, including relationships, lines of communication, structure and clarity of advice, degree of proactivity, or feedback on recent assignments or new team members. To get a client talking, ask open-ended questions. Be prepared for frank replies!

You can quiz your clients on-the-go as assignments progress informally over coffee or lunch. You can run a survey[7] or a formal interview. You can do this yourself or pay a consultant. The best way is to do it yourself: this is what your clients will expect and appreciate most. 'You' may not, of course, refer directly to the professionals working on the client in question. Informal discussions might be undertaken by professionals engaged on the relevant client, but for more formal and less regular client listening or feedback discussions, there is merit in having some degree of independence from the engagement team, to allow and encourage the client to speak frankly.

PSFs, ideally, should send a partner (not the client engagement partner) to the client briefing. For very important clients, it should be the managing partner. Business development professionals could and should attend such meetings, but in a support role to a partner. Do not over-engineer the client feedback process. Keep any questionnaire/survey, especially if sent in advance, to an absolute minimum. It is all about the conversation with the client and encouraging them to speak their minds freely, especially about relevant relationships.

Some professionals find all sorts of reasons for *not* directly asking their clients what they expect from them as advisers. Perhaps some PSF-based professionals fear this will create an opportunity for the client to try to negotiate fee discounts. Maybe, maybe not. Either way, you need the feedback. Other professionals may fear bad news about quality of work or relationships. Again, either way you still need the feedback. In fact, you need to seek feedback from dissatisfied clients to stop them becoming ex-clients. In the words of Bill Gates, 'Your most unhappy customers are your greatest source of learning.'[8]

Some professionals may take the view that it is wrong to hassle clients and to waste their time seeking feedback for the adviser's benefit. Provided you go about the listening process the right way, and don't over-cook it, most clients will be ready and willing to provide feedback. Your competitors will be trying to meet with your clients to ask them whether they are being properly serviced by your firm. You would be crazy not to hear the feedback your clients are sharing with your competitors.

A younger professional working in a PSF should take their lead from more senior members of the firm on when and how to solicit feedback from clients. If this doesn't seem to happen in your firm, or if it happens infrequently or in ways that are unsatisfactory, try to work up the courage to raise the subject diplomatically. Done well, this should be a career-enhancing rather than a career-limiting move.

Another good way for PSFs to get feedback from clients is to enter recognised competitions designed to solicit insights from the marketplace at large. In my first career, I was a big fan of the annual Client Choice Awards organised by the Beaton Research + Consulting group. My firm, Greenwoods & Herbert Smith Freehills, entered these Awards each year and did pretty well. Entrants can subscribe to a Beaton Benchmarks report to see how the market perceives their brand and client service performance, and to see how they compare with their competitors.[9]

What will clients want in the future?

At a fundamental level, your clients will want what they have always wanted: valuable advice that solves their problems and satisfies their needs provided by professionals they trust and respect. I would be surprised if this or the analysis set out in this chapter were to change hugely in the future.

However, as the Fourth Industrial Revolution takes off there are likely to be huge changes in *what* clients ask you to do, *how* they ask you and *interact* with you, and *how often* they do so. AI and other aspects of technology will be key to this. As machines get smarter clients not unreasonably will expect you to use the latest and greatest technology when you service them. This is because machines will do some (not all) things better, faster and much more cheaply than humans.

In a sobering analysis directed at lawyers in the United States but relevant to professionals worldwide, Dennis Horn and Ira Meislik, in their 2018 paper 'How to Ride the Coming Tidal Wave of Technology and Competition'[10], noted that at least these four trends will affect the legal landscape severely in the future:

- **Online information**. Clients with access to legal information through the internet will translate into less market power for the legal industry.

- **Competition**. Clients will increasingly have access to alternative sources for their legal needs, such as accounting firms, in-house lawyers, overseas legal research providers and internet-based legal talent.

- **Disaggregation**. Clients are disaggregating and will continue to disaggregate their legal needs, especially for complex litigation and due diligence, using technology for discovery, thus reducing the legal hours required for those tasks. You and your firm may only do 'bits' of an overall project if the client can get other pieces done more cheaply by means of technology and/or by humans in cheaper locations. Cost is important.

- **Cost pressures**. As clients seek lower and more predictable legal costs they are increasingly revolting against straight hourly billing.

Even if you are not a lawyer based in the United States, does this sound familiar to you? Trends like these will have an impact on the needs clients will have in the future and how you will service those needs.

Horn and Meislik suggest four broad courses of action for lawyers planning to set themselves up for success in the changing legal environment. These ideas make a lot of sense to me, and I think they would be useful for any professional anywhere to consider and reflect on. If you are not a lawyer, then whenever the word 'lawyer' appears, think about the suggestion from the perspective of your own profession.

1. **Adapt**. Success will require a strategic focus on the firm's core practices and an expansion of its client base. Those lawyers

who now primarily provide commodity advice and products will need to adapt and produce those products and deliver that advice in a very efficient manner, price-wise and cost-wise, or expand their offerings to include bespoke products for which clients are willing to pay.

2. **Acquire new skills**. For lawyers, legal knowledge will not be sufficient. They will need an ability and willingness to understand and harness the power of existing and emerging technology. To take advantage of the expanded disaggregation of legal services, lawyers will need to manage a legal supply chain and to use both law and technology to solve their clients' problems.

3. **Understand clients' needs**. For firms of all sizes, in the future the 'real money' will go to lawyers who know their clients' needs and how to market themselves. Intelligence and knowledge of the law will be no more than the table stakes a lawyer needs to get into the game. Rainmakers and problem solvers will continue to prosper, but the tools they need to succeed will increasingly include technology, organisational and communications skills.

4. **Satisfy client demands**. The customer is always and will always be right. If clients demand different billing models or the use of technology to perform certain tasks, successful lawyers will honour those demands. Lawyers who satisfy their clients' changing needs will thrive despite the disruptive forces bearing down on the industry.

A note of caution on Horn and Meislik's statement that the 'customer is always right'. As I have made clear in this chapter, clients are *not* always right, especially when it comes to ethical and behavioural issues.

In case you are thinking that Horn and Meislik's 2018 paper may be outdated, its key observations were echoed in a very interesting document released by Westpac Banking Corporation in conjunction with Beaton Research + Consulting in October 2024, 'How AI is Changing Client Relationships'.[11] The report foresees that 'as technology takes over more low-value tasks, higher value will be placed on problem-solving and human interactions that require emotional intelligence. Communicating with clients, and building long-term client relationships through empathy, will be the most crucial skills for professionals to develop.'

As we will see in chapter 8, these themes are reflected in how professionals should go about establishing their Prime Capabilities and Enablers.

In play

Looking back on my first career, and as I service clients in my second career, I have increasingly tried to be responsive. One of the things that drives most clients crazy is advisers who not only miss deadlines but don't advise the client *in advance*. Always meeting deadlines, and explaining any occasional blips beforehand, seems kind of obvious, but it is amazing how many professionals just don't understand this. Yet there is much more to responsiveness than being on time. When a client sends you something by email, let them know as soon as you can (always within 24 hours) that you have received it and are on the case. Also, take the time to read and respond clearly to questions the client may have raised in their email which are capable of a quick response. In client meetings, and especially at business development–type lunches and coffees, I would often promise to do something or provide something to an existing or potential client. Ideally, I would write down my commitments straight away or immediately afterwards I would make a note in writing that would ensure action and follow-up.

Early in my first career I worked in-house in Westpac's Group Taxation Department. My previous position had been with Price Waterhouse, which meant I found it easy to treat people in the business units as clients who needed advice and help. What took me longer to master was the need not only to ensure I wrote in plain English but to be brief in written correspondence. As anyone who has ever worked with me would attest, brevity is not one of my strong suits! But my boss, John Brodie, Head of Group Taxation at Westpac, provided some quick and courteous feedback on my writing style.

Late in my first career, I became particularly obsessive about being on time for meetings, especially those involving clients. If I had a client meeting at, say, 10 am, I adopted the practice of being at reception on the client floor just before 10 to wait for my client. If I had to wait a few minutes because the client was late, I figured this was better than the client turning up on time, perhaps having to queue at reception and then wait while I was found and made my way to the client floor. Unsurprisingly, clients loved this attentiveness.

I realised early on that like most people, clients love free stuff, provided it is useful, relevant and not just dressed-up marketing material. Accordingly, I spent a lot of time over the years not just contributing to regular firm newsletters on the latest tax developments but creating and sending more tailored and targeted material to individual clients, as well as providing update seminars and client-specific workshops. If clients don't always send you immediate return emails thanking you for such efforts, do not be surprised. However, it is a good idea to check in with clients occasionally when you chat to them to see if your business-development initiatives are hitting the mark. Ask them how they can be improved and what other topics they would like addressed in your missives and meetings.

In my second career as an executive coach, mentor and leadership consultant I have created a service code that I give to new clients.

My client service code

I greatly value the opportunity to be of assistance to my clients, whether through coaching, mentoring, facilitation, training or consulting or in any other manner.

In order that my service to my clients is always at the highest level, I am committed to the following standards:

1. **Respect.** I will always treat you with the highest respect. At times, as your coach/mentor, as well as supporting you, I may need to challenge your thinking. I will always do this with your best interests in mind!

2. **Ethics and integrity.** I will always act in your interest and with the highest of integrity, being mindful of, and in compliance with, the Codes of Ethics of the various industry and professional associations of which I am a member.

3. **Professionalism and competence.** I will always serve you to the best of my ability and with the highest level of professionalism and competence. If you ask me to coach/mentor/assist you on a subject outside of my experience and expertise, I will let you know. I will always be fully prepared, as appropriate, for our coaching/mentoring sessions.

4. **Commitments and timeliness.** I will do what I say I will — on time. I will meet any agreed timelines and deadlines.

5. **Communications.** I will acknowledge emails, phone calls and texts at the earliest opportunity, and within 24 hours.

This is *my* client service code. It is not a universal code that everyone should follow. Think about creating one for your clients that resonates with you and that you think will make you stand out in your marketplace. Tell them they can and should hold you accountable in the event that you don't live up to your commitments. Very few professionals ever think to create a simple code that lets clients know what they can expect of their advisers, and yours will be seriously impressed.

Key takeaways

- **Ask clients what they want.** Yes, it is that simple, at least in theory. Different clients want different things. You and/or senior professionals in your organisation should do the asking, rather than delegating the job to internal business development people or external consultants.

- **Clients of professional service firms.** They want lots of things, including always being treated with respect. There are many ways you can unwittingly disrespect your clients.

- **Clients of in-house professionals.** They too want lots of things, including respect. This includes your displaying good business acumen and understanding your organisation's business *very* well. They want you to communicate clearly and in plain English, and they want you to meet deadlines.

- **Client service charter.** If you don't already have a charter, think about creating one.

- **'Let me take care of that'.** Be inspired by former US President Barack Obama.

- **Clients are not always right.** You and your organisation need strategies to deal with clients whose behaviour falls into one or more of these categories:
  - ✓ unethical (or worse)
  - ✓ dysfunctional
  - ✓ plain old nasty.

- **Working on the best clients and best matters.** If you work in-house, you may not have much choice. If you work in a PSF, put yourself in the shoes of the more senior professionals in your firm who choose which more junior professionals get delegated to what types of work and on which clients. Do you have a good reputation and good relationships with these people? Do they know you, trust you, respect you? Do they think you like, trust and respect *them*? Do they think *you* are competent? Does a good reputation precede you?

- **Which clients would you prefer, if you could engineer some choice?** Your natural reaction may be to seek work on big-name clients — well-known companies, household names. But is this just about your ego? Are these really the best clients for you at this stage in your career?

- **What will clients want in the future?** At a fundamental level, your clients will want what they have always wanted: valuable advice that solves their problems and satisfies their needs, provided by professionals they trust and respect. That's the easy bit. These are just four trends that will affect your professional landscape in the future, if not right now:
  - ✓ online information
  - ✓ competition
  - ✓ disaggregation
  - ✓ cost pressures.
- **What to do to satisfy client demands in an ever-changing world.** You and your organisation need to do at least the following things on a continuing basis:
  - ✓ adapt
  - ✓ acquire new skills
  - ✓ understand clients' needs
  - ✓ satisfy client demands.
- **What if you don't do the above?** Maybe you will end up having a short career as a professional adviser.

Chapter 4

What employers want (and should do)

Maybe your employer wants you to be: accountable, adaptable (of course), agile, authentic, caring, client-focused, collegial, confident, consistent, creative, culturally sensitive, curious, digitally savvy, diligent, efficient, emotionally intelligent, energetic, flexible, friendly, hard-working, honest, humble, inclusive, innovative, intelligent, numerate (even if you are a lawyer), proactive, productive[1] (especially if you are a lawyer), relationship-focused, reliable, resilient, respectful, responsible, solution-focused, technically excellent (yes, this still matters), tolerant and trustworthy. They may also want you to have great judgement, business acumen and excellent business-development abilities, and a range of skills that include communication, conflict resolution, continuous learning, critical thinking, design thinking, interpersonal, lateral thinking, leadership, management, negotiation, presentation, time management and writing skills. And preferably you won't pester them with promotion prospects and pay ambitions. Whew.

Despite this chapter's title, I am not going to say much more about what employers *want*. They all want slightly different things, probably including a bunch of the qualities and skills listed. Your task as an employed professional, whether you are in a current job or looking for a new one, is to figure out what really matters to your current or prospective boss. This means more than checking out websites and glossy promotional publications. As I've suggested earlier, there are often unwritten rules around what counts and how to get ahead in most workplaces. You only find out what they are by asking pertinent questions, listening carefully and reading between the lines.

Because I am hoping that the odd (so to speak) employer might read this book, as well as employed professionals, the rest of this chapter is devoted to how employers *should* be behaving towards their staff members. These comments are directed towards professional service firms as well as organisations that hire in-house professionals. In the Introduction, the third of the modest goals I set for this book was that it would start a global revolution for better management of employed professionals.

Some things employers should be doing are super obvious and shouldn't really need recounting, but I will mention a few of them anyway. Come the revolution, they will do more inspiring and coaching and less managing. They will foster an inclusive workplace culture, provide a psychologically safe[2] work environment that has zero tolerance for bullying and sexual harassment, counteracts all manner of conscious and unconscious biases, does not overwork employees and pays them properly. They will treat everyone with courtesy, care and respect.

In recent times it has become a real thing for employers to focus on employee 'wellbeing'. And don't get me wrong, this is a great idea. However, in at least some cases, it has seemed as though wellbeing development has been outsourced to the employee. Some organisations invest in providing training in mindfulness, meditation and various positive psychology interventions[3] apparently in the hope that such initiatives alone will result in happier, more resilient staff who are less likely to burn out. If only it were that simple. A 2024 Oxford University research project involving 46 336 workers from 233 organisations in the United Kingdom found employer-sponsored wellbeing 'interventions', such as resilience training, mindfulness and wellbeing apps, saw no improvement in employee wellbeing.[4]

Rather than, or ideally as well as, fostering individual mindfulness, it would be better if employers were to implement mindfulness at a team level. And yes, this will include leaders and managers themselves getting their heads around some core principles of mindfulness rather than delegating the task to human resources, learning and development departments and to employees. A practical place to start thinking about this is this 2020 *HBR* article, 'Why Your Team Should Practice Collective Mindfulness'.[5]

Employers can help employees achieve greater levels of wellbeing and resilience and lower levels of burnout by fostering an inclusive workplace culture, providing a psychologically safe work environment, showing zero tolerance for bullying and sexual harassment, ferreting out and counteracting all manner of conscious and unconscious biases, and ensuring employees are not overworked, are paid properly and are treated with courtesy, care and respect. There would be less need for specific wellbeing programs because wellbeing would be incorporated into everyday interactions within an organisation, especially those between the employee and their immediate boss.

Employee engagement

I admire the Gallup organisation and in particular the various workplace surveys and reports it produces. In its 2023 *State of the Global Workplace Report*[6], Gallup found that only 23 per cent of employees worldwide are 'engaged' in their jobs. An engaged employee finds their work meaningful and feels connected to the team and their organisation. They are proud of the work they do and take ownership of their performance, going the extra mile for teammates and customers. Workers in Australia and New Zealand were bang on the global average of 23 percent. Europe's engagement level was a desultory 13 per cent, the lowest of any regional area, while the level in the United States and Canada was 31 per cent.

When Gallup released its 2022 *State of the Global Workplace Report*, it noted that improving the lived experience of employees in workplaces should not be 'rocket science', but:

> ... the world is closer to colonizing Mars than it is to fixing the world's broken workplaces. The real fix is this simple: better leaders in the workplace. Managers need to be better listeners, coaches and collaborators. ... In environments like this, workers thrive.[7]

In short, if you are not feeling engaged at work, if you feel you are not developing and being suitably challenged, the problem may lie more with your current employer's mismanagement and underdevelopment than with you as an employee.

A core function of any employer, and every leader and manager, is to understand how best to engage their employees. They need to formulate and implement appropriate actions rather than leave resolutions to gather dust in a planning document after yet another online pulse survey has been inflicted on overworked staff members.

Gallup has found that there are five primary drivers of employee engagement:

1. *A caring manager who is a good coach* — one of Gallup's 'biggest discoveries' is that the manager or team leader alone accounts for 70 per cent of the variance in team engagement
2. *Purpose* — people want purpose and meaning from their work
3. *Ongoing conversations* — not just annual performance reviews
4. *Development* — the employer is invested in helping employees to learn and grow
5. *A focus on strengths* — helping employees to achieve mastery using their greatest skills.[8]

Gallup has also found that, unsurprisingly, there are different ways of best engaging with employees of different ages and generations, and especially with what they describe as younger workers.[9]

The bare minimum employers should do to engender engagement of employees of any age is to ensure they do not burn out. Once again, Gallup is helpful. I recommend employers review not just the sobering and compelling data Gallup has assembled on the reality of employee burnout but their useful and practical suggestions for preventing it.[10]

As well as being burnt out, employees are also not going to feel especially engaged if they don't feel respected by their immediate boss and other managers and leaders in their organisation. After significant research involving data collected from more than 4800 employees, renowned leadership consultants Jack Zenger and Joseph Folkman identified seven leader behaviours that led to the overall impression of respectful treatment of employees:

1. valuing diversity
2. staying in touch with individuals' issues and concerns
3. being trusted
4. resolving conflicts
5. balancing getting results with a concern for others
6. encouraging open discussion of problems and differences of opinion
7. giving honest feedback in a helpful way.[11]

As Zenger and Folkman say, great leaders are well respected in their organisations. However, more importantly, they take deliberate, thoughtful steps to show respect for their employees.

As we noted in chapter 3, treating clients with respect is a core requirement for any professional. The same goes for employers' treatment of employees.

Humility

One way for employers to ensure the respectful treatment of their employees (and clients and everyone else) is for employers to have an appropriate level of humility – one of the key characteristics of a true professional discussed in chapter 1. In 2022 I taught a subject called Law, Regulation & Ethics in the MBA program at the Australian Graduate School of Management at the University of New South Wales. I was privileged and lucky enough to interview for my class leading Australian businessman David Gonski AC, who was also the Chancellor of that university. I asked David what he judged to be the most important attributes of a leader. This is what he told my class:

The first thing a leader must have, an absolute must, is humility.
I have absolutely seen people destroyed, mainly men I have to say, by their inability to keep humble. They lost their humbleness and thought they could do incredible things. Vanity doesn't allow you to hear what's going on. It doesn't allow you to listen to what others are saying. It doesn't allow you to value people and the most important thing, if somebody is vain, it is so easy to win in any battle with them. I love tennis, and it is the same as not having a backhand. You just put the ball on the backhand side in any negotiation and a vain person falls for it every time.

Humility should be the default position for leaders. In some countries and cultures, humility may be seen as a sign of weakness and thus an undesirable trait for a leader. Do your homework very carefully before abandoning humility.

Performance reviews

Do those two words cause a knot in your stomach? If so, you are not alone. Australian-based company Culture Amp quotes research into employee experience that found that, 'according to benchmarks, performance management systems are, on average, more despised than cable companies, internet service providers, and health insurance plans'[12], though maybe less so than politicians, banks or Qantas. Gallup research finds that, in many organisations, traditional performance reviews may do more harm than good and that only 14 per cent of employees strongly agree reviews inspire them to improve.[13]

In recent years, there has been an international debate about whether employee performance reviews are a good idea, and if they are, how often they should be held and how they should be administered. It is beyond the scope of this book to wade into this murky area, other than to quote a key conclusion from recent (post COVID-19) research into performance management practices in Australian organisations conducted jointly by the Australian Human Resource Institute and the University of Sydney Business School[14], which concluded, 'Except for ongoing feedback, no practice — traditional or new — was rated as being particularly effective in improving employee performance.'

Bullseye. You should be getting lots of good-quality ongoing feedback from more senior professionals in your organisation.

If you are also the subject of formal, periodic performance reviews, they don't have to be as bad as going to the dentist. Here are some tips.

1. Get in the right frame of mind

Preparation is key. You may not have much control over when the session will be held, but do your best to have it held on a day and at a time that works for you. Try to block out 20 or 30 minutes before the appraisal meeting to get in a good head space. Do some breathing and, if they work for you, some mindfulness or meditation practice. The last thing you want to do is to rush from a stressful client meeting straight into a performance review. It would be better for you and your boss to reschedule.

2. Minimise adverse surprises

Seems pretty obvious right? Regular feedback sessions with the people you report to should minimise the risk of unexpected messages in a formal review.

3. Don't let your job goals, objectives and KPIs gather dust

Guess what? During your review meeting, your manager is likely to pull out a piece of paper, or point to something on a screen that says what you should have been doing since your last review. Ideally you have been actioning those goals, objectives and KPIs and have come prepared to discuss and negotiate those for the year ahead.

4. Come armed with evidence

Assume your boss will have data they really care about, such as your billable hours or other measures of your productivity. Keep a brief written record of your other achievements during the review period and present it to your manager, possibly ahead of the review meeting. If you have received praise from people in your organisation or clients, humility should not prevent you from making sure that your boss is aware of the feedback.

5. Get good at receiving feedback

This is one of the Seven Accelerants discussed in chapter 9. As we will see, having an open, non-defensive mindset when receiving feedback is critical. Also, thank your boss as sincerely as you can for any feedback you receive.

6. Ask for specific assistance if you need it

Senior professionals in some organisations see their role in providing performance feedback to more junior professionals as one-way traffic, especially when it comes to improvement. The person being reviewed is told they are not up to scratch in one or more areas and then instructed to go off and 'improve'. With any luck, you don't work in such an environment. If you do, think about and ask for any help you think your employer could and should reasonably provide. That might entail more coaching, mentoring or training, or maybe you would benefit from working on different types of assignments or clients and with a greater variety of more senior professionals.

7. Keep a balanced, written record of proceedings

Most organisations typically require key things discussed in performance review meetings, especially action items, to be documented and filed appropriately. In theory, the onus may be on your boss or someone from human resources to make this happen, with your review of and input into the document. In practice, people are busy, and this may not always happen. Make sure that the paperwork is completed. You want a clear record of the outcomes, especially if you received unsettling news and commitments were made by you and the organisation as to what will happen next.

8. Face-to-face really is best

It is very tempting in a post-COVID-19, work-from-anywhere world, for some bosses to try to conduct performance reviews online. This is generally a bad idea, even if nothing of a contentious nature is to be discussed. Review meetings are a vital part of the development of the relationship between you and your boss. Nothing is better for relationship building than all parties being in the same room.

Ongoing feedback

In the previous section I quoted recent research so important for employees and employers that it warrants repeating here: 'Except for ongoing feedback, no practice — traditional or new — was rated as being particularly effective in improving employee performance.' If you are an employer, the rest of this chapter, and chapter 9, especially the part on feedback and advice, are particularly important. There I refer to Douglas Stone and Sheila Heen's *Thanks for the Feedback: The Science and Art of Receiving Feedback Well*. Despite its title, this book includes an excellent guide on how to *give* feedback. It explains that feedback (ideally ongoing) takes three broad forms[15]:

1. appreciation (thanks)
2. coaching (a better way to do it[16])
3. evaluation (here's where you stand).

The type of feedback being given, sought or expected in any particular situation demands the giver and receiver of feedback be on the same wavelength.

Appreciation, praise and recognition are *really* powerful

In recent decades there has been much discussion in academia and elsewhere around whether and when employers should 'appreciate'[17], 'praise' or 'recognise' employees.[18] At a practical level, mix it up. Use them all as and when appropriate.

When it comes to the power and importance of giving praise, I can't do better than quote the wise words of Dr Bob Murray and Dr Alicia Fortinberry in *Leading the Future: The Human Science of Law Firm Strategy and Leadership*:

> *If we could instil one simple skill into a law firm to pack the biggest punch, it would be praise. More research has been done on the impact of this skill than on any other aspect of management.*

Organisations with a culture of praise are 25 per cent more productive, and profitable, than others. ... praise releases the powerful reward and motivational neurochemical dopamine. We often say, not totally in jest, that by using praise you can not only get people committed to you but literally addicted to you.[19]

Although Murray and Fortinberry refer to law firms, in my experience their observations hold true for all the types of organisations I have come across.

A few tips on doing praise well

- Praise should be provided as soon as feasible after the relevant behaviour or activity and not saved up until a formal performance review months down the track.
- It should be as specific as possible to what was achieved or attempted rather than blandly generic.
- Commendable efforts that fail still deserve praise.
- Whenever possible, deliver praise in person, face-to-face.
- Make sure you praise everyone involved in a team effort.

At the risk of stating the obvious, praise is misused when it is not genuine or, worse, when it is used to manipulate the recipient into acting. Don't misuse praise.

If employers need any more data on the power of appreciation, praise and recognition in the workplace, or tips on practical implementation measures, I highly recommend Gallup and Workhuman's two 2023 reports, *Empowering Workplace Culture Through Recognition*[20] and *From Praise to Profits: The Business Case for Recognition at Work.*[21]

Coaching

In 2019 Gallup published a book linked to their work on employee engagement. *It's the Manager*[22] is based on their largest global study on the future of work. A central proposition is that, 'if leaders were to prioritize one action, Gallup recommends that they equip their managers to become coaches'.

Happily, many enlightened organisations now follow Gallup's recommendation. However, one company's efforts stand out. When Google was still a relatively young and brash company, a research team had tried to prove that managers don't really matter[23], which is to say the quality of a manager has no bearing on team performance. Some of Google's early leaders and engineers had regarded managers as either a necessary evil or an unnecessary layer of bureaucracy. By looking at employee feedback and performance ratings data, the research team quickly discovered that managers really *did* matter. Teams with great managers were both happier and more productive. In 2008 Google set up Project Oxygen, a detailed data-driven analysis, to figure out what makes a manager 'great' at Google. The single most important behaviour of Google's best managers was being 'a good coach', followed by a series of behaviours linked to teamwork and communication skills. Some at Google had assumed that computer coding (technical) skills would come out on top of the list of behaviours of Google's best managers. However, being a good coach topped the list, with technical skills coming in at number eight.

If you are still not convinced, then how about this. One of the articles in the *Australian Financial Review*'s 70th anniversary magazine included an interview with Tim Cook, chief executive officer of Apple, one of the world's largest, most successful and most admired companies. The article reported Cook's 'philosophy of leadership is to be a good coach'.[24]

How can organisations help their leaders and managers to be more coach-like without requiring them to undertake a Master of Science in Coaching Psychology? When I undertook that degree at the University of Sydney, I was fortunate enough to be part of the last class taught by the remarkable Anthony Grant, the founder of the university's, and the world's, first Coaching Psychology Unit, before his passing in 2020. Grant and his colleagues produced a treasure-trove of very helpful, practical, evidence-based coaching-oriented materials.

One of my favourite papers by Grant is right on point when it comes to helping managers and bosses to become more coach-like: '*The third "generation" of workplace coaching: creating a culture of quality conversations*'.[25] At the time of writing, this paper is freely available online[26], and I would strongly advise anyone who is serious about creating a coaching culture in their workplace to read it. I particularly like his reference to 'quality conversations' and the fact that he highlights the importance of employee wellbeing being considered as part of coaching conversations.

As Grant explains, meaningful workplace coaching cannot be limited to annual or semi-annual performance reviews, if indeed an organisation still has them.[27] Much greater agility is needed. Grant suggests leaders and managers be trained to have quality coaching conversations, and he proposes the Quality Conversations Framework (see figure 4.1).

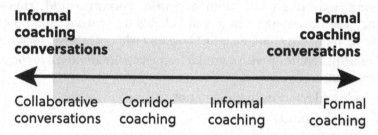

Figure 4.1 the Quality Conversations Framework

On the left of Grant's model are informal everyday 'collaborative conversations' that are part and parcel of organisational life. Next is 'corridor coaching', which involves short, three- to five-minute, on-the-run coaching opportunities that often occur in the workplace. They may arise before or after face-to-face or Zoom meetings or in transit between meetings. As Grant says, the key point is for the manager or leader to be able to recognise the coaching moment when it presents itself, ask the right questions and respond in a way that moves the conversation forward to an agreement on specific actions.

Next on the continuum are opportunities for unplanned, goal-focused informal coaching conversations of about 10 to 15 minutes. Perhaps a manager is in a meeting that has veered off course. Sensing the need to be more goal-focused, they might say something like, 'We have about 15 minutes left. What's the key thing we need to focus on?'

Having time-framed the conversation and set a specific goal, they could then use a common coaching model such as GROW (Goals, Reality, Options, Wrap-up) to guide the discussion. At the right end of the framework are the traditional planned 'formal coaching' sessions of, say, 30 minutes to an hour. Not every manager would utilise each approach with each team member. Instead, with training, the framework helps managers to identify different types of coaching opportunities and conversations that are fit for purpose for their employees and for their workplace. Grant explains:

> *The key principles underpinning this approach are simplicity, deep personalisation, and effectiveness. If we want to create genuine organisational or cultural change through workplace coaching, then the training methodology itself needs to be simple and accessible.*

Grant's article was written before COVID-19, and the notion of 'corridor coaching' may seem quaint in a hybrid working world. However, the increase in remote work has not changed the need for workplace coaching. What has changed is just how and when it is undertaken.

Gallup has come up with a similar framework it calls 'the five coaching conversations':

1. role and relationship orientation
2. quick connect
3. check-in
4. developmental coaching
5. progress reviews.[28]

Another excellent resource for a leader or manager is Michael Bungay Stanier's bestseller *The Coaching Habit*.[29] This book is framed around seven questions and some practical tools to help leaders and managers in their journey to becoming better coaches. Here are the seven questions:

1. The Kickstart question: What's on your mind?
2. The AWE question: And what else?
3. The Focus question: What's the real challenge here for you?
4. The Foundation question: What do you want?
5. The Lazy question: How can I help?
6. The Strategic question: If you're saying 'yes' to this, what are you saying 'no' to?
7. The Learning question: What was most useful for you?

Of course, as well as asking good questions, a leader or manager wishing to become more coach-like will need to ensure that their listening skills, and their ability to respond effectively to what they hear in response to the above seven questions, are up to scratch. Bungay Stanier's book can help here as well. It is very readable and well worth the investment of your time before you begin coaching your potentially bemused employees. Another terrific coaching book is Karen Stein's *Be Your Own Leadership Coach*.[30]

Artificial intelligence tools are already beginning to help time-poor managers to be better coaches, and this trend is likely to strengthen as the tools get better.[31]

We will return to coaching as a key component of 'deliberate practice', one of the Seven Accelerants discussed in chapter 9.

Mentoring

Mentoring is another of the Seven Accelerants in chapter 9, so I will be brief here. Wise professionals will seek out mentors from within and outside their organisation to maximise the breadth of their contacts and extend the perspectives they can access and tap into. As will be clear in the 'In play' section for this chapter, it is part of the employer's role to ensure employees have access to mentors within the organisation. The best resource I have come across on mentoring, for mentors, mentees and organisations, is *Make Mentoring Work*[32] by Peter Wilson, a leading Australian executive and previously the National President of the Australian Human Resources Institute (AHRI).

Artificial intelligence

Here are two key questions every professional should ask when searching for a job in the age of AI. First, has the prospective employer embraced investing in AI to make client service as efficient as possible? Second, is the organisation training professionals in the use of appropriate AI tools? Professionals should be wary of joining an organisation that cannot offer compelling and positive answers to these questions.

If you are the prospective employer trying to recruit the best and brightest young professionals into your organisation, how will you answer these two questions?

Curiosity, creativity and innovation

It should go without saying that curiosity is an important attribute in any field of human endeavour, but there has been an explosion of interest and research into curiosity by psychologists and social scientists in recent decades. Much of this has focused on the importance of curiosity in the workplace and its links to creativity and innovation.

This commentary in a 2023 academic research paper on curiosity echoes similar views in the business world:

Organizations nowadays are facing a complex environment with several challenges. Staying complacent has never been riskier since organizations and sectors undergo rapid changes ... Organizations that foster and encourage curiosity and focus on new ideas are better positioned to be creative.[33]

This paper sets out five areas organisations and leaders should be aware of when fostering an environment that encourages the curiosity, learning and growth that enable creativity:

1. **Training**. To encourage curiosity, employees must be able to access relevant training programs.

2. **Recruitment**. Select curious candidates because curiosity is contagious. Provided the organisational culture encourages it, curious newcomers will encourage greater levels of curiosity in their co-workers.

3. **Culture**. As you create a culture built on curiosity, analyse how the organisation's employees have been affected to date by elements such as fear, preconceptions, technology and their surroundings. Once individuals are aware of the things that have held them back, it becomes easier for them and their organisations to overcome those barriers and adopt a more curious mentality.

4. **The organisation as a whole**. Performance and creativity depend on curiosity at all levels as managers and their staff learn to respond with creative solutions to changing market circumstances. This is true for both creative and routine jobs in every sector.

5. **Mindfulness**. Employee mindfulness plays a key role in linking curiosity to employee creativity to create better outcomes. As we've discussed, mindfulness can be implemented at a team level. Developing humility in leaders is essential for employee mindfulness to be effective.

Joy and fun at work

There is a growing body of research that backs up the proposition that humour at work is a good thing. For example, in an *HBR* article Stanford researchers Jennifer Aaker and Naomi Bagdonas write:

When we laugh, our brains produce less cortisol (inducing calm and reducing stress) and release more endorphins (which give us something like a runner's high) and oxytocin (often called the 'love' hormone). It's like meditating, exercising, and having sex at the same time. Plus, it's HR-approved.[34]

How good is that?

But the power of humour is not limited to its impact on the individual. Emotions, good and not so good, are contagious. With the speed of a virulent COVID-19 variant, we spread our emotions to those around us and we pick up theirs, responding to behaviour, smiles, frowns and other facial and physiological reactions.[35]

Ask yourself these questions

Whether you are an employer or an employee, ask yourself these three questions *right now*:

- Am I adding to or detracting from the fun and joy my colleagues are experiencing in the workplace?
- How are they affecting my experience?
- What am I going to do about any suboptimal answers to the first two questions?

Purpose and meaning

In chapter 6, we will look at the role of purpose and meaning in work from the perspective of the individual professional. Recognition of the importance of a strong shared sense of purpose at an organisational level is growing. As we've seen, Gallup has found purpose to be one of the five key drivers of employee engagement. However, a global survey by *HBR* and the EY Beacon Institute found that, although there is near unanimity in the business community about the value of purpose in driving performance and staff retention, fewer than half the executives surveyed said their company had articulated a strong sense of purpose or used it to make decisions and strengthen motivation. Only a few companies appear to have so embedded purpose that they have reaped its full potential.[36]

A professional may want to work in an organisation whose purpose and values are aligned with those of the individual. Whether you are an employee or an employer, can you, right now and without resorting to a website, state the purpose and values of your organisation? Okay, if you must turn to a website, can you find those characteristics easily?

As Simon Sinek says in *Start with Why*, 'Profit isn't a purpose, it's a result. To have purpose means the things we do are of real value to others.'[37] Tim Cook, CEO of Apple, puts it this way: 'People are not looking to be told what to do; they're looking for inspiration, and they're looking to be part of something larger than themselves. They're looking for purpose.'[38]

In 2021 the US arm of PwC, one of the world's largest professional service firms, stated in its annual Purpose Report that its 'North Star' is 'to build trust in society and solve important problems'.[39] By and large, however, PSFs have lagged behind publicly listed corporations when it comes to clear statements of purpose. This is ironic given the plethora of surveys and reports that PSFs have produced over the years extolling the virtues of organisational purpose statements.

For leaders of PSFs looking to get their act together on the purpose front, a great place to start is *How to Lead a Values-Based Professional Services Firm* by Don Scales and Fran Biderman-Gross.[40]

Now, having said all this on 'purpose', as Stephen Friedman argues in a 2024 article in *HBR*, it may be 'Your Career Doesn't Need to Have a Purpose'.[41] He argues there is little actual evidence that a single, defined 'purpose' is necessary for a rewarding career. In fact, it's surprisingly common for people to go after what they think is their 'purpose', only to realise they hate it. Instead, he recommends shifting focus from 'purpose' to 'meaning', by asking questions like these:

- What do I like, prefer or enjoy doing? Let go of yearning for a career purpose.
- What am I good at?
- Would this role provide growth and learning I can use later?

So you don't *have* to have a 'purpose' or even seek 'meaning' in your work or your life more generally. If it isn't a big deal for you, that's fine.

Energising eight motivational factors

Beyond coaching and mentoring, purpose and meaning, employers seeking to attract and retain the services of the best young professionals would do well to understand and appeal to their motivational drivers.

What drives someone not only to join an organisation but to stay there, thrive and succeed? We will assume, perhaps heroically, that the employer fosters a great inclusive workplace culture, provides a psychologically safe work environment, has zero tolerance for bullying and sexual harassment, ferrets out and counteracts all manner of conscious and unconscious biases, doesn't overwork employees, pays them properly and treats everyone with courtesy, care and respect. And the employer avoids the kind of generational mindset that assumes Generation X, Gen Y or Gen Z employees have the same wants and needs. These are baseline or must-do factors but they are not enough. We need to get more personal.

If you are an employer, how do you ensure each of your employees feels a sense of purpose/meaning, autonomy, mastery, relatedness, status, certainty and fairness, and how do you ensure appropriate *feedback* is provided to each of them? At any given moment, each employee will have their own perceptions of how their employer is meeting each of their needs, but you are busy running a business and can't be constantly checking in let alone sorting out, say, real grievances from ambit claims. So, what to do?

One approach is to explicitly build the energising eight motivational factors, discussed in more detail in chapter 6, into various coaching conversations where appropriate and into employee goal-setting and performance management systems, processes and paperwork. Even organisations that no longer have formal annual appraisals are likely to document what is required of employees, whether in the form of specific goals or key performance indicators, as well as a welter of general policies and rules that employees must follow. What appears less common are employee-specific commitments by the employer. Yes, there may be an employee development plan, but too often these are unstructured, like afterthoughts from an appraisal meeting.

A concrete way to focus on the energising eight motivational factors would be to create a short statement of commitments on an employee-by-employee basis.

Mutual employer/employee commitments

The employer and employee each agree to concrete actions they will take to enhance each of the energising eight motivational factors*, where relevant to the specific circumstances of the employee. These commitments will be reviewed and renewed from time to time.

*The energising eight motivational factors are discussed in chapter 6.

Notes:

1. Not every factor may be important or relevant for any particular employee. If so, fine, just leave the boxes blank or delete them. This is not intended to be a 'box ticking' exercise. If an employee really doesn't care about one or more factors, then don't sit around creating unnecessary commitments.

2. By the same token, if an employee is highly motivated by some other factor not listed below (apart from money, which is a given) then add it into the mix.

	Employer commitments	Employee commitments
1. Purpose/meaning		
2. Autonomy		
3. Mastery**		
4. Relatedness/relationships		
5. Status		
6. Certainty		
7. Fairness		
8. Feedback		
Current Prime Capabilities		
Current Enablers		

**Mastery should include deliberate practice and on-the-job coaching (see chapter 9) of the relevant Prime Capabilities and Enablers discussed in chapter 8.

As we will see in chapter 8, professionals discover their Prime Capabilities and Enablers by quizzing their clients. Because this might seem a bit intimidating at first, more senior professionals, especially employer professionals, should offer guidance and support to their more junior colleagues.

A statement of commitments can be set up as a 'best endeavours' project based on mutual trust and respect rather than as something legally binding. It should be reviewed and updated from time to time. Of course, if the employer fails to live up to its commitments, employee engagement is likely to plummet. The idea is that the employer and the employee each make commitments. As an employee (and to radically misquote former US President John F Kennedy), ask not (only) what your employer can do for you but what you can do for yourself (okay, and for your employer). In terms of the feedback commitment, remember that this should include appreciation, praise and recognition, as well as areas for improvement, to paraphrase self-development pioneer Dale Carnegie.[42]

Is all this a bridge too far for your organisation at present? If so, here are six paths of change suggested by the originators of self-determination theory (discussed in chapter 6). Their research suggests these tips will help managers foster competence, relatedness and autonomy — and, as a result, employee motivation[43]:

1. Questions: ask open questions and seek employee involvement in problem solving.
2. Listening: actively listen and recognise employee viewpoints.
3. Choice: supply a menu of individual choices and responsibilities.
4. Feedback: furnish sincere, positive feedback (a constant theme throughout this book).
5. Controls: minimise coercive controls and go beyond financial rewards to motivate employees.
6. Development: share knowledge and provide employee development opportunities to foster autonomy and competence.

In play

My daughter Elizabeth was a nurse in a leading Sydney hospital when I was managing director of Greenwoods & Herbert Smith Freehills. One evening over dinner I asked her what active coaching and mentoring she was receiving in her job. Sadly, her answer made it clear there was plenty of room for improvement. Then it occurred to me to think about what I might hear if I were a fly on the wall in the dining room of one of my own staff members while they had a similar conversation. What would my employee say to their father or mother? Would I like their answer? And I began reflecting on the state of my firm's coaching and mentoring for its staff members.

After discussions with my fellow directors and some staff members, I concluded that our on-the-job coaching, while not perfect, was in reasonable shape, but the same could not be said of our mentoring efforts. There was no overarching program, so it was all a bit slapdash and uncoordinated. Some staff members, mainly on their own initiative, had mentors within the firm, but many did not. We did two things. First, we provided training in how to be a good mentor. For various reasons, not all directors became mentors. Second, we made sure that every staff member who wanted a mentor within the firm had one allocated. As far as practicable, staff were able to choose their own mentors.

I won't pretend that this revamped mentoring program was a total success. Not all directors and staff members took the program as seriously as I would have liked, and the ever-present demands of client work meant that well-intentioned and scheduled mentoring sessions did not always occur. Nonetheless I was proud of the system we had put in place and participated as a mentor to some of the firm's younger Associates. The enjoyment and reward I got from this led me into pro bono mentoring through professional bodies for young tax professionals working in other firms. This helped me to crystalise plans for my second career, including writing this book.

Looking back on my management and leadership style, I can see that I was not always cognisant of the importance of the energising eight motivational factors in my dealings with staff members and fellow partners and directors throughout my first career. No doubt some of them are reading these words, shaking their heads, and thinking that 'not always' is far too generous a description. On reflection, I had many failings on the *autonomy* front. Through most of my career, I was very keen to provide detailed instructions on how I wanted things done, which meant I didn't allow sufficient room for employee freedom of thought. Yes, okay, at times I was a micro-manager. It is no defence, but I didn't really appreciate the full importance in practice of all eight motivational factors until I undertook my Master of Science in Coaching Psychology. That knowledge came too late to be of use in my first career. Note to employers: do not make the mistakes I made.

And no, my firm never adopted anything like the suggested employer/employee statement of commitments set out earlier in this chapter. This is a case of do as I say, not as I did. If I had my time over in an organisational leadership role, this is something I would aspire to.

Key takeaways

- **What employers *want*.** They all want slightly different things. Ask questions and figure out what really matters to your current boss or prospective employer.

- **What employers *should do*.** They should foster an inclusive workplace culture, provide a psychologically safe work environment, show zero tolerance for bullying and sexual harassment, ferret out and counteract all manner of conscious and unconscious biases, not overwork employees, pay them properly, and treat everyone with courtesy, care and respect.

- **Performance reviews.** You should be getting good-quality ongoing feedback from more senior professionals in your organisation. If you are also the subject of formal, periodic performance reviews, make sure you prepare for them, ask for feedback and become skilled at receiving it well.

- **Ongoing feedback.** Both employer and employee need to be clear about what is intended and expected. Feedback takes three main forms:
  - ✓ appreciation (praise/thanks)
  - ✓ coaching (here's a better way to do it)
  - ✓ evaluation (here's where you stand).

- **Appreciation, praise and recognition are powerful, *really* powerful.** Appreciation, praise and recognition are important forms of feedback. They should be provided as soon as feasible after the noteworthy activity, not saved up until a formal performance review months down the track.

- **Coaching.** This is another type of feedback. Based on their largest global study on the future of work, Gallup was convinced that highest on the list of priorities for leaders was educating managers to become coaches.

- **Mentoring.** Employers should see it as their role to make sure that employees have access to mentors within the organisation.

- **Artificial intelligence.** As an employer, how would you (honestly) answer these two questions, if they were posed in an interview:
  - ✓ Have you embraced the need to invest in AI, to make client service as efficient as possible?
  - ✓ Is your organisation training its young professionals in the use of appropriate AI tools?

- **Curiosity, creativity and innovation.** Okay, you don't need me to tell you that these three things are important to the future of your organisation, but where do you stand on the following five ways to support the curiosity that should lead to creativity and innovation?
  - ✓ training
  - ✓ recruitment
  - ✓ culture
  - ✓ whole of organisation focus
  - ✓ mindfulness — at individual and team levels.
- **Joy and fun at work.** Humour, joy and fun in the workplace are evidenced-based ways to support happy, productive workers and profits.
- **Purpose and meaning.** A professional typically (but not always) wants to work in an organisation whose purpose and values are aligned with their own. Whether you are an employee or employer, can you right now, and without consulting a website, state the purpose and values of your organisation?
- **Energising eight motivational factors.** A concrete way to focus on the energising eight motivational factors (*purpose/meaning, autonomy, mastery, relatedness, status, certainty, fairness* and *feedback*) is to create a short 'statement of commitments' on an employee-by-employee basis, as set out in this chapter.

Part II

Playbook

Part II sets out 'A Playbook to Unleash Your Potential and Futureproof Your Success'. I have designed it to assist professionals to adapt constantly as they face the four interlinked challenges set out in the Introduction. Of those challenges, artificial intelligence requires *urgent consideration* by all professionals, given how quickly the technology is developing and reshaping workplaces around the world.

If you follow this Playbook, you should be assured of a successful and satisfying professional career. You will add value to happy and grateful clients as you harness and work with the latest and greatest AI tools at your disposal. And you will not be replaced by AI.

This Playbook is a practical document to be read and then actioned. It's dynamic, a resource you can return to time and time again for answers and strategies. It includes questions for reflection, templates and tools to enable you to put the ideas into action in your own career. And yes, as I noted in the Introduction, you should be able to have fun at work as you develop your career.

Futureproofing your success means applying the Five Factors (see figure II.1, overleaf) in the Playbook on a consistent, long-term basis to help you answer these two questions, first posed in the Introduction:

- How can I become my best possible professional?
- How can I add the most value in the age of artificial intelligence?

As you work through Part II, you'll find some overlap between the Five Factors. They have been numbered for convenience and ready reference and are listed in what seems a logical order for professional self-development. But they are all important and should be addressed together on an ongoing basis.

When creating any model or framework, an acronym is useful as a memory aid. Sadly, the best I can do here is CALMS, for **C**apabilities, **A**ccelerants, **L**earning, **M**otivation and **S**elf-care. Even then it is a fairly contorted acronym, because the factors end up out of order. This can (fairly) be viewed as acronym cheating, but so be it.

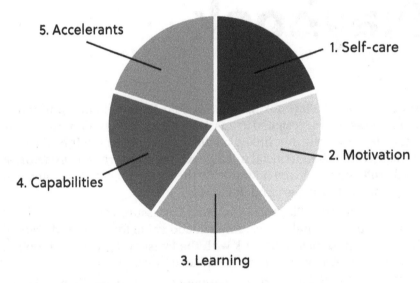

Figure II.1: the Five Factors (CALMS)

1. **Self-care.** Even the hardest working and most conscientious professionals are allowed to look after themselves! The first factor, self-care, is covered in chapter 5.

2. **Motivation.** You are most likely to succeed at anything if you are highly motivated to do so. The second factor is discussed in chapter 6.

3. **Learning.** Although you have one or more university degrees and professional qualifications, learning should never stop. We look at the third factor in chapter 7.

4. **Capabilities.** You will want to spend your precious time developing the right capabilities that will best assist you in the age of artificial intelligence. The fourth factor is addressed in chapter 8.

5. **Accelerants.** These are seven proven ways to get ahead in professional life. This fifth factor is covered in chapter 9, which deals with the first six Accelerants, and chapter 10, which explains the final Accelerant.

After the Five Factors are teased out you will be ready for chapter 11 and an interrogation of success.

Chapter 5

Fit your own oxygen mask first

This chapter focuses on the first of the Five Factors in the Playbook: *Self-care*. Legendary British actress and UNICEF Goodwill Ambassador Audrey Hepburn puts it like this: 'Remember, if you ever need a helping hand, it's at the end of your arm. As you get older, remember you have another hand: The first is to help yourself, the second is to help others.'[1]

The notion of self-care is broad and there is a limit to what I can cover in this slim chapter. I will assume you know that you need to eat and drink the right stuff and do a reasonable amount of exercise. I won't cover these 'basics', although it is clear that many people haven't yet got the memo on this subject. There are many sources of information on diet and exercise[2] produced by people much more qualified than me. This chapter also does not address topics like self-confidence[3] and the very common professional sector issue of so-called impostor syndrome[4], or mental health issues such as depression and anxiety.

When you settle into an aircraft seat, the safety briefing reminds you to fit your own oxygen mask first in the event of an emergency before helping others. The same principle applies throughout your professional career and indeed your life generally. Care for yourself first, so you can better care for your clients, colleagues, family and friends.

Complexity

In the Introduction, *complexity* in all its many guises is listed as the first of four interlinked challenges facing professionals now and into the future, yet, as you will have noticed, no chapter is specifically devoted to it. This is because complexity is so pervasive and personal that the whole Playbook, and especially this first factor, is designed to help you address the complexity in your life. From personal experience over 40 years, and watching many other people grappling with complexity, I am convinced, without any need to cite evidence-based research, that properly looking after yourself is an excellent step on your journey to address complexity as you experience it.

Of course, earnest self-developers reading the above paragraph may well be yearning to know more about complexity and how to address it, apart from following the self-care suggestions that follow and implementing the rest of the Playbook. Be careful what you wish for. There is a vast and, yes, complex pool of resources available on the subject of complexity in the modern world generally and in the business environment in particular. My suggested starting point for you is Amy Edmondson's authoritative book *Right Kind of Wrong: How the Best Teams Use Failure to Succeed*.[5] Edmondson's book, especially chapters 4 and 7, will help you think about complexity in a logical, considered way. In particular, chapter 7 provides an excellent overview of systems and systems thinking and their interaction with complexity, which are topics beyond the scope of this book.

Burnout

I will say a few more things on burnout, which is mentioned in various places in this book. In chapter 1, one of the listed hallmarks of a great professional is the ability to say no as needed to clients. To avoid burnout, you will also need to develop the capacity to say no to your employer. Getting your work–life balance right is a very personal thing. Pilita Clark observes, 'The thankless, invisible work that eats into time and career priorities is overwhelmingly done by women.'[6] Based on my observations over some decades, that is a reasonable and most unfortunate assessment.

Of course, with your employer, you won't just say 'no', whether you are a woman or a man. Author and communication expert Joseph Grenny advises, 'Don't simply say "no." Share your logic. Share your facts. Share the reasoning behind your decision. And most important, share the values that motivate your conclusion.'[7]

You will decide how many late nights and weekends you are prepared to work, if any, and just how much a slave you will be to any billable hours target you have been given. You will then carefully explain your current workload and commitments that may have been made to multiple partners or senior professionals in your organisation without their having a grasp of your overall load. You will state that you don't want to let anyone down. Ask that the senior professionals agree among themselves on what your priorities should be. Yes, I know, easier said than done. But smart young professionals increasingly adopt this strategy and find it does not turn into a career- or job-limiting move. The sooner in your career you can start applying this technique, the better. An excellent resource on tackling burnout is Melo Calarco's book *Beating Burnout Finding Balance*.[8]

What *is* self-care?

I agree with Professor Alyssa Westring from DePaul University's Driehaus College of Business who says there is no single 'right' way to do self-care.[9] Westring recommends you challenge your assumptions about self-care and find an approach that works for you. We'll now discuss just five areas of self-care. A resource I recommend, with links to many other ideas and articles, is the self-care page of the Beyond Blue website.[10]

'The Making of a Corporate Athlete'

My all-time favourite *HBR* article is 'The Making of a Corporate Athlete'.[11] I just love this article. Although now more than 20 years old, like a fine bottle of big Aussie red wine, it just gets better with age. If I was commencing my career today, this article[12] would be the first thing on self-development I would read, after this book of course. The authors of this insightful work, Jim Loehr and Tony Schwartz, originally coached world-class athletes to help them achieve their 'ideal performance state'. Then they realised that the same principles applied equally to business executives and professionals. As anyone who has read enough papers on business theory, coaching, psychology and other social sciences knows well, the proponents of theories and models love to use 2x2 matrices, cubes, circles with rings or pieces of pie, or pyramids to represent their ideas visually. Like many who have sought to build on Abraham Maslow's famous Hierarchy of Needs[13], Loehr and Schwartz are pyramid people.

They use a 'high-performance pyramid', with four levels of capacity, starting at the bottom with your *physical* capacity, then your *emotional* capacity, followed by your *mental* capacity, with your *spiritual* capacity at the pointy end. Their key insight is the need for 'rituals' to help you oscillate between periods of stress and high workload, and recovery time. A ritual is a meaningful habit[14] done deliberately to achieve a certain outcome. Rituals such as vigorous exercise, meditation[15], mindfulness, spending time in nature and prayer help you move up the pyramid. Loehr and Schwartz described in 2001 how the best world-class tennis players of the day followed precise recovery rituals between points on court. They hooked up players to heart rate monitors and found those with the most consistent rituals had the best recovery in terms of heart-rate drop between points. Since that article was written, Spanish tennis ace Rafael Nadal developed rituals[16] into a new art form, becoming the regular subject of the men's GOAT (greatest of all time) debates, at least before Novak Djokovic won his fourth US Open and 24th Grand Slam title in 2023.

As Loehr and Schwartz observed, the average professional athlete spends most of their time practising and relatively little time competing, with a typical career spanning a decade or two at most. By contrast, it is 'game on' for most business executives and professionals, hour after hour, day after day, year after year and decade after decade. Just like athletes, the best long-term performers in the business world use rituals to help them tap into positive energy at each level of the performance pyramid.

I often encourage my coaching and mentoring clients to read 'The Making of a Corporate Athlete' and improve their own rituals to prime progression up the performance pyramid. Among other benefits, it will help them optimise their productivity and minimise the risk of burnout. If you pack out your calendar with work, you won't be able to avoid burnout and oscillate between periods of stress and high workload and recovery. When he was CEO at Microsoft, Bill Gates used to fill up every minute in his calendar, until he saw the schedule of his good friend and bridge partner Warren Buffett, which had days without any appointments at all:

> Buffett's method — which is essentially 'work smarter, not harder' — is actually backed by science. Workers' proficiency steeply declines when they work more than 50 hours per week, a 2014 Stanford University study found.[17]

Research also shows[18] that engaging in appropriate rituals within workgroups can enhance the meaningfulness of work and a sense of team cohesion. However, care needs to be taken with the rituals you choose as a group activity, so you are suitably inclusive and respectful. Your colleagues are likely to hold a myriad views on what is and is not acceptable in the workplace though they will probably agree on ruling out the sacrifice of goats, chickens, other live animals, or the boss, in the office kitchen.

Sleep

Good sleep patterns seem to be eluding many people in the 21st century, not least busy professionals. At the same time, there has been an explosion in sleep-related research, much of which is both depressing and inspiring at the same time. Nine in ten people do not enjoy a good night's sleep, while suboptimal sleep is associated with a higher likelihood of heart disease and stroke.[19] At the same time, this research estimated that seven in ten of these cardiovascular conditions could be prevented by improved sleep. Inadequate sleep negatively impacts alertness and attention and is the largest preventable cause of motor vehicle accidents.[20]

Recent research[21] confirms what many people experienced during the COVID-19 pandemic — the desire to reward yourself with some 'me time' at the end of the day, which translates into putting off bedtime. Unfortunately, such procrastination is often neither productive nor satisfying, involving things like Netflix bingeing or mindless scrolling on phones and iPads. Even worse, research confirms what most people know intuitively: sleep deprivation can cause anger-management issues.[22]

Steven Lockley, Associate Professor of Medicine in the Division of Sleep and Circadian Disorders at Harvard Medical School, believes the importance of sleep has been significantly underrated compared to exercise and nutrition when it comes to wellbeing and optimal functioning.[23] As Lockley says, if you don't sleep, you don't perform at your best or make good decisions and you don't learn. Like many sleep experts he says that adults need a minimum of seven hours' sleep every night and that people who say they can get by on less are kidding themselves. Here are Lockley's top tips for getting more sleep:

- Actually make sleep a priority — put it in your daily calendar.
- No pets in the bedroom.
- Dim the lights two or three hours before bedtime.
- Stop using electronic devices as long as possible before bedtime — at least 30 minutes — and leave the devices outside of the bedroom.
- No caffeine after lunch and limit alcohol intake.

In good news for insomniacs, another sleep expert, Russell Foster, Professor of Circadian Neuroscience at Oxford University, says that the Western world has become fixated on the idea of seven or eight hours of uninterrupted sleep. He says that waking up in the middle of the night is quite normal and that people get overly worried about doing so.[24]

Okay, many professionals reading this mini-lecture on the importance of sleep have just done some massive eye rolls. And to be fair, when I was younger, I used to think I was pretty much indestructible and didn't need much sleep. Looking back, I can recall being overtired and not always performing at my best. In recent years, I have woken up (pun intended) and I now treat sleep as a priority and generally get seven good-quality hours a night.

I sense that some readers, especially high-flying lawyers working on international mergers and acquisitions, are still not convinced. You are telling yourself what I am saying is simply unrealistic, as deals keep rolling on and you need to do regular all-nighters for the sake of a transaction. Well, I am here to tell you that you do have a choice. Think about it again. Even hyper-frenetic serial entrepreneur Elon Musk has conceded that he needs to get at least six hours of sleep a night: 'I've tried [to sleep] less, but ... even though I'm awake more hours, I get less done,' he said in an interview. 'And the brain pain level is bad if I get less than six hours.'[25]

Self-compassion

Self-compassion involves several components:

- being kind to yourself rather than harshly self-critical
- seeing your own suffering as part of the larger human experience rather than seeing your experiences as separating and isolating
- being mindful and able to hold painful thoughts and feelings in balanced awareness rather than over-identifying with them.[26]

Ask yourself these questions

As you read that admittedly formal and somewhat stiff definition of self-compassion, what thoughts went through your head?

- Is self-compassion a meaningful concept for me?
- Am I regularly compassionate towards myself?
- If so, great. If not, why not?

Self-compassion is, along with meditation and mindfulness, a traditional Buddhist-influenced concept with which Western culture has been playing catch-up. It involves being open to your own suffering rather than avoiding or disconnecting from it, and healing yourself with kindness. It means understanding without judgement your own pain, inadequacies and failures, and seeing that suffering as part of the larger human experience.[27]

How do you 'do' self-compassion? Well, you won't be surprised that there is no single guaranteed pathway, but you might start by investing 20 minutes in watching a TEDx talk by self-compassion guru Dr Kristin Neff.[28] She explains the difference between self-compassion and self-esteem, and notes some of the downsides of too strong a focus on self-esteem. You could also read her book on the subject[29] or visit her website[30] for tips and exercises to improve and promote self-compassion.

Without self-compassion, Neff says in her TEDx talk, when things aren't going well, we may say things to ourselves we would never say to someone we cared about. In fact, we say things to ourselves that we wouldn't even say out loud to someone we didn't like very much:

> ... self-criticism releases a lot of cortisol. If you are a constant self-critic, you have constantly high levels of stress and eventually, to protect itself, the body will shut itself down and become depressed in order to deal with all the stress.[31]

With self-compassion we reverse this pattern and start treating ourselves as we treat our good friends. This is the baseline practice for self-compassion. We include ourselves in the circle of people we care about and to whom we offer kindness, care and concern. We offer encouragement, understanding, empathy, patience and gentleness. Yes even, or especially, if you are a tax lawyer[32] who is having a really bad day with an obnoxious client who thinks your charge-out rate is too high.

But self-compassion isn't just a private pursuit; rather, we should create 'compassion-centred workplaces'. Psychologist Justin Henderson, who specialises in mindfulness, acceptance and compassion-based therapies, argues:

> Our work environments must change. As our economy and society have often been insensitive to the natural order — taken her for granted and assumed an infinite supply of materials to consume. Our work has followed this basic assumption as well — that people will continue to give endlessly of themselves.[33]

Henderson goes on to say that change is possible, starting with the creation of 'compassion centred workplaces'. Any employers reading this section, please note and action accordingly!

Resilience

I spent more time reading, reflecting and researching this section than any other part of this book. Resilience is a keenly contested space in psychology and other social sciences. One reason that resilience is prized, especially by employers, is that the more resilient someone is, the lower the perceived risk of burnout.[34] There are many competing views and perspectives on what resilience means, how important it is and how to build it. The stresses surrounding the COVID-19 pandemic supercharged interest in the debate, especially in workplace settings.

One of many definitions of resilience is that it is the *process* of adapting well and even growing in the face of adversity, stress or trauma.[35] I italicise 'process' because research shows that although resilience is genetic to a small degree, it is not a fixed trait or characteristic that you either have or don't have. Rather, resilience fluctuates[36] and can be developed over time by individuals, ideally with the support of their employer, or other organisations, and of course of family and friends.

In research published in 2024, it was found that people who have higher levels of mental resilience can live as much as ten years longer than those not so blessed.[37] So how can we get some of this resilience stuff, especially at work?

Kathryn McEwen is an Adelaide-based psychologist and key member of *Working With Resilience*[38], an international consortium of practitioners and academics researching what resilience means in relation to our working lives. In an article, *Building Resilience at Work: A Practical Framework for Leaders*[39], McEwen addresses components of workplace resilience, many of which are addressed throughout this book, from the perspective of the *individual*:

1. **Live authentically.** Know and hold onto personal values, deploy strengths, and foster emotional awareness and regulation.

2. **Find your calling.** Seek work that has purpose in an environment that aligns with your core values and beliefs and in which you feel you belong.

3. **Maintain perspective.** Reframe setbacks, maintain a solution focus and manage negativity.

4. **Master stress.** Employ work and life routines that help manage everyday stressors, maintain work–life balance and prioritise time for relaxation.

5. **Interact cooperatively.** Seek feedback, advice and support (see chapter 9) and provide support to others.

6. **Stay healthy.** Maintain a good level of physical fitness and eat a healthy diet.

7. **Build networks.** Develop and maintain personal support networks.

McEwen talks about the importance of resilience at the team level in the workplace and the vital role that leaders have in creating conditions that allow individuals to flourish and be resilient. Employers often stress the importance of their new recruits exhibiting high levels of resilience, without always explaining what *they* will do to foster it. How does your team and its leadership measure up against these seven factors?

1. **Robust** — solid intention with agility. Having shared purpose, meaning and goals. Being adaptable to change and proactive when issues arise for the team.

2. **Resourceful** — optimising resources and processes. Harnessing team-member strengths and resources against priorities and building a culture of continuous improvement.

3. **Perseverance** — persisting despite setbacks. Persisting in the face of obstacles and having a solution, rather than a problem, focus.

4. **Self-care** — ensuring sustainable performance. Promoting and deploying good stress management routines and supporting life-work integration.

5. **Capability** — delivering in a changing landscape. Continually building capacity through accessing the networks, supports and advice needed.

6. **Connected** — having a sense of belonging. Being cooperative and supportive with each other and with the team in a way that creates cultural and psychological safety.

7. **Alignment** — sharing motivation for success. Aligning to create the desired outcomes. Being optimistic, noticing progress and celebrating success.

At a more basic level than these seven factors, employers can do two things that will go a long way to helping their staff become resilient. First, they can really care about their employees. If you are an employer reading this, imagine being a fly on the wall at a family dinner of Sally, one of your employees. Sally's father asks her whether anyone at her workplace really, truly cares about her? What answer do you hear Sally give her father? Second, employers can encourage resilience by not imposing intolerable and burnout-inducing workloads on their staff. If leaders tick off all seven factors above, but work their people into the ground and do not care about them as human beings, it is hard to expect too much in the way of individual or team resilience.

The health and effectiveness of workplace relationships are critical components of resilience. A survey of 835 employees in the UK[40] found that the biggest single drain on the resilience of both women and men is not work–life balance, as the researchers had expected, but the challenge of managing difficult relationships and workplace politics. Three out of four survey respondents identified 'managing difficult relationships/ politics in the workplace' as a reason for reduced resilience (rising to four out of every five at executive level).

As an employed professional, find out what you can about the politics in your organisation and how it may affect you — then stay out of them as far as possible until you are more senior. The more you can avoid engaging in office politics, at least in your younger years, the greater will be your workplace resilience.

As you get more senior, it may suit your career development to better understand and work with office politics. If so, let Stanford University's Jeffrey Pfeffer's book *7 Rules of Power* be your guide.[41] A useful discussion of the role politics inevitably plays in professional service firms may be found in Laura Empson's article 'How to Lead Your Fellow Rainmakers'.[42]

Ask yourself these questions

- How do I ensure my short- and long-term resilience in the workplace?
- How do I ensure that I do not detract from, and ideally enhance, the resilience of my colleagues?
- How can I help my team leader to strengthen resilience at a team level?

Breathing

I know what some of you are thinking: why a section on breathing? Surely he doesn't think we need help with what is after all an automatic function? Well, maybe some of us do.

Yes, we all breathe all the time, from the moment we are born until the moment we die. Many people don't give a lot of thought to *how* they breathe and whether some methods are better than others. Even the idea of there being different methods of breathing may seem odd.

But anyone with any training in meditation, mindfulness and/or yoga will know just how important breathing is to achieving a desired state of mind. Eastern religions, philosophies and medical practice have emphasised the importance of correct breathing for thousands of years, and Western science and culture have been slow to catch up.

After a doctor recommended he attend breathing classes to help strengthen his failing lungs, journalist James Nestor spent years learning everything there is to know about the importance of breathing. *Breath – the New Science of a Lost Art* was published in 2020 just as the world was focusing on breathing through masks to avoid the spread of COVID-19.

Nestor summarises much ancient Eastern wisdom as well as cutting-edge Western research on optimal breathing patterns. His website has links to a collection of short instructional videos from a range of experts, including Johns Hopkins School of Medicine's Dr Neda Gould's 'Reducing Stress through Deep Breathing'. Gould explains how to do slow, deep, diaphragmatic breathing to activate the parasympathetic nervous system and assist with stress reduction. As Gould advises, the many benefits of slow, deep breathing include:

- lower heart rate
- lower blood pressure
- increased energy levels
- decreased muscle tension and pain
- improved sleep
- a more focused mind.

What's not to like about breathing optimally? Being able to consciously control and regulate your breathing is not just useful for meditation and mindfulness. It can be beneficial in workplace situations such as preparing for potentially stressful presentations or interactions, and in their aftermath. It can assist in the moment if a conversation goes off the rails and your freeze, fight or flight responses kick into gear.

Gould's video and Nestor's book each emphasise the importance of breathing in through the nose rather than the mouth and Nestor cites numerous research studies that confirm the wisdom you may have been taught as a child. As Nestor explains:

Mouth breathing, it turns out, changes the physical body and transforms airways, all for the worse. Inhaling air through the mouth decreases pressure, which causes the soft tissues in the back of the mouth to become loose and flex inward, creating less space and making breathing more difficult. Inhaling from the nose has the opposite effect.[43]

Nestor also summarises some common breathing methods:

- **Box breathing**. US Navy Seals use this simple technique to stay calm and focused in tense situations: inhale through the nose to a count of 4; hold 4; exhale 4; hold 4. Repeat. Longer exhalations will elicit a stronger parasympathetic (relaxing) response.

- **4-7-8 breathing**. Nestor says he uses this technique, made famous by Dr Andrew Weil[44], for relaxation and to help fall asleep, but the benefits require this technique to be practiced and mastered over time:

  - Take a breath in through the nose, then exhale through the mouth with a *whoosh* sound.

  - Close the mouth and inhale quietly through the nose for a mental count of four.

  - Hold for a count of seven.

  - Exhale completely through your mouth, with a *whoosh*, to the count of eight.

  - Repeat this cycle for at least four breaths, or until you fall asleep.

Are you awake and still reading? Good. Ask yourself: could you perhaps reassess whether you are in fact breathing in an optimal fashion after all these years on the planet? If you still have doubts, I recommend you visit James Nestor's website with its instructional videos.

In play

I am not going to pretend that I was a model of self-care in my first career as a tax adviser. At times I prioritised work at the expense of relationships and my health. Looking back, I recognise this was a mistake. There was no compelling reason for my poor choices in terms of self-care and private relationships. I was very focused on my career, on promotion and on making money. If I had my time over, I like to think that I would choose a more balanced life and make some better decisions.

These days all five main topics in this chapter are very much front of mind for me in my role as an executive coach, mentor and leadership consultant. Each topic comes up regularly with my clients and in the interests of being as authentic and useful as possible to them, I aim to practise what I preach.

For example, and inspired by 'The Making of a Corporate Athlete', I have consciously developed various rituals to help not just to maximise my workplace performance but to enhance my overall high-performance pyramid. One of those rituals involves working out at the gym three times a week. One of these involves an intense session with a personal trainer, Ed. I also make time daily for prayer and self-reflection, both of which tended to be spasmodic in my first career. Most weekdays I take a walk in the Royal Botanic Garden across the road from my tax-deductible man cave (office). I am conscious of my weight and of what I eat and I sleep better and for longer than I did.

As part of my self-reflection, I consider my own self-compassion and resilience. Happily, I love my second career and it is far less stressful than my career as a tax lawyer and managing director, so I don't find self-compassion or personal resilience problematic.

On the breathing front, and partly inspired by James Nestor's book, I have heightened awareness of breathing more slowly and deeply. Breathing techniques, especially for stress management, are a regular feature of my work with clients. It is fun and interesting to swap notes with my clients on which breathing methods and tips seem to work best for different people in different circumstances.

Key takeaways

- **Burnout.** Decide your boundaries and learn to say no, but don't *just* say no:
  - ✓ Carefully explain your current workload and commitments, which may have been made to various partners or senior professionals in your organisation without any one of them having a grasp of your overall load. Explain that you do not want to let anyone down.
  - ✓ Ask that the senior professionals agree among themselves on what your priorities should be.
- **'The Making of a Corporate Athlete'.** This classic article sets out a 'high-performance pyramid', with four levels of 'capacity': physical, emotional, mental and spiritual.
  - ✓ Rituals can help you oscillate between periods of stress and high workload and recovery time.
  - ✓ A ritual is a meaningful habit undertaken deliberately to achieve a certain outcome. Rituals such as vigorous exercise, meditation, mindfulness, spending time in nature and in prayer also help you move up the pyramid.
- **Sleep.** The importance of sleep has been significantly underrated compared to that of exercise and nutrition when it comes to wellbeing and optimal functioning.
  - ✓ If you don't sleep, you don't perform at your best or make good decisions and you don't learn.
  - ✓ Most adults, including ambitious young professionals, need a minimum of seven hours' sleep every night. People are kidding themselves when they say they can do well on less.
- **Self-compassion.** Be open to your own suffering rather than avoiding or disconnecting from it. Generate a desire to alleviate personal suffering and to heal yourself through kindness. Self-compassion is a good and necessary thing!
  - ✓ It also involves understanding without judgement your own pain, inadequacies and failures, and recognising them as part of the larger human experience.
  - ✓ Treat yourself as you treat your good friends. This is the baseline practice for self-compassion. Speak to yourself as you would to a good friend — with encouragement, understanding, empathy, patience and gentleness.

- **Resilience.** This is the *process* of adapting well and even growing in the face of adversity, stress or trauma. The COVID-19 pandemic supercharged interest in resilience, especially in workplace settings. Like self-compassion, resilience needs to be fostered in the workplace and not outsourced.
- If you haven't already done so, ask yourself these three questions:
  - ✓ How can I ensure my own resilience in the workplace over the short and the long term?
  - ✓ How can I ensure that I do not detract from but, ideally, enhance the resilience of my colleagues?
  - ✓ How can I help my team leader to strengthen resilience at a team level?
- **Breathing.** Believe it or not, there are good and not-so-good ways to breathe. It is never too late to become a better breather.
  - ✓ Slow, deep breathing can lead to stress and anxiety reduction, lower heart rate, lower blood pressure, increased energy levels, decreased muscle tension and pain, improved sleep and a more focused mind. What's not to like?

Chapter 6

What gets you out of bed in the morning?

This chapter addresses the second of the Playbook's Five Factors to help you achieve a successful career: *Motivation*.

Ideally, you work for more than just the money. Maybe you are completely motivated and are totally satisfied with your current job. You have a clear picture of the future and a strategy for upskilling and achieving your goals as you go. If so, great, go ahead and skip this chapter. If this doesn't sound like your situation, then read on. You are hardly alone.

As noted in chapter 4, in its 2023 'State of the Global Workplace Report'[1] Gallup found that only 23 per cent of employees worldwide describe themselves as engaged with their job. An employee was regarded as engaged if they found their work meaningful and felt connected to their team and their organisation. They felt proud of the work they do and took ownership of their performance, going the extra mile for teammates and customers. Workers in Australia and New Zealand were at the global average of 23 per cent. The average in Europe was 13 per cent engagement level. Employee engagement in the US and Canada was 31 per cent.

Purpose and meaning

As was noted in chapter 4, you don't *have* to have a 'purpose' or even seek 'meaning' in your work, or your life more generally. If this isn't a big deal for you, then don't feel anxious if you can't articulate the purpose of your work or life at large.

Nonetheless, there is a vast body of research on the meaning of work that you may find useful.[2] It tells us, for example, that most people see their work as one of three things[3]:

- a **job**. The focus is mainly on financial reward and necessity rather than pleasure or fulfilment. It is neither a major part of life nor an end in itself.

- a **career**. The focus is on advancement, social standing and increased self-esteem.

- a **calling**. The focus is on fulfilling, socially useful work. The work activities themselves may be, but are not necessarily, pleasurable.

How do you view your current and future work? Your answer may help you decide how much purpose or meaning, if any, you expect to derive from your work. Take time to reflect occasionally on what you seek to achieve, now and in the future. A wise, experienced mentor can be very helpful. Are you trying to change the world? If so, how exactly? Is your goal to help others? Is the establishment of trusting, supportive relationships important? How do you prioritise financial and non-financial goals?

How about this remarkable example of an employee's commitment to their employer and to clarity of purpose? Guinness World Records announced in April 2022 that 100-year-old Brazilian Walter Orthmann had worked for the same company for a record-breaking 84 years and nine days. In 1938, when he was 15 years old, he began work as a shipping assistant for a Brazilian textile company, Industrias Renaux SA (now known as RenauxView) in Santa Catarina. Walter told Guinness 'the best part about having a job is that it gives you a sense of purpose, commitment, and a routine' and his 'best professional advice' was 'to work for a good company and in an area where you feel motivated'.[4]

If you are struggling to articulate your purpose, I recommend Adam Leipzig's TED talk 'How to know your life purpose in 5 minutes'.[5] It is based on these five questions and concludes with advice on creating your own elevator pitch.[6]

1. Who are you?

2. What do you love to do?

3. Who do you do it for?

4. What do those people want or need?

5. How do those people change as a result of what you give them?

Given his emphasis on discovering purpose by focusing on helping others, Leipzig's approach is well suited to those working in professional services.

During my tax career, I came across many people working in the Australian Taxation Office (ATO) who clearly were deriving great purpose from their jobs. Although some of them could have earned considerably more money in the private sector, they enjoyed their work in the ATO because they were making a difference to the operation of the Australian taxation system. Although I never asked any of them Leipzig's five questions, I suspect that many might have responded with greater speed and clarity than their much more highly paid peers working in professional service firms. Is your purpose just 'show me the money'?

Another resource to help you reflect on your work–life purpose is Nick Craig and Scott Snook's *HBR* article 'From Purpose to Impact'.[7] They recommend grappling with purpose by means of structured peer-group discussion, but you could work through their useful and practical suggestions on your own. If you set up or join a discussion group of like-minded professionals, as recommended in the *Suggested reading and viewing lists* section at the end of this book, then this would be an ideal opportunity to put Craig and Snook's suggestions into practice.

If you are looking for greater meaning and purpose in your life more generally, then a superb starting point is Viktor Frankl's classic *Man's Search for Meaning*[8], based on his experiences in Nazi death camps. Frankl said, 'There is nothing in the world, I venture to say, that would so effectively help one to survive even the worst conditions as knowledge that there is a meaning in one's life.'

Recent research[9] has found that, across age groups, a strong sense of life purpose is associated with lower loneliness, as well as greater intentions to engage in COVID-19 protective behaviours.

An important driver for many professionals is the opportunity to undertake pro bono work for deserving causes as part of their employment. A warning to employers reading this book: I know professionals who have resigned from organisations because they were not afforded sufficient scope to participate in pro bono assignments.

Passions and skills

There are various schools of thought on which matters most: a pre-existing passion for your work or a passion that develops out of the process of building skills until you're really good at what you do.

In a famous address to the Stanford University graduating class of 2005, Apple co-founder Steve Jobs told his audience that because work fills such a large part of our lives, we are only truly satisfied when we do what we believe to be great work. And the only way to do great work is to 'love what you do'.[10] He advised the graduates if they hadn't found that love yet, they shouldn't settle but should keep looking.

Georgetown Professor Cal Newport, in *So Good They Can't Ignore You*[11], instead argues that skills trump passion in the quest to find work you love. He reinforces his position with his reading of Jobs's life in the early days of Apple when he didn't seem to be passionate about computers. Newport points out, backed by research findings, that the 'passions' of many people are for things that will probably not lead to successful, financially rewarding work. The gist of Newport's argument is that passion comes *after* you have put in the hard work to develop skills and become excellent at something useful and valuable, and not before.

Dan Cable, Professor of Organizational Behaviour at London Business School, agrees. He has been studying and writing about job choices and career successes for 25 years, and far from 'follow your passion' his bumper-sticker career advice is 'follow your blisters'.[12] Persist until your skin toughens up. Eventually, through use and practice, the activity 'marks you' and you develop a special competence.

There are dangers in following your passion. In her article 'When Passion Leads to Burnout'[13], Jennifer Moss warns of the danger that if we equate work we love with 'not really working', we may come to believe that if we love it so much, we should do more of it — all the time, actually. This can lead to burnout, and the consequences can be both dire and hard to detect.

The always perceptive Professor Scott Galloway has interesting things to say in a highly entertaining two-minute video clip, part of an interview titled *Galloway on follow your passion*.[14] The gist of Galloway's opinion is that telling young people to 'follow their passion' is very bad advice. Instead, people should find something that they are good at and then apply themselves through perseverance and sacrifice, so as to eventually become great at whatever their chosen occupation happens to be. Then the prestige and sense of self-worth of being great at something will cause passion to ignite. As we will see in the 'In play' section at the end of this chapter, Galloway thinks that such an approach even applies to tax lawyers.

There are many books that can help you think through how to approach the challenge of finding work you will enjoy and how and when to change careers, including the grand-daddy of the genre, *What Color Is*

Your Parachute?[15] This book, which has been updated most years since it was first published in 1970, is well worth reading if you are struggling to find what type of work most suits you. The famous Flower Exercise, which involves a detailed self-inventory, will take some work but will really get you thinking about your career.

Most young professionals decided in high school to go to university or college and get a degree because at the time, for whatever reason, it seemed like a good idea. As I discuss in 'In play', it can take a while for love to grow so some patience may be needed.

Motivation: the energising eight

Are you highly motivated? Do you leap out of bed every morning, eager to get to the office or your workspace at home or your local cafe and join Zoom meetings and videoconferences? Do you feel that your chosen career has meaning, and that you are developing skills and a love for your work? Even if you do feel like this, do you sometimes feel demotivated? Well, read on! Here are what I have termed the energising eight factors of motivation, assembled from a variety of sources.

1. Purpose/meaning

Daniel Pink includes purpose as one of the three elements of motivation in his bestselling book *Drive*.[16] He recalls famed Hungarian-American psychologist Mihaly Csikszentmihalyi telling him, 'purpose provides activation energy for living' and 'evolution has had a hand in selecting people who had a sense of doing something beyond themselves'.[17]

The 19th-century German philosopher Friedrich Nietzsche famously said, 'He who has a why to live for can bear almost any how.'[18] That's good enough for me. Purpose leads my list of the energising eight factors of motivation.

There are more theories and models about human motivation and what drives us than you can poke a stick at, but one stands out. Since the 1970s, self-determination theory (SDT) has been used to explain, predict and foster human motivation much better than old-school carrot-and-stick approaches. It certainly explains a lot of the functional and dysfunctional behaviour I observed in my first career. According to the proponents of SDT[19], three fundamental psychological needs or nutriments are essential for optimal functioning and personal wellbeing. These needs, which help individual intrinsic motivation to flourish, are the next three of my energising eight factors of motivation.[20]

2. Autonomy

To be autonomous is to have a sense of initiative and ownership of our actions and to act out of choice, volition and self-determination. It does not mean independence, because people may depend on others and still act autonomously. It is to have control over whatever it is we are doing, whether in the workplace or outside it. It is supported by the awareness that you are valued, and undermined by external controls such as rewards or punishments.

3. Competence (mastery)

For SDT purposes, competence 'refers to the experience of mastery and being effective in one's activity'. [21]

The need for competence is best satisfied within well-structured environments that afford optimal challenges, positive feedback and opportunities for growth. Given that one of my criteria in chapter 1 for someone to be a true professional, was to *strive for mastery and not mere competence*, the use in SDT of the word 'competence', rather than 'mastery' or excellence, is perhaps unfortunate. Daniel Pink uses mastery rather than competence as one of his three elements to explain motivation. I will go with Pink on this.

4. Relatedness

Relatedness connotes a sense of belonging and connection, and the experience of satisfying and supportive relationships. Facilitated by mutual respect and caring, it connotes caring about others and having them care about us.

Thwarting any of these three basic needs damages motivation and wellbeing. A young professional starting out on their career will typically have little autonomy, because while they may have deep theoretical knowledge they will necessarily have only the beginnings of competence and be only just starting to develop business relationships. The good news is that, as I noted in chapter 4, a thoughtful employer can greatly accelerate a young professional's self-determination.

Impressed as I am by SDT theory, research and its usefulness in understanding how the workplace functions, it did not explain *all* my observations of motivation and demotivation in my first career. Other factors include those David Rock identifies in his SCARF model for collaborating with and influencing others.[22] The model encompasses five fields of human social experience: status, certainty, autonomy, relatedness and fairness. There are obvious overlaps with SDT, so here are brief notes on the other aspects of SCARF, which I have included in my energising eight.

5. Status

Status designates our relative importance to other people. What is our level of seniority and where are we in the pecking order?

6. Certainty

Certainty concerns our ability to predict the future. Our brains crave certainty and are pattern-recognition machines that are constantly trying to make predictions.

7. Fairness

Fairness concerns our perception of fair exchanges between people. At the extreme (probably not in most workplaces), people are prepared to die to right injustice. If you want to see just how deeply fairness is ingrained not just in humans but in other species, then I recommend a hilarious and thought-provoking three-minute video clip[23] in which two capuchin monkeys in captivity are given unequal rewards for performing the same task.

I need to include one more thing, to complete my list of the energising eight motivational factors.

8. Feedback

Feedback is implicit in some of the preceding seven factors, but in practice it is so important it is worth a specific mention. Feedback comes in all shapes and sizes, as we saw in chapter 4. When done well, with well-timed, specific recognition, praise or carefully crafted constructive encouragement, for example, feedback can be a huge motivator. On the other hand, a lack of feedback, or feedback that is poorly delivered, can be highly demotivating. Feedback is so important that it is one of the Seven Accelerants I discuss in chapter 9.

• • •

Looking back at my first career, I can see with the marvellous benefit of hindsight that many great and not-so-great things I did and observed others do can be understood by a combination of purpose, SDT, SCARF and feedback. If employers enable people to feel appropriate purpose/meaning, autonomy, mastery, relatedness, status, certainty and fairness, and provide appropriate feedback, good outcomes can be achieved.

Take away just one of these eight factors, and some highly dysfunctional behaviour is on the cards. Employed professionals are entitled to seek satisfaction of all eight factors as they progress through their careers. As mentioned in chapter 4, smart employers who want to retain their staff would do well to fully understand and accommodate those needs.

Having said all this, it's not as though the energising eight factors of motivation are inscribed on stone tablets brought down from the mountain top. They are just a bunch of things the evidence shows are important for many people. Maybe you are motivated by some or none of these factors, and other things as well.

Ask yourself these questions

Reflect on questions like these periodically:

- What really motivates me in the workplace?
- Does my current job sufficiently satisfy those needs?
- If not, why not, and what am I going to do about it?

Other theories on motivation

There are many other models and approaches to motivation.[24] For example, Canadian-American Albert Bandura's self-efficacy theory (SET) studied an individual's belief in their capacity to undertake actions necessary to achieve goals. Self-efficacy beliefs affect self-motivation and action through their impact on goals and aspirations. They influence what challenges someone chooses to pursue, how much effort they are prepared to expend and how long they will persevere in the face of difficulties. When faced with obstacles and setbacks, those who doubt their capabilities may slacken their efforts, give up prematurely or settle for poorer solutions, while those who believe in their capabilities are likely to redouble their efforts. According to SET, one of the strongest ways of achieving self-efficacy is through gaining mastery in one or more domains[25], which as we have seen is also a key aspect of SDT. It is a virtuous circle. The more you begin to master your chosen profession, the stronger your self-efficacy and motivation are likely to be, leading to a higher level of enjoyment as you strive for higher levels of mastery.

Dr Bob Murray and Dr Alicia Fortinberry[26] have adopted the acronym CATS, for the basic human drivers of certainty, autonomy, trust and status. To keep my list to a manageable length (and sadly without a cute acronym) I resisted the urge to include trust, but I accept that it is an important building block of relationships, and thus relatedness.

People are motivated by all sorts of things in addition to trust and the energising eight needs noted above. Things like love, kindness and charity. And money, greed, power[27] and lust. We will not dwell on these motivators but they obviously influence our behaviour and shouldn't be ignored in the workplace. Especially money. In my experience, particularly in the professional services and financial services sectors, I came across people who were highly motivated by and focused on how much money they were earning. Often this was about perceived status and fairness. They wanted to be paid at least as much as the colleagues they thought of as their peers. Of course, some people have sadly inflated views of their real worth and the value they add to their organisation. This, combined with a strong sense of fairness, could lead to unrealistic pay demands.

Setting goals

Do you set goals for yourself together with clear action plans to achieve them? In my experience many people do, but a surprising number do not. Or, more accurately, often goals have not been well thought through and remain little more than vague ideas of possible future achievements. Research has produced overwhelming evidence that setting sensible, achievable goals with clear action plans and accountability measures is a very sound method of motivation and personal development.[28] Ideally, goals and their accompanying action plans should be SMART (Specific, Measurable, Attainable, Realistic and Time-bound).[29]

Goals can be very powerful. On 25 May 1961 US President John F Kennedy announced what was in my view the most inspirational, SMARTest goal of all time: 'I believe that this nation should commit itself to achieving the goal, before this decade is out, of landing a man on the moon and returning him safely to the Earth.'[30] Kennedy's assassination on 22 November 1963 drove the American people to achieve their national goal.[31] In fact, they overachieved: Apollo 11 and Apollo 12 landed not one but four men on the moon and returned them safely to Earth before the end of 1969.

On a more terrestrial level, retired Australian tennis superstar Ash Barty believes in the power of goal setting. However, because setting goals can be daunting, it was only in 2019 that she worked up the courage to actually write her goals down on paper. One of those goals was that she wanted to be ranked in the top 10 players in the world.[32] She too overachieved, becoming the world number one women's tennis player for more than two years.

Maybe your goals are a tad less ambitious than Kennedy's or Barty's. That's okay, they will probably also be cheaper and perhaps easier to achieve. But that's the thing. You do want to achieve them, and maybe you dream of overachieving. A coach or mentor can be invaluable not only in assisting with goal setting, but in helping you develop concrete action plans and, most importantly, holding you accountable for the outcomes. We will return to goal setting and mentoring in chapter 9.

Although I can't recommend working yourself up into a state of anger, recent research has found that anger can be a powerful motivator for reaching challenging goals.[33] The researchers noted that anger did not appear to be associated with reaching goals when the goals were easier, and in some cases amusement or desire were also associated with increased goal attainment.

Goals are not everyone's cup of tea, and many professionals have successful and happy careers without being too goal focused. Adam Alter, Professor of Marketing at New York University's Stern School of Business, describes goal setting as a hamster wheel type process. He advocates setting a system rather than a goal.[34]

UpSideDown coaching

Sydney-based health-sector professional and coach Dr Nickolas Yu has devised UpSideDown coaching as an effective and elegant way to help people cultivate purpose, passion and perspective through exploring meaning, values and goals.

The benefits are that it:

- taps meaning and values, which are drivers of motivation in addition to the energising eight factors
- helps 'chunk down' big goals and identify connections and relationships between goals
- supports more informed choices about what people really want, including recognising potentially competing goals
- can aid seeing bigger and broader perspectives.[35]

UpSideDown coaching is ideally performed by a skilled coach working directly with a client. However, if you were to follow the following steps, which are set out in the way a coach would go through the process with a client, you could do this on your own. That is, you would be both the coach asking the questions and the client responding to them.

Step 1: Up

The 'Up' part of the process taps into motivation. The coach asks the client to name a significant goal, and to write it down. The coach then asks: 'When you have achieved this goal, *what will this make possible?*' The client writes down one or more responses, *above* the initial goal, as the initial branches of a tree. Say the client provides four responses to the question. The coach then helps the client to select the one or two most significant responses and again asks the client what achieving this goal will make possible. The client again writes down one or more responses to help the tree grow. This cycle is repeated until the client stops, repeats themselves or starts to get confused. The top-level responses will likely reveal deep-seated personal values and motivations. The coach helps the client in this process by making perceptive reflections and choosing which responses to pursue further as the tree branches up. At or towards the top of the tree, the coach will help with meaning making by asking questions like, 'What are you becoming aware of when you look at your goal map/tree? What are you noticing?'

Step 2: Side

The 'Side' part of the model explores multiple pathways to success. The client returns to the original goal and goes up one level to what that goal will first make possible. The coach then asks, a number of times: 'How else could you achieve this outcome?' Each response, being a potential new goal, is written down next to the first response to the original goal, and the 'Up' part of the process is then repeated for each such new response.

Step 3: Down

The 'Down' part of the model focuses on the details of making the dream a reality. This involves helping the client to plan and write down concrete actions to achieve one or more SMART goals that have been prioritised through the Up and Side steps, thus completing the goal map/tree.

In play

Professor Scott Galloway observed:

> No one grows up thinking, 'I'm passionate about tax law.' But the best tax lawyers in this nation fly private and have a much broader selection of mates than they deserve. Then they get to do interesting things. Which by the way makes them passionate about tax law.[36]

Okay, I will confess that as a six-year-old I was not running around saying I wanted to be a tax lawyer when I grew up so I could help big companies pay the correct amount of tax.

In my final year of high school, I decided to study Law and Economics at university, but I didn't know what I was going to do after graduation. After summer vacation work and experience at both KPMG (known then as Peat Marwick Mitchell) and Price Waterhouse I decided that a career in tax would be a good way to spend my working life. I know what some of you are thinking. Remember this was *my* life, not yours.

Truth be told, in the early years I didn't always enjoy my job as a tax adviser. In SDT terms it took me quite a few years to develop what I perceived to be some level of competence, let alone mastery, to get some autonomy over how I operated and to develop some great relationships with clients and most (not all) of my colleagues and professional peers. On various occasions I thought of doing other things with my life as far removed from tax law as possible. However, and with the benefit of hindsight, I am very glad I stuck with my choice of career. Not only did it pay well, but it was intellectually challenging and rewarding, and I was able to meet and work with some extremely interesting and clever people. And yes, I have a much broader selection of mates than I deserve.

When I started my tax career, I didn't really aspire to leadership. It took me a while to grow into the job (just ask any of my former colleagues), but I ended up greatly enjoying my role as managing director of the firm.

Although I liked both client work and my leadership roles over the years, I was driven from early in my career to try to improve both tax law itself and its interpretation and administration. Yes, this will sound super dull to many readers, but it was highly energising for me and gave my work purpose and meaning.

Over the course of 30 years I was involved in all manner of efforts to have Australian tax laws either rewritten or interpreted differently in accordance with my views. One rather lengthy episode stands out. It started in 1990. I was 29 and had been at Westpac for about a year. Among other responsibilities, I managed a team charged with preparing Westpac's annual tax returns. By then, due to financial deregulation and innovation in the 1980s, Westpac was trading at full tilt in a plethora of new-fangled derivative financial instruments such as swaps, futures, forwards and options over interest rates, foreign currencies, credit risk and various other 'underlying' products and risks. The sums involved in these trades were in the many, many billions of dollars and dealing with their tax implications was unnerving. Being stuck in the horse-and-buggy era, tax law at that time was totally unsuited to such instruments and there was great uncertainty on how the law applied. So very strange tax outcomes could and did arise.[37]

I got it into my young head that it would be simpler, as well as more certain, equitable and efficient for everyone, including the ATO, if the tax laws could be reinterpreted or, if necessary, rewritten to have taxable income from these complicated instruments deemed to be whatever had been recorded as profit or loss in a bank's audited financial statements. Happily, my boss at Westpac (John Brodie) and our peers in other banks were thinking the same thing. Sadly, the ATO was unable to interpret the existing law to our liking. Thus began a quest for new tax laws, which after endless proposals, submissions and rounds of consultation, were enacted in 2009. During its torturously slow gestation, the reform project was almost scuppered each time there was a change of federal government. If, as many people say, the new rules are totally incomprehensible, they are consistent with the rest of Australian tax law. Certainly the new law resulted in much more sensible and predictable tax outcomes than had the previous regime.

My role in this 19-year rewrite of taxation of financial arrangements (TOFA) lasted for more than half my first career. Not only did it (and numerous other tax reform projects) help to give my work a great sense of purpose and meaning, but I got to meet and work with a terrific bunch of people in other banks, the ATO and Federal Treasury.

Many people asked during the TOFA journey why it was taking so long—more than twice the time taken to put a man on the moon.[38] There were many reasons for the delays, but the complexity of both the subject matter being tackled and tax law itself didn't help. After all, as Albert Einstein said 'the hardest thing in the world to understand is income taxes'.[39]

Key takeaways

- **Purpose and meaning.** How do you view your current and future work? Your answer will help you decide how much purpose or meaning, if any, you expect to derive from your work. Make some time to reflect occasionally on what you seek to achieve with your work, both now and in the future. This is where a wise and experienced mentor can help.

- **Passions and skills.** There are various schools of thought on the relative importance of inherent passion or love for your work and focusing on skills building in the expectation you will eventually fall in love with what you do. At a practical level, most young professionals decide in high school to go to university or college and get a degree in something, because at that time, for whatever reason, it seems like a good idea. It can take a while for love to grow, so some patience in your early years as a practising professional may be needed.

- **Motivation.** The eight energising factors of motivation are: purpose/meaning, autonomy, mastery, relatedness, status, certainty, fairness and feedback. These are not inscribed on a stone tablet. Maybe you are motivated by some of these factors, and other things as well. Reflect on them and from time to time ask yourself questions such as these:
  - ✓ What really motivates me in the workplace?
  - ✓ Does my current job sufficiently satisfy those motivations?
  - ✓ If not, why not, and what am I going to do about it?

- **Setting goals.** Do you set goals for yourself and clear action plans to achieve them? You don't need to set goals, but the research shows overwhelmingly that setting sensible, achievable goals with clear action plans and accountability measures is a very sound method of motivation and personal development. One approach is to set SMART goals: goals and action plans that are specific, measurable, attainable, realistic and time-bound.

Chapter 7

Lifelong learning, development and curiosity

In this chapter we consider the third of the Five Factors in the Playbook for futureproofing your career: *Learning*. The following view is attributed to pioneering American industrialist Henry Ford: 'Anyone who stops learning is old, whether at twenty or eighty. Anyone who keeps learning stays young.' I think that is very wise counsel.

The World Economic Forum (WEF) agrees. In *The Future of Jobs Report 2023*[1], based on a global survey of 803 companies, the WEF listed 'curiosity and lifelong learning' as one of the five most useful skills for the jobs of the future.

What are *you* going to keep learning throughout what will be, God willing, your long life? And *how* will you learn? How will you keep developing and what will you develop into? Are you a curious person and, if so, how will you sustain that curiosity as you get older? These are of course highly personal questions to which each of us will have our own answers. All I can hope to do in this chapter is to sow some seeds while covering a few things I and others have found useful, inspiring and interesting.

The key point I will make is that thinking about and planning your own learning and development is a very good idea. Take charge of this yourself. Don't leave it to the vagaries of the employers you work for in the course of your career or careers. Research shows that people who engage in lifelong learning tend not only to be happier and more fulfilled[2], but to live longer.[3] Surely a significant bonus!

Curiosity, which we first encountered in chapter 4, may have killed the cat but a good dose is increasingly important for humans seeking to make their way in the world and in their careers. Having a curious mindset is a vital asset for lifelong learning.

How much do you care?

That's right, how much do you care about your own learning and development? The fact that you are still reading this book should tell you something.

Ask yourself these questions

- What will I do when I finish this book?
- Will I change my approach to my own learning and development?
- Will I develop a detailed plan and strategy?
- Am I, or will I develop into, a lifelong learner?
- How will I cultivate and maintain curiosity?

The default position for many professionals goes something like this: They put a fair bit of time and attention into learning and development of their primary technical skills, especially at the start of their careers—the so-called hard skills, to which we will return in chapter 8. The soft skills, typically, are lower on their list of priorities when it comes to planning and strategising. Maybe they get picked up along the way, maybe not, depending on the job and the whims of and occasional programs provided by employers. As you will see in chapter 8, I prefer to use the expressions Prime Capabilities and Enablers, rather than hard skills and soft skills.

The need for professionals to take charge of their own learning and development has been underscored by the post-COVID remote-working revolution: the third of the interlinked challenges facing professionals I set out in the Introduction. Many professionals now spend little time in face-to-face contact with more senior professionals with expertise to share. This means fewer spontaneous opportunities for coaching and mentoring. Don't expect your employer to have necessarily either recognised or appropriately responded to this situation. If you work remotely, even part of the time, take the bull by the horns and make sure your learning and development are not overlooked.

Adult learning

How do adults best learn new things? How do *you* best learn new things? While we're all different, recent decades have seen much research on the adult learning process that is worth knowing about.[4]

I finished high school in 1978, and I guess I became an adult around that time. In that same year, American sociologist Jack Mezirow published his first paper on transformative learning theory for adults.[5] I became aware of the importance of this theory only in 2019, by which time I was 58. I am still learning new things and now I am trying to do so in a way that is transformative.

Mezirow's eight-page paper 'Transformative Learning: Theory to Practice'[6] is a great introduction to understanding and applying transformative learning. At the time of writing, it is freely available online.

The purpose of transformative learning is to help equip us to develop autonomous thinking, which is to say the ability to make our own decisions rather than acting according to the beliefs, judgements or feelings of others. The importance of autonomous thinking in transformative learning dovetails with the role of autonomy as one of three fundamental psychological needs or nutriments essential for optimal functioning and personal wellbeing, as espoused by self-determination theory (discussed in chapter 6).

Transformative learning involves changing our frames of reference. By adulthood certain frames of reference are deeply entrenched — the values, feelings, conditioned responses and assumptions shaped by our upbringing and experience. There are two kinds of frames of reference. The first are 'habits of mind', those habitual ways of thinking, feeling and acting that are influenced by internal assumptions that may be unconscious. These are fundamental and the hardest to change. The second are points of view on specific matters, including beliefs and value judgements.

At the heart of transformative learning is a willingness to transform our frames of reference through critical reflection on the assumptions on which our interpretations, beliefs, habits of mind and points of view are based. When circumstances permit, transformative learners move towards frames of reference that are more inclusive, discriminating and self-reflective.

Individual self-reflection, which is also critical to emotional intelligence, as we will see in chapter 9, can lead to significant personal transformation. However, transformative learning holds that this is generally insufficient. When we are learning new things that involve understanding purposes, values, beliefs and feelings, we really need to engage in discussions with others to test and debate evidence, arguments, competing interpretations and alternative points of view. Setting up a professional discussion group (book club) is one way to ensure you have a suitable forum for such discussions (see the suggested reading lists section at the end of this book).

Mezirow equips educators with the tools they need to facilitate discussion between learners and to teach in a transformative way that assists learners to become aware and critical of their own and others' assumptions and to recognise their own frames of reference. This enables learners to imaginatively, creatively see problems from other perspectives. And educators can play a vital role in facilitating discussions between learners.

Ask yourself this question about someone whose job it is to teach you new things: *Do they teach in a transformative manner?* If not, is there a way you might encourage them to do so? Here is another question: *How can I best learn in a transformative way if I am trying to learn things by myself?* A set of questions later in this chapter offers some tips and ideas.

Having got my head around Mezirow's transformative dimensions of adult learning, I dove into Benedict Carey's 2014 *How We Learn*.[7] I expected to find lots of references to practical aspects of transformative dimensions of adult learning and responses to Mezirow's theory, but I was disappointed. *How We Learn* comes from a different perspective. It is a masterful summary of recent research into how our brains absorb and retain information. Carey reminds us that for much of human history our brains foraged for information, strategies and learning based on the imperative of survival as we went about our daily tasks of finding food and mates and avoiding predators. Ideas about what we now think of as education have developed only relatively recently.

If you want refreshing, evidence-based pushback to traditional modern education, then *How We Learn* is your go-to book. Carey is a journalist and not a scientist, but he has his head around current research and has pulled it together for the layman. Here are just two of many at times counterintuitive ideas and tips. We are often told that it is important to have a dedicated study area and time. According to Carey, the research shows that most people do better over time if they vary their study or practice locations, and the time of day. We are also commonly told to practise one skill at a time. Carey reports on evidence to show mixing or 'interleaving' multiple skills in practice sessions in fact sharpens our grasp of all of them. Many of the capabilities and skills I address in this book are highly interconnected and would benefit from mixing and matching in their practice and development.

70:20:10 learning and development

The 70:20:10 Institute explains the principle of learning and development as follows:

- 70 per cent of learning comes from experience, experiment and reflection.
- 20 per cent derives from working with others.
- 10 per cent comes from formal interventions and planned learning solutions.[8]

These numbers remind us that, in the workplace, we learn most from working and interacting with others (70 + 20). Of course, the specific ratio in any given situation will vary, depending on the work environment and the organisational results required. But in my experience, 70:20:10 seems about right. Certainly, formal planned learning sessions (10 per cent) tend to be wasted unless followed up by the 20 per cent and 70 per cent components.

Nonetheless, in academic learning and development circles, the 70:20:10 concept has generated some controversy, including this comment from Richard Harding, Research Fellow of the Open University (UK)'s Department of Public Leadership and Social Enterprise:

> *The siren song of the 70:20:10 'rule' tempts the unwary, promising self-evident truth, efficiency and cost saving ... Contingent real-world phenomena generally defy such precise, immutable and generalized quantification and it's unlikely to apply so exactly in any organization — let alone across differing ones.*[9]

The 70:20:10 Institute website devotes considerable space to countering 'myths' around and objections to the 70:20:10 principle.

Learning in the age of artificial intelligence and complexity

In *Basic AI*[10] David Shrier argues that developing 'cognitive flexibility' will be vital for navigating the world of AI. He proposes that cognitive flexibility is one of the building blocks necessary for acquiring new knowledge and that 'if you want to stay competitive, and win at work in the age of AI, you need to retrain your brain so that you can learn faster and bring that learning to bear in a context relevant to your workplace.'[11]

In a section titled 'Remaking Your Brain', Shrier lists five principles that can assist with developing the cognitive flexibility necessary for knowledge acquisition:

1. the importance of practice
2. the benefits of reflection
3. sustained and gradual change
4. peer learning
5. creative exploration.

All these principles feature in various guises in this book.

A recent research study found, unsurprisingly, that humans use social information to guide their decisions, even when others' preferences differ from their own[12], and that 'it is our extraordinary capacity for social and cultural learning that has played a key role in the success of the human species. A better understanding of this ability could let us incorporate similar principles into AI, such as in virtual assistants or recommendation algorithms.'[13]

Complexity, which along with AI is one of the four interlinked challenges set out in my Introduction, will also have an impact on how and what you learn. Here I again refer you to Amy Edmondson's book *Right Kind of Wrong: How the Best Teams Use Failure to Succeed*, as a terrific resource to explore learning in the age of complexity.

The careful and wise use of artificial intelligence can assist individuals and organisations to address complexity and uncertainty, and to enhance learning. In a November 2024 report titled 'Learning to Manage Uncertainty, with AI', the researchers concluded:

Based on a global survey of 3,467 respondents and interviews with nine executives, our research quantitatively and qualitatively establishes a relationship between organizational learning, learning with AI, and the ability to manage rapidly changing business environments.[14]

The researchers offered suggestions on how AI-specific learning can substantially improve three areas of organisational learning: knowledge capture, knowledge synthesis and knowledge dissemination.

Growth mindset

Carol Dweck, a professor of psychology at Stanford University, is the leading guru on growth mindset vs fixed mindset. According to Dweck[15], people who believe their talents can be developed through hard work, good strategies and input from others have a growth mindset. Such people achieve more than those with a more fixed mindset, who believe their talents are innate gifts. People with growth mindsets worry less about looking smart and put more energy into learning.

Research by Dweck and others suggests that when companies pursue a growth mindset, not only do their employees report feeling more empowered and committed, but they also receive greater organisational support for collaboration and innovation. By contrast, people at primarily fixed-mindset companies report more cheating and deception among employees, presumably to gain an advantage in the talent race.

Dweck acknowledges it's not easy to attain a growth mindset. One reason is that we all have our own fixed-mindset triggers. When we are challenged or criticised or fare poorly compared with others, we can become insecure or defensive, which inhibits our growth. If an organisation encourages a fixed mindset, it is harder for people to practise growth mindset thinking and behaviour, such as sharing information, collaborating, innovating, seeking feedback or admitting to errors.

The idea of the growth vs fixed mindset has attracted plenty of controversy, including the claim that 'the foundations of mind-set theory are not firm and bold claims about mind-set appear to be overstated'.[16] Dweck has responded to this and other criticisms.[17]

Despite the controversy, if you are attracted to the idea of a growth mindset, then Dweck and others offer countless ideas on how to achieve this happy state. These suggestions from Oregon State University are a pretty good place to start:

- **Seek out new challenges**. Trying new things, even if you end up failing, helps you to stretch and grow. Being prepared to experiment, even if it is a struggle, can have a profound influence on how you approach challenges and difficulties in your life.
- **Be persistent**. Obstacles may appear and you won't always succeed, at least not immediately. Keep going and do not give

up. Seek assistance and guidance from other people including family, friends and mentors. Reflect on where you are and where you want to be.

- **When you receive criticism, do not ignore it**. You may receive polite feedback, and maybe not so subtle criticism on occasions. Reflect on what people tell you and decide what corrective actions, if any, you will take. Actively seek feedback/advice from others. Seeking and actioning feedback as appropriate is one of the Seven Accelerants we will explore in chapter 9.

- **Draw inspiration from the success of others**. When people you know succeed in their endeavours, offer them praise and congratulations. Be inspired and not envious of other people's success and try to avoid making comparisons. Everyone is on a different path and there are many paths to success. Chapter 11 will help you to reflect on what 'success' means for you.[18]

If you find that the voice in your head is not helping you in your quest to develop a growth mindset, don't despair. Help is at hand. For example, award-winning psychologist Ethan Kross's book *Chatter: The Voice in Our Head and How to Harness It*[19] introduces practical, evidence-based tools and has certainly changed the way I talk to myself. A number of my clients report having had the same experience with this book, and not just on fixed vs growth mindsets.

Adult development theory

Over the past hundred years or so psychologists have studied the way adults develop over the course of their lives and how they make meaning from their environment and from the people in their lives. The theory of adult development I have been especially drawn to is that of psychologist Robert Kegan, a professor at the Harvard Graduate School of Education. In his seminal work, *In Over Our Heads*[20], Kegan discusses the mental demands of modern life: 'the expectations upon us ... demand something more than mere behaviour, the acquisition of specific skills, or the mastery of particular knowledge. They make demands on our minds, on *how* we know, on the complexity of our consciousness'.[21]

What follows is a summarised and necessarily incomplete account of Kegan's adult development theory. My description of adult development theory is drawn largely from Jennifer Garvey Berger's 'Key Concepts for Understanding the Work of Robert Kegan'[22], which at the time of writing was freely available online.

According to Kegan, transformative adult development does not come from knowing more things. Rather, it comes from the *way* we know things. Kegan draws a distinction between those things that are Object and those that are Subject in terms of the way we make meaning from our surroundings, from the information we receive and from what we experience. Objects are those elements of our knowing that we 'can reflect on, handle, look at, be responsible for, relate to each other, take control of, internalize, assimilate, or otherwise operate on'.[23] In short, when things are Object, we *have them,* and we can view them as if from a distance. By contrast, things that are Subject *have us.* They are so deeply embedded that we cannot view them in any objective sense. A core part of adult development is moving more and more things from Subject to Object. The more in your life you reflect on and handle, the more complex and diverse your world view will become, because you can objectively see and act on more things.[24]

Kegan suggests that there are five *orders of mind*, five substantially different ways through which we make sense and meaning of the world and construct reality. Not everyone progresses through each order and no order is inherently superior to any other, but at each successive order of mind people can make more things Object and thus attain a more complex and diverse world view.

The first order, experienced mostly by young children, is a time of magic and mystery within which the notion of rules is hard to grasp and remember. In the second order, the Sovereign Mind, people are mostly self-centred. They are aware other people have feelings and desires, but they generally lack empathy. Rules are understood but the orientation is to avoid or get around a rule if possible. The second order is experienced by older children, adolescents, some adults (and perhaps a particular President of the United States, assuming he made it past the first order).

The third order, the Socialised or Traditional Mind, is that experienced by older adolescents and most adults. They are able to control the desires and impulses to which they were Subject in the second order; they are now Object in the third order. They can self-reflect and think abstractly but can sometimes find it hard to make discriminating decisions between their own interests and the demands of other people. Their self-esteem is highly reliant on the views of others. The fourth order (the Self-Authored or Modern Mind — some adults) sees people creating a sense of self that exists outside the needs and opinions of other people. They have strong internal rules and regulations and can feel empathy for others. They are able to accept and reflect dispassionately on feedback: feedback is now Object, whereas it would generally have been Subject at earlier orders.

The fifth order, the Self-Transforming or Postmodern Mind, is experienced by a very few adults, and not before later life. They have learned the limits of their own inner systems, and they now see the world in many shades and colours, rather than black and white. They are aware that other people have their own inner systems, and they look for similarities and not just differences. People at this level make great mediators.

Simply learning about Kegan's theory of adult development, and the notions of Subject/Object and Orders of Mind, has had a major bearing not just on my own world view but on how I perceive other people and their decisions and choices.

There are some common themes and overlaps between transformative learning and adult development. Here is a tool to assist you on both quests.

Transform your learning and development

As you go through life you learn new things and develop into the best version of yourself. The following questions are designed to challenge your thinking and assumptions as you follow that path. They will also help you address the complexity that, as I noted in the Introduction, is one of the four overarching challenges professionals face today and that they will face in the future.

Before you make a decision about a person or a course of action, ask yourself:

- What do I believe, *how* do I know this is true, and how could I be wrong?[25]

- What are my values and beliefs and how are they challenged by new ideas, people or events?

- What are my 'habits of mind' — my habitual ways of thinking, feeling and acting, influenced by my internal assumptions?

- What assumptions am I making about other people and their beliefs and motivations? Where did these assumptions come from? Are they evidence-based? Are they actually helpful in the present situation?

- What could be other interpretations or perspectives?

- How can I design some safe-to-fail experiments through which to try out new things?

- What am I prepared to give up and let go of in order to learn and develop?

- Who can I discuss new (or old) thoughts and ideas with to gain other perspectives?

- What things in my life, right now, might be Subject (things that 'have' me and that I can't really see) and how can I make them Object (things I can reflect on, handle, look at, be responsible for, relate to each other, take control of, internalise, assimilate or otherwise operate on)?

In play

In my first career, most of my deliberate learning and development involved keeping up with ever-changing taxation law and practice so I could be as useful as possible to my clients. I rarely stopped to think strategically about all the other capabilities and skills that would ensure I became the best possible tax adviser. Certainly I had no overall plan or roadmap. I picked things up along the way from random training courses, through experience and making mistakes, and through osmosis and watching others display assorted capabilities and skills, well or badly. I like to think that if I had my time over I would be more aware and focused on identifying key capabilities and skills and developing them, strategically and by 'deliberate practice', as I will discuss in chapter 9. In a sense, that is the reason for this book. It is like a long letter to my 24-year-old self.

After my first career, I enrolled in a Master of Science in Coaching Psychology at my alma mater, the University of Sydney. It was a fabulous experience. Freed from the daily challenges of keeping up with changes to tax law and filling in time sheets in six-minute increments, I revelled in having the time and motivation to learn about a whole new field of human knowledge, the emerging discipline of how the principles of psychology can be employed in an executive coaching context. As I noted in the Introduction, I learned all manner of things that would have been extremely useful in my first career. I have tried to capture some of those lessons and experiences in this book.

In my second career, I have a delightful tax-deductible man cave — oops, office — in Macquarie Street, Sydney, near the Royal Botanic Garden. On the wall above my desk, I have placed a copy of my own performance mindset mantra, which I reflect on regularly and indeed live by: 'I always strive to perform to the very best of my ability and I keep learning and improving. I do not compromise my physical, mental, spiritual or social wellbeing. And I have fun!' (I love exclamation marks! Sadly, my editor didn't allow me to use too many of them in this book.) The use of mantras has not only been found helpful to raise performance levels in all sorts of domains, but there is strong evidence that practising mantra meditation is effective in relieving stress and in coping with hypertension.[26]

As you can see, my mantra is quite wordy. Mantra gurus, and there are many of them, will generally advise that a mantra should contain only a couple of real words, or maybe some sound (like *om*) or a grunt of some sort. That might be fine and indeed necessary for high-performance athletes. But hey, I am an ex–tax lawyer so cut me some slack. I was very proud that I kept my mantra to only 33 words ... and one exclamation mark. As you can see, I have included continuous learning and improvement as part of my mantra.

Key takeaways

- **How much do you care?**
  - ✓ How much do *you* care about your own learning and development? If you don't care about it, no one else will either!
  - ✓ What will you do when you have finished reading this book?
  - ✓ Will you change the way you go about your own learning and development?
  - ✓ Will you develop a more detailed plan and strategy?
  - ✓ Are you, or will you develop into, a lifelong and curious learner?
- **Adult learning.** Adults learn differently from children:
  - ✓ Ideally, we transform our long-held frames of reference through critical reflection on the assumptions upon which our interpretations, beliefs, habits of mind and points of view are based.
  - ✓ Individual self-reflection can lead to significant personal learning and transformation. However, this is not enough. When learning new things that involve understanding purposes, values, beliefs and feelings, we need discussions with other people to test and debate evidence, arguments and alternative points of view.
  - ✓ A professional discussion group (book club), as discussed in the reading lists section at the end of this book, is one way to create a forum for such discussions.
- **70:20:10 learning and development.** The principle is that:
  - ✓ 70 per cent of learning comes from experience, experiment and reflection
  - ✓ 20 per cent derives from working with others
  - ✓ 10 per cent comes from formal interventions and planned learning solutions.
- **Growth mindset.** This somewhat controversial theory states that people who believe their talents can be developed (through hard work, good strategies and input from others) exhibit a growth mindset. Such people are believed to achieve more than those with a more fixed mindset, who believe their talents are innate gifts. This is because people with growth mindsets worry less about looking smart and put their energy into learning. Ideas on

how to achieve a growth mindset, if you are so minded, include the following:

✓ Seek out new challenges.

✓ Be persistent.

✓ When you receive criticism, do not ignore it.

✓ Draw inspiration from the success of others.

- **Adult development theory.** According to psychologist Robert Kegan, true adult development does not come from knowing more things. Rather, it comes from the *way* we know things. Kegan draws a distinction between things that are Object and things that are Subject in the way we make meaning from our surroundings, the information we receive and the events we experience:

  ✓ Things that are Object are those elements of our knowing that we can reflect on, handle, look at, be responsible for, relate to each other, take control of, internalise, assimilate or otherwise operate on.

  ✓ Things that are Subject are so deeply embedded we cannot view them objectively.

A core part of adult development is moving more and more things from Subject to Object. The more in your life you can take as Object, reflect on and handle, the more complex and diverse your world view can become, because you can see and act upon more things.

Kegan suggests five 'orders of mind' — substantially different ways through which people make sense and meaning of the world and construct their reality. Not everyone progresses through each order, and no order is inherently superior to any other. At each successive order of mind, people can make more Subject things Object and thus achieve a more complex and diverse world view.

Chapter 8

Prime Capabilities and Enablers: become AI-proof

This chapter addresses the fourth of the Playbook's Five Factors to help you build a successful career: *Capabilities*. In the previous chapter we explored the process of lifelong learning and development (L&D). It's now time to get more specific. Obtaining one or more university or college degrees and other necessary qualifications to join your profession of choice are steps on your journey of lifelong L&D, but what else are you going to learn, when and in what order? How are you going to develop? And how will you make yourself AI-proof? We need an appropriate collective noun for the things you are going to learn and develop. Assorted consultants, human resource and L&D professionals can tie themselves up in knots trying to define and differentiate terms such as skills, attributes, tools, competencies, capacities and capabilities in ways that generally don't equate with standard dictionary definitions.

Many organisations have now adopted capability frameworks. I will use the forward-looking definition of capability set out by Chartered Accountants Australia and New Zealand (CA ANZ) in their CA Capability Model: 'a capability establishes a high-level definition of the attributes (skills, knowledge, cognitive attributes and behaviours) that individuals and workforces need to succeed in the future'.[1]

You won't find this definition in the *Oxford Dictionary*, but it is perfect for the purposes of this book. I am going to explain two types of capabilities: Prime Capabilities and Enablers. But first I will recount the sorry tale of hard skills vs soft skills, and other efforts to categorise various types of capabilities.

Hard skills vs soft skills

In the old days (okay, still today for many people) hard skills were valued over soft skills. Hard skills were what mattered. These were the technical skills you learned at university or college, your core professional skills, kept up to date by continuing professional education. Everything else, including people skills, were soft skills. They were not that important and could be safely ignored, until you were given negative feedback that you lacked them. Even then you might not have bothered too much unless your pay, promotion or status were under threat.

The terms soft skills and hard skills and their relationship to each other are products of the US military. This is the same outfit that gave the world snafu and fubar (google them) and many other entertaining and not-so-entertaining expressions and acronyms.

The term soft skills had been in military use for some years when, in 1972, the US Continental Army Command (CONARC) sponsored the CONARC Soft Skills Training Conference. Apparently, the army's initial definition of the term—'job related skills involving actions affecting primarily people and paper, e.g., inspecting troops, supervising office personnel, conducting studies, preparing maintenance reports, preparing efficiency reports, designing bridge structures'—was not very helpful for analysing job requirements and *responsibilities*. Interestingly, the conference report concluded that 'no distinction should be made between hard skills and soft skills' and recommended that 'soft skills' be eliminated from systems engineering terminology'.[2]

The term persisted, however, and spread from the US Army into the business world and other walks of life, where it has come to encompass all manner of things including communication, relationships, emotional intelligence, teamwork and leadership skills. Over the years there have been numerous efforts[3] to persuade people that, despite the negative connotations of softness, soft skills are just as important and indeed sometimes more important than hard skills. But the connotations persist, with the result that many publications featuring lists of recommended skills to be acquired by executives and leaders don't mention soft skills.[4] For all that many or all of the listed attributes may in fact be defined as soft skills. Despite a great deal of research suggesting otherwise, the term soft skills retains a pejorative flavour, with the implication that they matter less than hard skills. Because soft skills has become a loaded term, there have been all manner of earnest attempts to come up with an alternative, such as people skills, which in their turn have been similarly derided.

Hard skills, soft skills, technical skills, people skills, human skills, social skills and a whole bunch of other descriptors abound in the business world and in the academic literature. The term soft skills is still widely used but is unloved. A replacement label is needed, but there's no agreement on a new appellation. Best-selling author and entrepreneur Seth Godin suggests soft skills should be rebadged as real skills.[5]

I now not only join the chorus proposing the abolition of the term soft skills; I suggest a fundamental rethink of the distinction between hard skills and soft skills, at least in a professional services context. As you will see, Prime Capabilities are not the same as what have been regarded as hard skills, just as Enablers are not the same as soft skills. My approach is more nuanced (I love that word) and more than a simple renaming exercise.

So, professionals, I want you to forget all about hard skills and soft skills. These are no longer useful terms, if indeed they ever were.

An introduction to Prime Capabilities and Enablers

Your clients typically don't care about distinctions between hard skills and soft skills, or what skills you may need to become a whole person. They don't care about your lifelong journey of learning and development. They just want first-class service and for you to understand their needs and solve their problems as quickly and as cheaply as possible. However, just because your clients don't differentiate between hard skills and soft skills, it doesn't mean you shouldn't think about the skills and capabilities you need to serve them to the best of your ability. Recall the two questions you considered in the Introduction:

- How can I become my best possible professional?
- How can I add the most value in the age of artificial intelligence?

Part of the answer to each question depends on your taking the time to figure out what capabilities will best serve you, and how you will go about developing or improving those capabilities in the future. I suggest you take a client-centric perspective. I would remind you that this book is intended for professionals working in-house across a range of organisations and not just for professionals working in professional service firms (PSFs). If you are an in-house professional, your clients are all those inside your organisation who rely on your expert advice and assistance.

Ask yourself versions of these questions:

- Why, exactly, are my clients paying me, or my organisation?
- What outcomes do my clients value and expect from me?
- Who am I providing services to and what are their key needs of me?
- How, exactly, do I add value to my clients?
- What are the core deliverables I am expected to produce?

The answers to these types of questions will help you to determine your Prime Capabilities, which I define as follows:

Prime Capabilities *are the* key *capabilities that enable an expert senior professional to add value for their clients by best servicing their needs and solving their problems. They are what you do/have now or aspire to do/have: what your clients expect that you will do and do well.*

Ideally, your Prime Capabilities should number no more than between four and six. The absolute best way to identify them is to ask the questions I've suggested, or similar questions, of some of your clients. If your clients simply say, 'Solve my problems as quickly and as cheaply as possible', buy them another coffee or beer and push for more details.

Prime Capabilities are aspirational. Thinking about your Prime Capabilities from the perspective of an expert senior professional in your profession will help you, if you are a younger professional, to decide on something to aim for.

Enablers are all the other capabilities that assist you in using your Prime Capabilities in the service of your clients.

Your clients probably won't mention what we've identified as Enablers when you put your questions to them. This is not because they are unimportant. It is because you asked your clients to nominate the top four to six *key* skills and attributes that best answer the five questions set out earlier. If asked, clients would likely say, yes, the Enablers are still important or that they were taken for granted. Accordingly, you may need to figure out your Enablers without as much client input as for your Prime Capabilities. However, you can still discuss the concept with clients and with colleagues within your organisation.

Pretty much every professional should have Enablers which include things like: emotional intelligence; self-management and personal accountability; teamwork, collaboration and delegation skills; communication, relationship and conflict resolution skills; critical thinking, decision-making and problem-solving skills; efficiency and meeting management skills. How you describe and prioritise such Enablers will be very much a personal thing.

Unlike Prime Capabilities, you may have any number of Enablers, but at some point you will need to prioritise them for the purposes of learning and development. I won't pretend that there will always be a neat and easy way to decide what is a Prime Capability and what is an Enabler. However, for reasons I will go on to discuss, it seems useful to try to make this distinction as best you can.

A key Enabler for most professionals will be knowing how to expertly prompt and otherwise use the latest and most applicable AI tools.

The fundamentals of being a true professional, as discussed in chapter 1, are assumed and shouldn't generally appear on lists of Prime Capabilities and Enablers. Client service type skills (see chapter 3) shouldn't generally be Prime Capabilities, but they might be Enablers.

This chapter explores capabilities from a client-facing perspective. Your Prime Capabilities and Enablers are likely to change over time as client needs and expectations change and as you become more senior and take on different roles. That is, Prime Capabilities and Enablers are not a set-and-forget thing. You should reassess them from time to time. As you take on leadership roles, your Prime Capabilities and Enablers are likely to differ in some respects from those you adopted for servicing clients.

As noted in chapter 4, some junior professionals may be a bit intimidated about asking clients to help them uncover their Prime Capabilities and Enablers. This is where more senior professionals, especially employer professionals, can assist.

Prime Capabilities and Enablers: why bother?

There are at least three reasons why it is useful to determine your Prime Capabilities and Enablers. First, doing so should make you a more successful client-serving professional. By definition, both types of capabilities are viewed from a client perspective.

Second, this assessment should assist you in planning your learning and development. You have only so much time to spend on structured L&D as opposed to learning on the job, and identifying your Prime Capabilities and Enablers will help you with L&D prioritisation.

Third, as we will discuss, knowing your Prime Capabilities and Enablers is a useful way of assessing how AI and machines may threaten and/or assist your career. For these purposes, a machine is any non-human device or tool.

Why distinguish Prime Capabilities from Enablers? Because it will help you prioritise and develop the capabilities that make you most valuable to your clients now and as automation and AI continue to develop.

Examples of Prime Capabilities and Enablers will make the concepts clearer. As you will see, the same skill or attribute may be a Prime Capability for one professional and an Enabler for another. It is likely those within a particular profession, sub-profession or sector will have similar Prime Capabilities because their clients are likely to have broadly similar problems and needs. At the same time and as the examples that follow show, professionals in different professions with differing client needs are likely to have different Prime Capabilities.

If you work in a PSF, don't automatically assume your employers (the partners or other owners of the firm) know exactly what *your* Prime Capabilities are or should be. They are not your clients. Of course, you will seek their input but also gain insights directly from your clients. If you ask senior professionals in a PSF what skills you need to develop to get ahead, they will perhaps name some firm-focused rather than client-centric qualities, such as business development prowess. That's fine and you should include such capabilities somewhere in your skills arsenal and L&D plans.

If you are a professional who works in-house, the organisation is both your employer and your client. In practice, you will have many individual clients within the organisation. You may get a range of views on what should be your Prime Capabilities. Seek input from colleagues in your in-house department in order to reconcile client priorities.

Don't assume that your university or college education, and any additional formal training for admittance into your chosen profession, even mentioned all relevant Prime Capabilities and Enablers (or all applicable hard skills and soft skills), let alone provided suitable training and instruction. Most educational institutions still seem to be struggling to fit all the perceived 'hard skills' of the relevant profession into their curricula.

Examples of Prime Capabilities and Enablers

Here are three examples that will help you better understand the concept of Prime Capabilities and Enablers.

Peter is an executive coach, focusing mainly on leadership development. He is a young-at-heart professional, having already had a lengthy first career as a corporate tax lawyer. Someone suggests he should work out his Prime Capabilities and Enablers. After overcoming his lawyerish scepticism, Peter does some research and reflection. After talking with some clients and fellow coaches he comes up with these Prime Capabilities:

- **Core coaching skills.** These include awareness, listening skills, asking questions, offering perspectives, and challenging and supporting clients in their quest for goal setting, achievement, and personal development.

- **Specialist skills**. Peter decides that getting a good handle on theories of adult development and complexity would be useful given his client base.

- **Emotional intelligence**. It becomes clear to Peter early in his second career that many of his clients have worked out that this is something they need help to develop. As a result, he figures that he should try, somewhat belatedly, to get on top of some of this stuff himself so he can be a role model.

- **Leadership skills**. These are important, given that Peter purports to coach and mentor people on such skills.

Peter also assesses his Enablers and comes up with negotiation skills to assist with obtaining and retaining clients, and awareness of technology and AI and their potential to render him obsolete early in his second career.

Having identified his Prime Capabilities, Peter embarks on an ongoing journey of learning, development and improvement in each area. This includes undertaking a Master of Science in Coaching Psychology, any number of other courses and programs on various specialist skills, and fostering emotional intelligence. Peter also decides to teach in the MBA program at the University of New South Wales's Australian Graduate School of Management (AGSM), which will maintain his understanding of leadership skills. As to his Enablers, Peter is sufficiently intrigued by the impact of AI on professionals that he decides to write a book that will include the topic.

Peter is so impressed by his discovery of Prime Capabilities and Enablers that he begins to encourage his clients to go through the same process, starting with Paul and Mary.

Paul is a Chartered Accountant working in the audit division of a mid-sized accounting firm. He reviews the CA Capability Model promoted by his industry body, CA ANZ, and has discussions with some clients as well as partners in his firm. He summarises his Prime Capabilities as follows:

- **Accounting and auditing skills.** An expert understanding of all the accounting and auditing standards, together with relevant aspects of corporation and other laws, is required.

- **Judgement and decision making.** Laws and accounting and auditing standards are not always crystal clear. Sound judgement and decision making are highly prized by clients.

- **Use of technology.** Clients expect Paul's firm to use the latest technology to deliver the best service for the lowest cost.

Paul also reflects on his Enablers and comes up with these, again after reviewing the CA Capability Model: communication, emotional intelligence, relationship, self-management, and team management skills. Senior professionals in Paul's line of business are expected to manage and lead large teams.

Of his Prime Capabilities, Paul decides the one that most needs specific attention is judgement and decision making. He includes this topic as an area for special focus in his mentoring sessions with a senior partner and he also pays close attention during his day-to-day work to how senior professionals make judgement calls. Paul is something of a computer nerd, so he is well on top of his 'use of technology' Prime Capability. In fact, he is streets ahead of most of the partners and is helping his firm to assess different external software tools and artificial intelligence platforms. As to his Enablers, Paul agrees with his reporting partner that his written communication skills need a lift. The firm has an internal L&D program to improve such skills and Paul signs up.

Mary is a high-flying mergers and acquisitions lawyer, working in the in-house legal team of a major multinational corporation. Mary starts the identification of her Prime Capabilities and Enablers with self-reflection on her experiences and client feedback in her career to date. Next she quizzes more senior colleagues in her team, including the corporation's general counsel. She then has some coffee catchups with several of her internal clients. After some further thought and reflection, Mary summarises her Prime Capabilities:

- **Legal knowledge** — a good understanding of corporate law and practice in the major countries in which the corporation operates.

- **Business acumen** — the ability to translate the law into sensible and commercially astute advice relevant to the corporation, its needs and risk profile based on the experience, judgement and wisdom of the professional.
- **Negotiation skills** — the ability to engage in effective and productive discussions with internal clients, external advisers, counterparties and regulators so as to maximise outcomes for the corporation while minimising risks and potential downsides.
- **Ability to meet deadlines** — the corporation runs a very tight ship, and timetables must always be met. Mary and her colleagues typically have multiple projects on the go with various business units. They must be adept at managing competing priorities and deadlines through regular and clear communication with internal stakeholders.

Mary comes up with quite a long list of Enablers, including written and verbal communication skills, collaboration with colleagues, emotional intelligence, self-management, project management and a good understanding of the latest developments in relevant AI tools.

After some further reflection and discussion with the corporation's general counsel, Mary decides that of her four Prime Capabilities, the one most needing extra attention in the short to medium term is her ability to negotiate. She designs an L&D program accordingly, with the help and support of the general counsel. Mary is happy that she is developing her other Prime Capabilities on a day-to-day basis, augmented by existing L&D programs that her employer and professional bodies provide. With her Enablers, and again in conjunction with the general counsel, Mary targets development of her emotional intelligence and her knowledge of emerging AI platforms relevant to her work for the corporation.

Prime Capabilities and Enablers in the age of AI

You have now determined your Prime Capabilities and Enablers. Here are further questions to ask yourself and, ideally, your clients:

- What can I currently do better than a machine?
- What tasks do my clients currently value my doing, either by myself or with some expert supervision of a machine?

How did you answer the first question? If your answer was 'nothing' or 'not much', your position is highly suboptimal. Perhaps you should reassess your Prime Capabilities or find a new career. You want to make sure that you are as AI-proof as possible.

As noted earlier, ideally you will reconsider your Prime Capabilities from time to time. The answer to the first question is likely to change, possibly dramatically, over the course of your career, or even over a year or two, and this will have an impact on how you can best add value for your clients. The more predictable, repetitive or routine a task is, the quicker it will be taken over by smart machines. The more a task requires judgement or an understanding of context including human feelings and emotions, the longer it will be before machines are stealing your lunch and your job. As we saw in chapter 2, most jobs involve repetitive, routine tasks as well as more cerebral ones, and machines will chip away at these low-hanging fruit first. If the Susskinds (chapter 2) are right, the things your clients will value you for will steadily decline in coming decades.

There are any number of recommendations, from people much more expert than I am, on the key capabilities you should develop if you are to be more useful to your clients than increasingly intelligent machines. Here is a compilation of key capabilities extracted from a range of reputable sources[6] (as ChatGPT and brethren become ever more sophisticated, these suggestions will inevitably change[7]):

- adaptability
- analytical thinking
- avoiding predictability
- coaching skills
- collaboration and teamwork
- communication skills
- continuous, adaptive, lifelong learning
- creative thinking and problem-solving skills
- critical thinking
- curiosity
- digital and data literacy
- emotional intelligence, including self-awareness, empathy and emotional control
- ethical compass
- flexibility
- humility
- influencing without authority
- judgement and decision-making skills

- leadership skills
- personal brand
- time management
- trust building.

Ask yourself these questions

- When looking at this list, what am I thinking?
- Which of these items will best assist me to keep ahead of AI?
- Which ones are or should be in my toolkit of Prime Capabilities and Enablers?

If you answer 'all' or 'lots of them' to the second or third questions, which ones will you prioritise for development, and when and how will you do this?

Even without taking into account advances in AI, a 2024 study by researchers at the CSIRO found that the kinds of interpersonal skills predominant in this list continue to grow in importance for employment in the post-pandemic, remote-work-friendly Australian labour market.[8] As David L Shrier advises in *Basic AI*, 'emotional intelligence and other "soft skills" represent key job capabilities that AI will have difficulty replicating'.[9]

However, in an interesting October 2024 article in the *Australian Financial Review* titled 'Office workers are losing social skills', Euan Black cited plenty of evidence from employers and researchers that 'awkward and badly behaved co-workers are on the rise (and) managers complain about a decline in social skills triggered in part by the isolation of working from home'.[10]

One notable absence from the rather earnest list of capabilities I've garnered is storytelling. Don't take my word for it. Here is what Professor Scott Galloway had to say on CNBC *Make It* in March 2024, well over a year after the launch of ChatGPT:

> *If I could give my 13- and 16-year-old one competence that I think would stand the test of time, it'd be storytelling ... The type of storytelling may not matter, because the platforms people use to communicate can rapidly change.*[11]

Tasks

So far we have been considering capabilities. A professional needs Prime Capabilities and Enablers to produce results in response to client requests for assistance. Professionals undertake various tasks to satisfy client demands. They have had non-human assistance in meeting those demands ever since there have been sticks, stones, donkeys ... and machines. On maintaining our client-centric focus, I will use these definitions:

- **Human tasks** are those that, at any given moment, your clients value humans doing, either in toto, or with some expert supervision of one or more machines.

- **Machine tasks** are those that, at any given moment, your clients value machines doing rather than humans, either in toto, or with some routine non-expert supervision of a machine.

- **Expert supervision** means supervision requiring substantial human domain-specific knowledge, experience, expertise, judgement and wisdom.

- **Machine** is any type of non-human device or tool.

In practice, over time it will be your clients and the marketplace, not lists in business magazine articles, OECD or World Economic Forum reports or peer-reviewed academic journal articles that will decide what is a human task and what is a machine task. As AI and other machines become more sophisticated, the range of machine tasks will increase and human tasks will decrease. Nonetheless, ask yourself: Do *my* Prime Capabilities and Enablers adequately equip me to perform human tasks for clients in my chosen profession, at least at present?

If your Prime Capabilities do currently assist you to perform human tasks, on the one hand this is good news. Remember, your Prime Capabilities are the key capabilities that add value for your clients, helping service their needs and solve their problems. Having these Prime Capabilities is why you got hired. However, who knows what the machines of the future might be able to do? Keep developing those capabilities but maintain a close eye on whether and how quickly machines are catching up.

It seems to me that for many years to come any sensible client seeking, say, legal advice of any significance will regard that need as a human task. The client will expect the appropriate use by their adviser of the best available AI tools, but we seem to be a long, long way from being able to rely totally on machines to perform what we've called human tasks.

Any clear-thinking client will want AI-type machines to be expertly supervised by a human. In the case of legal advice, the supervision will need to come from a human who has substantial domain-specific knowledge, experience, expertise, judgement and wisdom. In this case, that person is a lawyer.

In other fact patterns and domains, the person might be an accountant, actuary, banker, financial adviser or planner, management consultant, coach, mentor, architect, engineer, scientist, information technology worker, or someone working in the human resources, advertising, market research or public relations sectors.

The speed and nature of the impact of AI on professionals will vary greatly from sector to sector. Tim Hall is the founder of PrimeSolve, which produces software that uses AI to create financial plans. Hall says that the AI software can already do 'absolutely everything'[12] a human financial adviser can do, including making decisions, discussing options and comparing alternatives. However, because money is tied up with emotions, Hall thinks that the role of AI will be to work in tandem with, rather than replacing, a human financial adviser. In its October 2024 report titled *Beware the gap: Governance arrangements in the face of AI innovation*, the Australian Securities & Investments Commission (ASIC) provided the results of its analysis of 624 AI use cases in 23 companies in the financial services sector. ASIC concluded that, at present, 'AI generally augmented rather than replaced human decision making and there was only limited direct interaction between AI and consumers.'[13]

What if Enablers equip you to do human tasks? Great, but remember that Enablers are all the other capabilities that assist you in using your Prime Capabilities in the service of your clients. You generally don't get hired *just* because you have a great set of Enablers. You need some valuable Prime Capabilities. Nonetheless, you should still develop Enablers that equip you to do human tasks, because it could be that you get hired rather than another professional who has equivalent Prime Capabilities but lacks the relevant Enablers.

Let's look at just one of our examples: Mary. All Mary's four Prime Capabilities will assist her to undertake human tasks as defined above. Machines are getting better with legal knowledge but it will be a long while, if ever, before the CEO of a multinational company gives the details of a proposed (unfriendly and complex) global takeover plan of a major rival to a machine with legal capacity, let alone relies on its advice without vetting by one or more expert human lawyers. As for the corporation's obsession with deadlines, this is Mary's responsibility. If key deadlines are missed Mary, not a machine, will be fired. Meeting deadlines is very much a human task.

Although Mary's two other Prime Capabilities (business acumen and negotiation skills) do not feature regularly on generic lists of human skills, they are very much human skills that will equip her to undertake human tasks, at least at the time of writing this book. Mary would be well advised to continue honing her business acumen and negotiation skills. Having said that, she will need to maintain up-to-date legal knowledge in order to judge whether the machines are giving her accurate information. If Mary lets her own legal knowledge slide, there is a risk that her valuable business acumen and negotiation skills will be adversely impacted.

Bringing it all together: a practical template

Like any consultant, I love a good 2×2 model and I was determined to include one in this book. Figure 8.1 shows a practical tool that will enable you to periodically map your capabilities against typical tasks your clients give you. Identify your Prime Capabilities and Enablers and ask yourself how they assist you to perform human or machine tasks for clients and complete the template accordingly.

Like most such models, the top right quadrant is the best place: lots of human tasks requiring your Prime Capabilities. If you don't have much in this quadrant, decide what you are going to do about the situation, and quickly.

As noted earlier, according to the CA Capability Model of CA ANZ, a *capability* establishes a high-level definition of the attributes (skills, knowledge, cognitive attributes and behaviours) that individuals and workforces need to succeed in the future.

Prime Capabilities are the *key* capabilities that enable an expert senior professional to add value for their clients by best servicing their needs and solving their problems. They are what you do/have now or aspire to do/have: what your clients expect that you will do and do well.

Enablers are all the other capabilities that assist you in using your Prime Capabilities in the service of your clients.

Human tasks are those that, at any given moment, your clients value humans doing, either in total, or with some expert supervision of one or more machines.

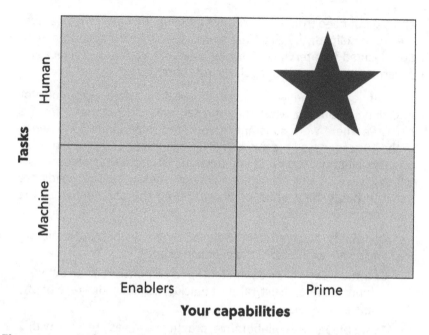

Figure 8.1: professional capabilities and tasks template

Machine tasks are those that, at any given moment, your clients value machines doing rather than humans, either in toto, or with some routine non-expert supervision of a machine.

Expert supervision means supervision requiring substantial human domain-specific knowledge, experience, expertise, judgement and wisdom.

Machine is any type of non-human device or tool.

In play

In 2022 I was asked to assist the New South Wales Bar Association with some professional development for its barrister members. The title of the session was 'Working with solicitors and their clients'. Various topics were up for discussion, including 'Understanding what your solicitors need from you and what they do not need'. Now, I had been a solicitor in my first career, which involved many experiences with numerous barristers, so I had a very clear idea about what *I* needed and did not need from the barristers I briefed. However, that was just me — one solicitor, by this time some years into my second career. So I decided to interview 18 senior solicitors from both private and government sectors who regularly brief barristers.

Without leading the witness, so to speak, I asked each solicitor questions, including what they needed and did not need from a barrister. There were constant themes and remarkable consistency in the 18 responses I received. This is a summary of the key insights into the 'what do and don't you need' question from my interviews, which I gave to the barristers in my presentation. The needs are listed in descending order of priority, from the perspective of the solicitors interviewed:

- **Deadlines**. Always meet deadlines, or get in contact to explain any delay (well) before the deadline expires.
- **Communication**. Be contactable and responsive; be an active listener; develop trust/rapport quickly; acknowledge receipt of briefs and emails.
- **Team player**. Be collaborative, practical and easy to work with.
- **Mindset**. Focus on strategy and solutions. Look and think two steps ahead.
- **Your requirements**. Be clear on what you need and when.
- **Legal and advocacy skills, and work ethic**. Although required, they were largely assumed and rarely mentioned by the solicitors interviewed.

When I interviewed the solicitors, I used none of the jargon from this chapter, such as Prime Capabilities and Enablers. Nonetheless, by speaking to solicitors, being the people who typically select them, brief them and pay their fees, I had effectively compiled a generic, first-cut list of some likely Prime Capabilities for New South Wales barristers.

The *Australian Financial Review* reported in June 2024 that Australia's most expensive lawyer apparently was Mark Robertson KC. Mr Robertson, who is of course a tax barrister, was reported to charge $6250 an hour, or $50 000 a day. The article said: 'Mr Robertson is a clear market leader on fees for tax advice because of his *business acumen* and *communication skills* (emphasis added) — a trait not widely evident with tax lawyers. "He's just so good with clients," said one solicitor. "Boards love him."'[14]

Key takeaways

- **Hard skills vs soft skills.** This was never a useful distinction. Just forget about it.
- **Prime Capabilities and Enablers.** This is a more useful way to think about your capabilities now and into the future:
  - ✓ Prime Capabilities are the *key* capabilities that enable an expert senior professional to add value for their clients by best servicing their needs and solving their problems. They are what you do/have now or aspire to do/have: what your clients expect that you will do and do well.
  - ✓ Enablers are all the other capabilities that assist you in using your Prime Capabilities in the service of your clients.

  To ascertain your Prime Capabilities, ask yourself, *and your clients*, these questions, or something similar:
  - ✓ Why, exactly, are my clients paying me, or my organisation?
  - ✓ What outcomes do my clients value and expect from me?
  - ✓ Who am I providing services to and what are their key needs of me?
  - ✓ How, exactly, do I add value to my clients?
  - ✓ What are the core deliverables?
- **Prime Capabilities and Enablers: why bother?** There are at least three reasons why it is useful to determine your Prime Capabilities and Enablers:
  1. Doing so should make you a more successful client-serving professional. Both types of capabilities are viewed from a client perspective.
  2. This assessment should assist you in planning your learning and development.
  3. Knowing your Prime Capabilities and Enablers is a useful way of assessing how AI and machines may threaten and/or assist your career.
- **Prime Capabilities and Enablers in the age of AI.** At least at present, before the arrival of artificial general intelligence, well-trained humans have big advantages over machines in many areas including: emotional intelligence, communication, critical thinking, curiosity, judgement, decision making,

problem solving, understanding context, leadership and ethics. Make yourself as AI-proof as possible.

- **Tasks.** Clients want you to undertake tasks to solve their problems and satisfy their needs. Here are some definitions:
  - ✓ *Human tasks* are those that, at any given moment, your clients value humans doing, either in toto, or with some expert supervision of one or more machines.
  - ✓ *Machine tasks* are those that, at any given moment, your clients value machines doing rather than humans, either in toto, or with some routine non-expert supervision of a machine.
  - ✓ *Expert supervision* means supervision requiring substantial human domain-specific knowledge, expertise, experience, judgement and wisdom.
  - ✓ *Machine* is any type of non-human device or tool.
- In time it will be your clients and the marketplace that will decide what is a human task and what is a machine task, rather than lists in business magazine articles, OECD reports or peer-reviewed academic journal articles. Nonetheless, ask yourself, *Do my Prime Capabilities and Enablers adequately equip me to perform human tasks for clients in my chosen profession, at least for now?*
- The professional capabilities and tasks template in this chapter will help you to periodically map your capabilities against human and machine tasks. Like most such models, the top right quadrant is the best place, with lots of human tasks requiring your Prime Capabilities.

Chapter 9

The Seven Accelerants to supercharge your career

In this chapter and the next, we consider the fifth of the Five Factors in the Playbook: *Accelerants*.

We have already looked at basic requirements for professional success, which include intelligence, integrity, skill, competence and diligence. But in today's ultra-competitive and AI-charged world, these are no longer sufficient. My experience, training and reading have convinced me that there are Seven Accelerants that will help anyone (including professionals) to get ahead in their careers and become leaders in their fields. This chapter introduces these interlinked Accelerants, aspects of which we have already encountered:

1. **Planning**. Create and periodically update a personal, professional and business development plan and ask one or more people to hold you accountable.

2. **Feedback/advice**. Actively seek feedback/advice from others, with a non-defensive mindset, and act on that feedback as appropriate.

3. **Deliberate practice**. Undertake career-long 'deliberate practice' and development of your Prime Capabilities and Enablers.

4. **Mentors**. Aim to have at least two mentors and become a mentor yourself to others in due course.

5. **Emotional intelligence**. Actively work on your emotional intelligence. Like technical competence, it's a skill you'll never cease to work on.

6. **Executive presence**. Work on building this highly prized if somewhat nebulous quality from the start of your career.

7. **Personal brand**. Begin creating your professional personal brand at the start of your working life. This Accelerant is treated separately in chapter 10.

None of the Seven Accelerants are new ideas, but that doesn't mean they aren't important. If I were starting out today, I would develop and employ all of them. In fact, I am using each of them right now, in my second career.

You may be thinking, *I'm a busy person with limited time and there are seven of these damned things. Where do I start?* Start with Planning, because it will require you to figure out which of the other six Accelerants to focus on and when. *Hint:* Although the above seven are not in priority order (okay, apart from Planning), since all professionals need feedback/ advice, you might place that high on the list.

Remote work

I will make just a few comments on the dramatic increase in working from home (WFH) and other forms of remote working in the post-COVID era, given I have what now seem to be old-fashioned ideas. In the Introduction, I identified remote working as one of the four interlinked challenges facing professionals. As with complexity, another of the four challenges that was discussed in chapter 5, I haven't devoted a lengthy discussion of remote work; it comes up throughout the Playbook as part of the plan to help you become your best possible professional whether you are working in the office, remotely or a mix of the two.

If I could turn back time and restart my first career today, I would be in the office as much as possible, four or five days every week. I think close proximity to more senior professionals, colleagues and clients, would provide the best platform not only to develop my Prime Capabilities and Enablers but also to activate the Seven Accelerants. I can't imagine developing at a good pace, let alone an accelerated one, if I was spending many hours a week at home, even if I were deeply involved in videoconferencing. In my world, face-to-face matters for a host of relationship, learning and feedback reasons. It really matters. Of course, there wouldn't be much point in my commuting to the office if the senior professionals I hoped to learn from were working from home. If that was the case, I would find myself a new employer whose senior professionals chose to be in the office as much as possible in order to mentor younger professionals.

If, for whatever reasons, you do decide to WFH multiple days a week, ask yourself and senior professionals in your organisation whether this is putting you at a disadvantage in terms of career development and/or promotion prospects. If so, figure out how to best meet the challenges while retaining what for you are the benefits of WFH.

Planning

Yes, I know it's a cliché, but if you don't have a plan, how do you know where you are going? How do you keep track of what is the best use of your precious and limited time and energy? The best laid and most motivational plans are written down.

And I get it: many professionals hate thinking about, let alone spending time writing out, a plan unless it's one they are being paid to do as part of billable client work. Many regard them as a total waste of time. I have been creating annual personal, professional and business development plans for almost 30 years, ever since I became a partner at Price Waterhouse in 1996. At first, I thought they were a hassle, mainly because a more senior partner instructed me to do them. When I became managing director at Greenwoods, I had to cajole my fellow directors to do them. I am now a true believer and I do them for my own one-man micro-business. They help motivate me and keep me focused.

I've designed a six-part template to help get you started, with suggestions for what to include in each section (table 9.1, overleaf). Review and update your plan and progress at least annually and ideally more often — say, on a quarterly basis.

Here is my definition of business development, which is relevant to professionals working inside organisations as well as those employed in professional service firms:

Business development consists of all the daily activities and deliberate actions that build your relationships and reputation so you are front-of-mind (and on lists and panels) to provide valuable services when existing or potential clients (including people you have yet to meet) have problems that need solving.

Yes, okay, the idea of business development planning will be of greater interest and relevance to professionals working in PSFs than to those employed in in-house roles. In fact, I can visualise many overworked, underpaid and underappreciated in-house professionals rolling their eyes at the thought of trying to generate more work.

You also need to think about accountability. Who will you share your plan with to achieve some measure of accountability for your intended actions? I know, along with feedback, responsibility and performance reviews, accountability is one of the most feared words in the business world. Maybe you are completely self-motivated and don't need anyone looking over your shoulder. In well-run organisations there is oversight, transparency and sharing of plans and mutual accountability. However, perhaps your workplace is not into planning, or you don't trust anyone in your organisation enough. If you need external accountability (not everyone does), then recruit someone to share your plan with — maybe a life partner, a friend or ideally one or more mentors. Ask them to hold you accountable, and update them periodically.

Table 9.1: Professional and business development planning template

1	**Values, principles and purpose.** They may be work related or personal (we discussed these in chapter 6). Write them down here.
2	**SMART, motivational goals.** Record your short- and longer-term goals, ambitions, hopes and dreams (we discussed these in chapter 6).
3	**Accelerants.** Write down plans for how you will action or develop one or more of the other six Accelerants in the coming year. You can't do them all at once, so prioritise what is most important to you for the period covered by your plan: – Feedback/advice – Deliberate practice – Mentors – Emotional intelligence – Executive presence – Personal brand

4   **Professional development**. Write out your plans for the coming year for achieving your professional development goals:

- What continuing professional development (CPD) will you undertake?

- Which Prime Capabilities and Enablers will you learn, develop and practise deliberately (Accelerant #3)?

- In which area(s) of practice will you increase your technical skills, and how will you do this?

5   **Business development (BD)**. Record plans for the coming year to achieve your goals:

- What are your golden rules for daily BD activities* and your practice?

- What specific, concrete, deliberate BD actions* are you going to undertake? Put them in your calendar as appropriate.

6   **Accountability**. Who will you discuss/share your plan with so you're accountable?

*The notions of 'daily activities' and 'deliberate actions' in the context of building your personal brand are discussed in chapter 10. Similar principles apply in business development.

In a perfect world, you would also have a longer-term plan. Executive coach Mary McNevin's 'How to Develop a 5-Year Career Plan' offers a useful roadmap.[1]

Feedback/advice

Feedback was one of the 'energising eight' factors of motivation discussed in chapter 6. Many people have a love–hate relationship with feedback. Does the word fill you with dread? While we know we can grow and benefit as a result of good feedback, we fear being told we are not up to scratch, or receiving feedback that is simply unfair or badly delivered.

When you are a young professional, you will typically be on the receiving end of feedback, and as you become more senior you will provide it to others. You will give and receive feedback in your private life, probably every day. So the sooner you know how to seek and receive feedback in an effective way, as well as provide it to others, the better. Unfortunately, most people, including professionals, are never taught how to do it well. Make it your business to learn the art of feedback as soon as possible. It will stand you in good stead as you become more senior. Being unable to either receive or provide feedback in an appropriate manner has derailed many a career. Personality psychologist Dr Robert Hogan explains that for every star athlete there are nine or ten who are just as skilled but will never become stars because they don't listen to feedback: 'they don't allow themselves to be coached'.[2]

Do you seek out feedback? Do you listen and allow yourself to be coached by others? Remember, the perceptions others share with you as feedback are their reality, even if you think they are on another planet. If you need help with listening to feedback, then head to a book called *Becoming Coachable*.[3] That book and of course this one, with a sticky note directing the lucky recipient to chapter 4, would make terrific Secret Santa gifts for many partners in professional service firms.

If I were starting my career today, one of the first self-development sources I would read (after 'The Making of a Corporate Athlete', discussed in chapter 5), would be Douglas Stone and Sheila Heen's *Thanks for the Feedback: The Science and Art of Receiving Feedback Well*.[4] I have read a great deal on feedback, and nothing comes close to the wisdom, tools and practical suggestions in this book. And, despite the title, you will learn how to *give* as well as *receive* feedback. It is well worth the investment of your time. The authors point out, as I noted in chapter 4, the giver and receiver of feedback must be on the same wavelength on the type of feedback being given, sought or expected:

> *Part of the problem is that the word 'feedback' can mean a number of different things. ... The very first task in assessing feedback is figuring out what kind of feedback we are dealing with. Broadly, feedback comes in three forms: appreciation (thanks), coaching (here's a better way to do it), and evaluation (here's where you stand). Often the receiver wants or hears one kind of feedback, while the giver actually means another.*[5]

I have framed Accelerant #2 as feedback/advice, and so far I have focused on feedback. When someone has already decided to comment on an aspect of your performance, skills, dress sense or personal hygiene, maybe you don't care whether it is framed as feedback, advice or plain old negative criticism. But what about when you proactively approach someone? Should you ask them for feedback, advice or something else?

Some interesting research suggests that when we ask others for feedback, sometimes what we get is too vague to be useful in helping us to understand where or how to improve. This is in part because feedback is a loaded term, which means many people don't like giving it. Most people are happy to give advice, though. Researchers found people received more effective and actionable responses when they chose to ask for advice rather than feedback:

... when asked to provide advice, people focus less on evaluation and more on possible future actions ... if you ask someone for advice, they will be more likely to think forward to future opportunities to improve rather than backwards to the things you have done, which you can no longer change.[6]

But the research hedges its bets. A novice might ask for feedback rather than advice and so avoid demotivating criticism in favour of encouragement.

Whether you seek advice or feedback, it is *super important* not to be defensive or argumentative if you hear something you don't like. First, the person you approached won't bother trying to assist you again. Second, as discussed in chapter 7, defensiveness is a classic indicator of a fixed rather than a growth mindset. It limits our ability to listen, learn and grow. It is beyond the scope of this book to provide tips on not being defensive, but the best and most practical advice I have come across is contained in rule 27 of Dr Harriet Lerner's *Marriage Rules*.[7] This book is a gold mine of sensible relationship advice that is as applicable to the business world as it is to married couples. Before outlining 12 steps to reducing defensiveness, she reminds us:

We're all defensive a fair amount of the time, although we may be better able to observe defensiveness in other people. Just a little bit of anxiety is enough to reduce the listening part of the human brain to the size of a pinto bean. Once we're in defensive or reactive mode we can't take in new information or see two sides of an issue — or better yet, seven or eight sides. Defensiveness is normal and universal. It is also the archenemy of listening.

Are you defensive when you receive less than glowing feedback, and does the listening part of your brain shrink to the size of a pinto bean as a result? Try to monitor and moderate your defensiveness next time you get some feedback.

Deliberate practice

As well as being an aspiring professional, perhaps you have other skills. You might play the guitar like Jimi Hendrix, play tennis like Ash Barty, dance like John Travolta, or at least better than Justin Timberlake, or have any number of other talents outside of your day job. Let's assume you are talented at a particular pursuit. How did you achieve your level of skill? Even if you were a natural, it's because you practised. A lot. You may or may not have had lessons or formal coaching, but you spent many hours building your skills. Depending on your focus, resources and level of organisation, the granularity and specificity of the micro skills you practised will have varied. But you have done a lot of practice. Importantly, you were probably aware that you were practising and that the people around you who were learning the same skill were practising too.

But when it comes to professional careers, many people don't apply the same logic, principles and degree of rigour to the development of their skills or, in the jargon of this book, their Prime Capabilities and Enablers.

In a 2007 article in *HBR*, K Anders Ericsson, Michael J Prietula and Edward T Cokely reported on their research into expertise and outstanding performance in a wide variety of domains including surgery, acting, chess, writing, computer programming, ballet, music, aviation and firefighting. They concluded:

> *The development of genuine expertise requires struggle, sacrifice, and honest, often painful self-assessment ... It will take you at least a decade to achieve expertise ... you will need to invest that time wisely, by engaging in 'deliberate' practice ... that focuses on tasks beyond your current level of competence and comfort.*[8]

Think about the non-work skill you are very good at. Does the above quote ring reasonably true when you think about what it took to develop your expertise? Now ask yourself: do you engage in some similar, methodical 'deliberate practice' of your burgeoning professional skills? If not, why not? If you decide to become more 'deliberate' in the practice, development and honing of your Prime Capabilities and Enablers, what will you need to do that is specific to your profession and circumstances?

Ericsson and associates stress the importance of good coaches in the achievement of first-class performance in any domain. In this respect, professional services are no different from golf, chess, the guitar or limbo dancing. As these researchers point out, coaching should never stop, though with time you may become your own coach:

> *Self-coaching can be done in any field. Expert surgeons, for example, are not concerned with a patient's postoperative status alone. They will study any unanticipated events that took place during the surgery, to try to figure out how mistakes or misjudgements can be avoided in the future.*

If you need any further convincing that deliberate practice and coaching are good ideas in a professional services environment, watch American surgeon, researcher and writer Atul Gawande's TED talk 'Want to get great at something? Get a coach'.[9] In this inspirational talk, Gawande explains how he set out to improve as a surgeon by inviting a more senior surgeon to come into his operating theatre to observe him, take notes and provide feedback. Gawande said that after two months of coaching he felt himself improving, and after a year his surgical complications fell considerably. 'It was painful. I didn't like being observed, and at times I didn't want to have to work on things. I also felt there were periods where I would get worse before I got better. But it made me realize that the coaches were onto something profoundly important.' He also reported huge improvements in the survival of newborns in rural India after a major program of coaching for neonatal doctors and nurses.

There are four distinct features that separate deliberate practice from other forms of practice[10]:

1. It requires a clearly defined goal that identifies the specific Prime Capability or Enabler, or the targeted aspect of performance to be learned or improved on. It demands that challenge exceeds skill and focuses on tasks beyond your current level of competence and comfort.

2. It is actually deliberate! It requires complete concentration and effort in learning or improving on the identified skill or aspect of performance.

3. It requires informative feedback, preferably immediate through coaching. To improve learning and performance, the feedback must be constructive, even if it is sometimes painful. Feedback, the second Accelerant, facilitates the learning process and guides the selection, sequence and type of future practice activities.

4. It also requires repetition, but repetition alone is not enough. Mindless repetition of a task does not automatically lead to improvement. It must be focused, responsive and reflective.

Are you being sufficiently coached on a day-to-day basis by people more senior and experienced than you? If not, why not? What are you going to do about it? One great way to start is to ask for more coaching. If the senior professionals in your organisation can't or won't make the time to coach you competently, perhaps you need to consider changing jobs.

Another aspect of deliberate practice is to ensure that, over time, you get exposure to the working styles and knowledge of numerous senior professionals in your organisation. This diversity of experience will help make you a well-rounded and thoughtful senior professional yourself in due course. As far as possible, don't let yourself fall into the common trap of working with only one or two senior professionals in your organisation. More often than not, this ends up being career-limiting rather than career-enhancing. So put your hand up and ask to be moved around a bit.

As you practise and improve your professional skills, you will make mistakes. All humans make mistakes in any endeavour they undertake, whether it is learning to dance, to play a musical instrument or to become a first-rate engineer or architect. You will want to learn from your mistakes and to minimise them in future, but mistakes you will make. Own up as soon as you identify a mistake, whether it's yours or someone else's. In the first instance, inform a more senior professional in your organisation. What they do with the information you have provided — especially if it has an impact on advice that has already been provided to the organisation's clients — will be a good test of that person's character. If you need any convincing that even professionals need to accept that mistakes happen and that these are learning opportunities, head for organisational psychologist and best-selling author Adam Grant's *Hidden Potential: The Science of Achieving Greater Things*.[11] Grant warns of the dangers of perfectionism and goes so far as to recommend setting up a 'mistake budget'. Psychological safety guru Professor Amy Edmondson has popularised the idea of 'intelligent failure' in her *Right Kind of Wrong: The Science of Failing Well*.[12]

Mentors

Coaching, as discussed previously and in chapter 4, helps you build your Prime Capabilities and Enablers as you become the best professional you can be. Ideally, you will be being coached daily while you are working with more senior professionals in your organisation. Mentoring is different. A wise and experienced mentor can offer you a broader and longer-term perspective on your career. Peter Wilson, Australia's foremost authority on mentoring, explains:

> *Mentoring is a well-honed art and craft, and not a science. It is an intergenerational learning experience between two people in an environment that is private and trusting, and which engenders confidence for the big issues to be opened up, addressed and discussed. Mentoring is not, however, a forensic examination of a person's current performance gaps, with an accompanying requirement for hyper-intensive business fitness programs, designed to bring their subjects into superior shape in double-quick time.[13]*

Ideally you will have at least two mentors at any given time, one inside your organisation and one outside. Not only will this give you a broader perspective but your external mentor should be more objective when it comes to helping you assess whether your current organisation and role are the right fit for you.

Perhaps your organisation offers a mandatory or optional mentoring program. If so, great, but you may find yourself paired with someone poorly trained or insufficiently committed. Take the initiative and approach your preferred senior professional and ask them to mentor you on an agreed basis. Most will be pleased to be asked. Of course, they may already have one or more mentees, so you may not get your first pick. A rule of thumb is that an internal mentor should not be your boss, or a senior professional you work with closely on a day-to-day basis. Choose someone in the organisation you think cares about you as a person and who will offer a wider perspective and different insights into your organisation from those of your immediate manager.

An external mentor may or may not be a member of your profession, but they should have a good understanding of the business world, care about you as a person and grasp the essential elements of what it takes to be a good mentor.

There are endless desirable attributes for internal or external mentors. You want them to have been around the block a few times. They should both support and challenge you and your thinking as appropriate and required. Mentors should respect you, be great listeners, and provide useful and balanced feedback.

Business thinker and author Erika Andersen suggests these five qualities to look for in a mentor[14]:

- **Self-reflection**. You want someone who has experience and wisdom to share. However, that is not enough. You want a mentor who has self-reflected on *why* and *how* they achieved things, and why things they tried did or did not work. You want someone who is willing to share those reflections with you, so you can apply them to your own circumstances as appropriate.

- **Discretion**. For your mentor to be of most use, you need confidence to open up and be honest with what is going on for you. You need to be able to trust your mentor to keep confidences, in the same manner that you do with your clients. Recall that 'keeps confidences' was one of the indicia of a true professional discussed in chapter 1.

- **Honesty**. You need candour in both directions. You will be brave enough to seek counsel from your mentor. In return, and when requested to do so, you want your mentor to give you straight, unvarnished answers. For example, if you are contemplating changing jobs, you want to hear what your mentor really thinks about your options.

- **Curiosity**. You will generally set the agenda for discussions with your mentor. However, ideally your mentor will display curiosity and ask you questions about what is important to you, your goals and what you are seeking to achieve. By being curious, your mentor will be best positioned to offer you targeted rather than generic advice and wisdom.

- **Generosity of spirit**. A generous mentor will offer you all they reasonably can, through their words *and* actions, to help you succeed and achieve your goals. They will assist you to make connections, arrange introductions and share resources. They will not be threatened by or envious of your success. A generous mentor believes in you and your potential and will celebrate your triumphs.

With both internal and external mentors, it will help if there is some structure to the relationship, including a schedule of regular meetings and an upfront discussion of the ongoing needs and expectations of mentor and mentee. For example, if you have agreed during a mentoring session to take some action, send the mentor an email afterwards, thanking them for their time and recording your commitments and the timeframe for their completion. This will please your mentor and also help them to hold you accountable for progress.

You may end up formally or informally reverse mentoring on any number of things, including the views and perspectives of younger professionals and how to best deploy emerging developments in technology. This is what Peter Wilson termed an intergenerational learning experience.

As you become more senior, you will help mentor the next generation. This is an honour and a privilege. Mentor them well, even if you yourself were not so fortunate.

Emotional intelligence

Emotional intelligence became a thing after the publication of Daniel Goleman's 1996 book of the same name.[15] He acknowledges that the concept of emotional intelligence was first proposed by Peter Salovey and John Mayer in a 1990 academic paper.[16] They hypothesised that emotional intelligence is 'a set of skills that contribute to the accurate appraisal and expression of emotion in oneself and others, the effective regulation of emotion ... and the use of feelings to motivate, plan and achieve in one's life'. Research conducted since 1990[17] shows we can develop emotional intelligence by means of awareness, education and practice. You are not doomed to being emotionally challenged, even if you are a tax lawyer.

Here is my cheeky definition:

Emotional Intelligence is a modern, convenient and catchy collective noun for a bunch of personal awareness, relationship-enhancing, and decision-making skills that have been regarded as vitally important since before the dawn of humanity, under many guises and names.

Why do I say, 'before the dawn of humanity'? In *Wild Leadership*[18], Erna Walraven, former Senior Curator at Taronga Zoo in Sydney, documents her observations of wild animals over more than three decades. She concludes that successful long-term leaders in animal societies have the following characteristics:

- They are trustworthy.
- They keep the group safe.
- They resolve conflict quickly.
- They make productive decisions for the group.
- They share resources fairly.
- They have compassion and empathy.

In a nutshell, successful animal leaders display emotional intelligence along with many other attributes we sometimes believe, in our conceit, are peculiar to humans. For example, members of the four great ape species (chimpanzees, bonobos, gorillas and orangutans) have been observed to engage in intentionally provocative behaviour and play, often accompanied by playful teasing.[19]

Some researchers dispute the concept of 'emotional intelligence' (in humans) both because it is not a form of measurable intelligence and because it is defined so broadly and inclusively that it is meaningless.[20] Nonetheless, there are now many approaches and models dealing with emotional intelligence and the components said to comprise this set of skills. As I will extrapolate in the 'In play' section of this chapter, I am a fan of the Australian-developed Genos International approach to emotional intelligence[21], which comprises these six core competencies:

- self-awareness (ranging from an unproductive state of disconnection to a productive state of being present)
- awareness of others (ranging from insensitive to empathetic)
- authenticity (ranging from untrustworthy to genuine)
- emotional reasoning (ranging from limited to expansive)
- self-management (ranging from temperamental to resilient)
- positive influence (ranging from indifferent to empowering).

Of these, self-awareness is key. No self-awareness, no emotional intelligence. Dr Tasha Eurich has identified two broad categories of self-awareness.[22]

The first, *internal* self-awareness, refers to the degree to which we see our own values, passions and aspirations in relation to our environment, together with our reactions to these, including thoughts, feelings, behaviours, strengths and weaknesses, and their impacts on others. Her research reveals internal self-awareness to be associated with higher job and relationship satisfaction as well as personal and social control. Increased internal self-awareness may be achieved through self-reflection[23], self-observation, journaling, meditation and mindfulness.

The second category, *external* self-awareness, refers to our understanding of how others view us.

The research suggests that people who know how others see them are more empathic and make better leaders. The only way to really get a handle on your external self-awareness is to ask good questions of others who know you reasonably well. You can do this through a workplace feedback questionnaire put together by your organisation or a third party and completed anonymously online by your colleagues. Ideally it will solicit comments rather than mere box-ticking. Implementing such a question-naire and debriefing reports with participants requires care and skill.

Eurich contributes to a large body of research that highlights the importance of emotional intelligence in the workplace. A 2023 analysis of 150 research studies showed 'emotional intelligence was significantly related to career adaptability, career decision-making, self-efficacy, entrepreneurial self-efficacy, salary, career commitment, career decision-making difficulties, career satisfaction, entrepreneurial intentions, and turnover intentions'.[24] What's not to like?

It seems to me that emotional intelligence in the age of automation and AI is likely to be so important that it should be at least an Enabler and sometimes a Prime Capability for every professional, young or old. James Runde, vice chairman at US investment bank Morgan Stanley, nails it when he argues, 'If you can develop these traits — self-awareness and adaptability, collaboration, and empathy — early on, you'll be able to set yourself apart from your peers and build a life and career that is successful and satisfying.'[25]

Before we leave emotional intelligence, a reminder that self-awareness goes well beyond emotions. Any professional will want to be self-aware of their technical strengths and weaknesses along with many of the other attributes addressed in this chapter and throughout this book.

Executive presence

Executive presence, sometimes known as the 'it factor' or the 'X-factor', is a very loose concept that can mean different things to different people. Properly understood, it is much more than gravitas, charisma, the 'wow' factor or the ability to hold a room.[26] I like this definition from Bates Communication Inc: 'Executive presence is the ability to engage, align, inspire, and move people to act.'[27]

Bates[28] has come up with a useful, research-based model, the Bates Executive Presence Index (the Bates ExPI)[29], which has three dimensions — character, substance and style:

- *Character* is the behaviours at the core of who we are from the standpoint of our values, beliefs and emotional disposition. It is foundational to the leader as a person.

- *Substance* is the behaviours of good leaders. Substance behaviours, such as asking the right questions, displaying good business judgement, and the ability to inspire others, usually develop over time through leadership experiences.

- *Style* is those behaviours that engage others in meaningful two-way communication. Style focuses on both the quantity and quality of the conversations needed for the collaboration required to get business results. It is about the leader's ability to drive execution.

You may be asking yourself, *Why should I care about executive presence?* Well, all types of organisations are now demanding their leaders and senior executives have a sufficient level of executive presence and they will often offer at least some of them coaching to build the necessary skills. When, as part of a 2020 survey, CoachSource asked organisations about the four developmental areas where executive coaching is most requested, the top four responses were executive presence (54 per cent), emotional intelligence (48 per cent), influencing others (45 per cent), and vision and strategy (40 per cent).[30]

The US-based Human Capital Institute, in conjunction with the TRACOM Group, notes:

Executive presence is associated (often synonymously) with leadership. Of the more than 350 HR professionals we asked, 92% agree that executive presence is an important part of leadership ... Further, 77% of respondents agree that those with high levels of executive presence progress quickly in their careers.[31]

It's hard to nail down a definition, yet most people recognise executive presence, or its lack, in others. If you have been a professional for even a short period, you will have observed good and not-so-good examples. Some of those who exhibit this X-factor are senior professionals in your own organisation — people you know and trust. Ask them for some frank feedback on your current level of executive presence. Although we tend to be pretty good at assessing it in others, we are generally less aware of our own abilities in this regard. Probe those senior professionals in your organisation for feedback and suggestions.

When you ask a trusted colleague for tips, their response is likely to focus on what the Bates model describes as style, which includes such things as your level of gravitas, rather than elements of character and substance. Nonetheless, take the feedback and action it as appropriate.

Style includes but is not limited to how you sound: the quality, tone, pace and volume of your voice; eye contact or lack thereof; posture, gestures and body language. Different elements of style apply to online interactions, especially if your camera is switched off or is displaying just your face.

Being a great public speaker will boost your executive presence and your personal brand, as I will discuss in the next chapter. Ask people you trust for their frank assessment of your current oratory abilities. If you sense they are suboptimal, think about a course or training to lift your game. Early in my first career my then employer, Price Waterhouse, sponsored me for a number of years as a member of Toastmasters. This helped me enormously in building whatever skills I may have in public speaking.

Global investor Warren Buffett confesses that 'until the age of twenty, I was absolutely unable to speak in public. Just the thought of it made me physically ill. I would literally throw up'.[32] He had the sense and perseverance to enrol in a Dale Carnegie public-speaking course while he was studying at Columbia Business School. He says, 'that $100 course gave me the most important degree I have. It's certainly had the biggest impact in terms of my subsequent success'.[33]

On the style front, professionals and businesspeople can learn a lot from professional actors. When I was at Greenwoods, a team of actors from the Corporate Training section of the Australian National Institute of Dramatic Art (NIDA) ran an impressive workshop for us that included elements of executive presence. I asked the actors whether there was a bible for their industry when it came to developing such executive presence. Without a second's delay, they named Keith Bain's *The Principles of Movement*.[34] Bain was regarded as one of Australia's most influential theatre practitioners and a mentor to generations of actors, including Cate Blanchett, who, in her foreword to his book, said, 'there is no doubt Keith was and is the biggest single influence on my work as an actor'.

On presence, for an actor, Bain writes:

This attribute may be difficult to define in words, but we recognise its unmistakable quality when we meet it in another person. It begins with good alignment, releasing into the space around you qualities of your personality, authority and assurance. It registers as an aura that attracts our notice, a personal atmosphere that can be felt as well as seen, an air that radiates from within to surprising distances beyond the body's limits. It's a charismatic state that proclaims status, creates focus and demands attention.[35]

If you can't attend a NIDA Corporate Training session, then reviewing and implementing some of Bain's practical tips will help you improve at least some parts of the style component of your executive presence. But remember, there is more to executive presence than style. Reflect on the elements of character and substance I noted at the beginning of this section.

The Seven Accelerants are strongly interconnected. For example, the work you do on your executive presence will benefit from planning, seeking advice/feedback, deliberate practice, mentoring and working on your emotional intelligence. Improving your executive presence will boost your personal brand, as I will discuss in the next chapter.

In play

When it comes to the first Accelerant, I have admitted I was a bit late to the planning party but I am now a convert. On the feedback front, in the last seven years of my first 34-year career I received way more of it than I had in the whole of the first 27 years. During my time as managing director of Greenwoods & Herbert Smith Freehills, my fellow directors provided me with liberal amounts of solicited — and more commonly unsolicited — feedback. This ranged, in my humble opinion, from the highly perceptive and constructive to the destructive, bordering on deranged. I had to remind myself that feedback is a gift and that it was a good thing my fellow directors could and did express themselves so freely and so regularly.

Looking back, I made conscious efforts to improve a variety of professional skills, but I will not pretend that it was done in a way that K Anders Ericsson would have described as 'deliberate practice'. If I had my time over, I would be much more deliberate.

In my first career I was very fortunate to have had some terrific mentors at key stages. John Masters was my main mentor in my early years at Price Waterhouse, John Brodie took that role when I was at Westpac and Dr Alicia Fortinberry was a source of much wise counsel when I was receiving all that valuable feedback at Greenwoods. Each of them, and others, played a vital role in helping me to become the best possible professional I could be, and I am very grateful to them all.

To the ongoing amusement of family members and friends, I have a piece of paper of which I am very proud that says I am certified (some of them think in more ways than one) to administer (inflict?) the Genos Emotional Intelligence Assessment Scale on unsuspecting clients. More than one of them has helpfully pointed out that this does not certify that I myself have any particular level of emotional intelligence. This is factually correct. But to return to what I wrote towards the start of this chapter, I am always actively working on my emotional intelligence and my executive presence. It is a never-ending journey.

I recount some of my first-career personal branding endeavours in chapter 10.

Key takeaways

- To excel in today's ultra-competitive and AI-charged world, there are Seven Accelerants that will help anyone, including professionals, to get ahead in their careers and become leaders in their fields:

  ✓ **Planning.** Create and periodically update a personal, professional and business development plan and find one or more people to hold you accountable.

  ✓ **Feedback/advice.** Actively seek feedback/advice from others with a non-defensive mindset. Action it as appropriate.

  ✓ **Deliberate practice.** Undertake career-long 'deliberate practice' and development of your Prime Capabilities and Enablers.

  ✓ **Mentors.** Aim to have at least two mentors and become a mentor yourself in due course.

  ✓ **Emotional intelligence.** Always actively work on your emotional intelligence. Building your emotional intelligence, like your technical competence, is a never-ending journey.

  ✓ **Executive presence.** Start work on building this highly prized if somewhat nebulous quality from the start of your career.

  ✓ **Personal brand.** Begin creating your professional personal brand at the earliest stage of your working life. This Accelerant gets its own treatment in chapter 10.

- Where to start? Planning is most important and must come first. Planning will require you to figure out which of the other six Accelerants to focus on at any given time. *Hint:* Although the above seven are not in priority order (apart from Planning), concentrating on feedback/advice is a good idea for most professionals.

Chapter 10

Building your personal brand in the digital age

This chapter focuses on the last of the Seven Accelerants: *personal brand*. Like executive presence, one of the Seven Accelerants discussed in chapter 9, personal brand is a somewhat nebulous but nonetheless important concept. A strong and credible personal brand will help you fulfil your mission to become the best professional you can be.

We all know that successful companies like Apple have strong brands, typically built up over many years. In a famous 1997 article in *Fast Company* American writer and business management guru Tom Peters observed:

> *Nobody understands branding better than professional services firms. Look at McKinsey or Arthur Andersen for a model of the new rules of branding at the company and personal level. They have lots of soft assets ... people, preferably smart, motivated, talented people. And they have huge revenues — and astounding profits.*[1]

If you work or have worked in a professional service firm, maybe even the now defunct Arthur Andersen LLP if you are a baby boomer, can you relate to what Peters says? Okay, maybe not the 'astounding profits' bit, unless you have already made partner. As Peters points out, you too have a brand.

Your personal brand is related to your reputation, but these two concepts are often said to have slightly different meanings. As executive coach and author Harrison Monarth[2] observes, everyone has a reputation. This includes the first impressions you make, your communication style and the relationships you form. Your reputation comprises the opinions and beliefs others form about you based on your actions and behaviours, regardless of your intentions. He sees personal brand, on the other hand, as more intentional. It is proactive. It is how you *want* people to see you. Your reputation is about credibility but your personal brand is about visibility and the values you consciously display.

You can define your brand by aligning your intentions with your actions, which is to say by deliberately acting to influence how others see you and to help them connect both emotionally and intellectually to the image you portray.

It seems to me, there is an overlap between personal brand and reputation. Personal brand could be regarded as a trendy, modern name for intentional reputation building.

Assessing your personal brand

In chapter 1, I emphasised the importance of humility. There is nothing inconsistent in the notion of humility and curating your personal brand.

Like it or not, you will always have a personal brand — good, bad or indifferent. For all that you create it intentionally, it is not what you think it is. It is how other people assess it and you. To return to our fly-on-the-wall metaphor, imagine listening to a group of people who know you well and are speaking about you from a personal and a professional perspective. What do they say about how you present yourself, your character, your strengths and weaknesses, your special traits and attributes, what differentiates you from others ... and your reputation? The summary of their response is your personal brand.

Given you are not a fly on the wall, how can you get a handle on your personal brand? As discussed in chapter 9, self-reflection is central to self-awareness. However, self-reflection will get you only so far. One of the constant themes of this book is the usefulness of seeking and receiving feedback from other people. The best way to assess your personal brand is to ask some good questions of people you know and trust. Here is a handy definition that happens to include reputation. Personal brand 'relates to an individual's association in the minds of others, where the demonstration of skills and traits creates an impression, perception, and reputation about that person'.[3]

Here are some questions you might ask others, including your mentor(s):

- How would you describe my personal brand right now?
- What adjectives best sum up my personal brand in your mind?
- What could I start doing, continue doing or stop doing, to help me build a strong and credible personal brand?

If the people you approach are stumped by the term personal brand, replace it with 'reputation'.

You can ask questions like these in formal performance review sessions or informally with different people at different levels in your organisation. You could also ask clients you know well and trust, and even trusted competitors in your profession. And of course you can google yourself from time to time and see what pops up!

Project managing your personal brand

There is a lot to be said for approaching your personal brand from the perspective of a project manager. This list is based on suggestions Dorie Clark and Antonio Nieto-Rodriguez make in a 2022 *HBR* article[4]:

1. **Identify your purpose.** What do you want to be known for? What do you stand for? How will you differentiate yourself from other professionals? As you become more experienced and senior, part of this will include whether and how to promote yourself as a specialist in one or more fields or areas of expertise within your chosen profession.

2. **Decide on your investment.** Mostly this will be the amount of time you will spend on specific activities of the type discussed in the following sections of this chapter. An entry-level online presence is inexpensive in monetary terms. As you become more senior you may choose to create a personal website if your organisation is okay with that.

3. **Be clear about the benefits — and how you'll track them.** Creating a unique personal brand will take many years. So set up some SMART goals, actions and expected outcomes. Set up a mechanism to keep track of your progress. A mentor can be invaluable in holding you accountable.

4. **Identify your stakeholders.** You are one of them, but your employer is another. How does your organisation feel about your

developing a personal brand online or otherwise? What written or unwritten rules apply to personal brand building in your organisation? Identifying your target audience is important in both offline and online worlds.

5. **Lay out your resources and deliverables**. It is important to dedicate time for building and managing your personal brand, and to ensure you deliver on any commitments you make.

6. **Nail down your plan and strategy**. This brings us to another theme of this book. As discussed in chapter 9, if you don't have a plan and a coherent strategy, how do you know where you are going? How do you keep track of what is the best use of your precious, and limited, time and energy?

Clark and Nieto-Rodriguez advise that by project managing your personal brand, '... your chances of success in developing a reputation you can be proud of will be much higher.'

Your personal brand—inside your own organisation

Most discussion on personal branding focuses on how you present yourself to the wider world. However, your personal brand starts with how you wish to be perceived in your own organisation.

Ask yourself these questions before seeking feedback from others in your organisation:

- Am I sufficiently respectful of others in my organisation and do I know my place?
- Do I speak up when necessary—for example, to raise ethical issues, technical concerns, potential process improvements or opportunities to seek new clients or assignments?
- When appropriate, do I challenge how things are done in my organisation?
- Are other people sufficiently respectful of me?
- How brave am I? Am I willing to take appropriate risks, within some guardrails, when it is okay to make a mistake? (See discussion on deliberate practice in chapter 9.) Do I accept a willingness to fail from time to time in order to learn and grow? Are such mindsets acceptable in my organisation? If not, am I working at the right place?

In chapter 3 we discussed the importance of promptly calling out any unethical behaviour by your colleagues or clients. If you fail to do so and do not resign, your personal brand may be damaged. You may be tainted, fairly or unfairly, by association.

Building your personal brand the old-fashioned way

Because there is some overlap, I will now modify the general-purpose definition of business development in the professional services sector that I addressed in chapter 9:

> *Building your personal brand consists of all the daily activities and deliberate actions that build your relationships and reputation, so you are front-of-mind (and on lists and panels) to provide valuable services when existing or potential clients (including people you have yet to meet) have problems that need solving.*

Yes, this definition will resonate more with professionals in professional service firms than those employed in in-house roles, but in-house professionals who ignore internal business development, and development of their personal brand, do so at their peril. I could say a lot more about business development but will save it for the next book. And yes, I included the word 'reputation' in this definition.

The point of this definition is to make clear that all the 'daily activities' and 'deliberate actions' that build your relationships and reputation for purposes of business development will also build your personal brand.

What do I mean by 'daily activities'? Well, pretty much anything you usually do, day by day, to serve your clients and assist your colleagues in your organisation. Doing first-rate work, meeting agreed deadlines, building relationships, communicating well, and being a pleasant and cheerful human being will go a very long way towards building your personal brand. Not only do such activities not take any extra time, but you get paid to do them. Of course, such 'daily activities' have a relatively narrow reach, at least initially, because you are building your reputation and personal brand with people with whom you are in direct contact. Over time, however, your reputation (good, bad or ugly) will spread in the time-honoured way — by bush telegraph.

By contrast, 'deliberate actions' are the type of offline or online activities implicit in project managing your personal brand. There are any number of such actions you might take, depending on your profession, experience and seniority. I have listed some of these later in the chapter. To do these tasks well requires time and effort. Generally, your organisation will have a say in how much time they will allow you to expend on such activity within normal working hours (a rather quaint expression in the post-pandemic work-anywhere-anytime world) and how much support they will provide. Depending on the scale of your ambition, some deliberate actions will end up being done in your own time.

Deliberate actions, performed well and strategically, reach further and faster than daily activities, such as doing a great job on your client work, to build your name and reputation. The usual c-words apply to deliberate actions in both offline and online worlds: be credible, clear and consistent in your messaging, be committed and communicate well. And be sure to use relevant up-to-date and quality content.

In building a strong personal brand, ideally you will combine daily activities with deliberate actions. However, daily activities are much more important than deliberate actions. If you post stuff online incessantly and run around doing all manner of things listed in the 'Bringing it all together section' but drop the ball on your regular client work and other day-to-day tasks, you will end up with a pretty flaky personal brand. Promise.

This list of old-fashioned things, covered to varying degrees elsewhere in this book, will be helpful in building your personal brand:

- Enjoy the work you do.
- Be hard-working, resilient and open to new things while still having a life.
- Develop self-awareness of your traits, strengths and weaknesses.
- Be a collaborative team player.
- Keep studying and learning, formally and informally.
- Gain the necessary breadth and depth of technical competence over time in a specialised world.
- Seek out and act on feedback and advice.
- Cultivate the respect of your colleagues, peers, clients and competitors.

As we discussed in chapter 9, the tasks of building a personal brand and doing business development overlap. There is a similar overlap between personal brand and executive presence; your executive presence is a subset of your personal brand.

Building your personal brand in the digital age

A disclaimer: As noted in the 'In play' section for this chapter, I am an avid personal brander. However, most of my personal branding experience was conducted in the stone age, that distant period of human history before the internet became a thing. Here I am preaching rather than discussing my practice.

As I prepared to write this section, I surveyed the many books and online offerings by the ever-growing army of those who describe themselves as digital personal branding gurus. In the course of my reading I became a fan of William Arruda, who has for many years published widely on offline and online personal branding. Check out his page on the Forbes website and his LinkedIn page — I can attest that the latter is far more up-to-date and interesting than mine. You can of course also find him on X, Facebook and who knows where else. You will be able to glean a lot of useful and sensible ideas on digital personal branding directly from his online offerings. As a stone ager, I was reassured by an article Arruda published in *Forbes* in 2021 in which he proposed that the three most important tenets of personal branding — which he identified as authenticity, differentiation and delivering exceptional value — were just as relevant and important online as they were in the real world.[5]

I also spoke to some digitally savvy young professionals and reviewed their online offerings, together with the digital profiles of other professionals who seem to be at the forefront of such branding activity. Here are some practical insights I gleaned:

- The usefulness of an online presence will depend on your profession, job, organisation and circumstances. There is no one-size-fits-all.
- The two usual places for professionals to build an online presence are their own organisation's website and LinkedIn. Only when those two are working well is it worth exploring the multitude of other online platforms.
- Take your lead from those senior professionals in your organisation and in organisations similar to yours who appear to be digitally savvy. And look at what your peers and competitors are doing.
- Decide what you want to be known for. All the comments earlier in this chapter on project managing your personal brand apply equally in the online world.

- Don't simply repost your organisation's material. It will be of interest to no one, apart perhaps from the business development people in your organisation who like to keep statistics on these things.

- Come up with original material that is interesting and relevant to your clients, colleagues and competitors. This need not be lengthy. You should present as insightful and original. Perhaps comment briefly and incisively on some current development of interest in your sector.

- If possible, include pictures, infographics, charts. People are drawn to the combination of text and visuals. As the saying goes, a picture is worth a thousand words.

- Be modest, human — and humorous when the circumstances allow. And promote others as well as yourself.

- Producing quality posts can take time but be careful not to overinvest. In deciding how often to post, again, be guided by others in your sector.

- Seek out feedback occasionally from your colleagues and clients on what they value about your online efforts.

Sometimes you will see exhortations such as, 'Make a commitment to post every single day for at least one year'. If you think that is a great use of your time as a professional, knock yourself out. Frankly, I would rather commit to visiting the dentist every single day for a year.

Promote others as well as yourself

As you build your personal brand online and in the physical world, perhaps you are feeling uncomfortable with doing lots of shameless self-promotion. (I have never had that problem.)

Happily, research has found that dual promotion, in which you compliment a colleague or peer while also talking about your own accomplishments, can boost perceptions of warmth without harming perceptions of your competence. Others learn about your abilities and see you demonstrate respect for others. By talking positively about other people, you signal that you aren't self-centred — you're seen as a well-intentioned, warm colleague, even if you are an M&A lawyer or an investment banker. Practical tips on how to implement this practice may be found in a 2023 article published in the *HBR*, 'How to Self-Promote — Without Sounding Self-Centered'.[6]

Bringing it all together

Here is a list of offline and online deliberate actions to consider when building your personal brand. What's right for you will depend on your profession, experience and seniority, as well as on your organisation's degree of support. Taking a structured, project-management approach is a good idea, as suggested in the *HBR* articles I've referred to.

As I've noted in this chapter, while daily activities are more important than deliberate actions, both are valuable. And when embarking on deliberate actions, don't forget to bring to bear other recommendations, such as seeking out and acting on feedback.

- Write good-quality articles and papers as well as short, pithy comments in the right journals, periodicals and online publications, starting with your own organisation's website and LinkedIn. Maybe, in the fullness of time, write a book or two.

- Speak at organisation/client events and publicly at conferences. Co-present with clients/industry leaders or regulators for your profession. Even if you can't get speaking slots at such events, at least attend and network your socks off. This applies to both live and virtual events and conferences.

- Take the opportunity to be seconded to clients to maximise the diversity of your experience and client/industry knowledge, as well as to build relationships.

- Provide advice to leading players in one or more sectors.

- Get involved in one or more professional and/or industry bodies/associations. This will take lots of hard (usually unpaid) work on committees, writing submissions etc. Become the 'gun' or go-to person on one or more issues.

- Develop a media/industry presence as a thought leader on one or more issues.

- Establish a social media presence. Contribute pieces to your organisation's website with you named as author. Curate a compelling LinkedIn profile and/or a blog. Post original material rather than reposting, or commenting on, others' work.

- Develop wide and deep, mutually respectful, relationships with people in relevant regulatory/government bodies, ministerial advisers and the like in your area(s) of specialisation.

- Get involved in consultation bodies that interact with government/agencies on issues affecting your profession.
- Teach/lecture part-time at a university, college or other tertiary body in your field.
- Remember, your personal brand and your executive presence (see chapter 9) are closely intertwined.

In play

I started building my personal brand with gusto from the time I commenced my first career in late 1984, although this was before 'personal brand' had become a thing. If you had asked me what I was doing, I would have said I was trying to build a good reputation as quickly as possible. If you had asked my colleagues what they thought I was doing, they would have rolled their eyes and said something like 'Tony is doing more shameless self-promotion.'

In those pre-internet days I promoted myself the old-fashioned way. At one time or another I did all the things set out in the list above, apart from being seconded to a client. Although it took me a while to get used to public speaking on the rather dry subject of tax law, eventually I made regular podium appearances. In chapter 6 I recounted my role in a 19-year project to reform the taxation of financial arrangements. This provided countless opportunities to present and to write all manner of lengthy and tedious articles and papers, as well as my first book.

During my time at Greenwoods & Herbert Smith Freehills, the firm punched well above its weight in making submissions to Government, Treasury and the Australian Taxation Office on all manner of policy and administrative aspects of Australian tax law. I loved being involved in this activity, especially after I became the firm's managing director. I tried to persuade myself that such outsized consultation efforts helped the firm's brand as much as my own. Of course, the firm didn't get paid to be involved in all this never-ending consultation. Some of my fellow directors, quite rightly, would query me from time to time on whether we were overcommitting in our Sisyphean efforts to help with tax reform.

For many years I was a lecturer in the University of Sydney's LLM tax program, where I enjoyed explaining to students how Australia's tax laws tried to grapple with transactions denominated in foreign currency and modern financial instruments. I stopped teaching only when I became the firm's managing director.

Fairly late in my first career I became a fan of sending the firm's staff and sometimes its directors on secondment with our clients. I was reticent at first because about 50 per cent of the time the client would poach the secondee. Eventually, I concluded I would rather have one of our happy alumni working in a client organisation than someone who had worked for a competitor. In addition, when secondees did return to Greenwoods not only were their personal brands enhanced, but they had gained useful insights into life on the client side of the fence.

Spending the best part of five years in Westpac Banking Corporation's tax group relatively early in my career strengthened my personal brand. In one sense it was like being on a very long secondment. When I returned to public practice at Price Waterhouse, I noticed an increase in my perceived credibility as a tax adviser to the banking sector. I had been there and done that.

Key takeaways

- **Personal brand.** Whether you like it or not, you always have a personal brand, good, bad or indifferent.
  - ✓ Importantly, your personal brand, although intentional, is not what you think it is. It is how other people assess it and you.
  - ✓ Imagine you are a fly on the wall, listening to a group of people who know you well. They are speaking about you from a personal and professional perspective: how you present, your character, your strengths and weaknesses, your special traits and attributes, how you are differentiated from others ... and your reputation. The gist of what they say is your personal brand.

- **Assessing your personal brand.** Here are some questions you can ask people you know and trust, to help you assess your personal brand:
  - ✓ How would you describe my personal brand (reputation) right now?
  - ✓ What adjectives best sum up my personal brand in your mind?
  - ✓ What could I start doing, continue doing or stop doing to help me build a strong and credible personal brand?

- **Project manage your personal brand.** Do these things:
  - ✓ Identify your purpose and decide on your investment.
  - ✓ Get clear on the benefits — and how you'll track them.
  - ✓ Identify your stakeholders.
  - ✓ Lay out your resources and deliverables, and nail down your plan and strategy.

- **Your personal brand — inside your own organisation.** Ask yourself these questions before requesting feedback from others in your organisation:
  - ✓ Am I sufficiently respectful of others in my organisation and do I know my place?
  - ✓ On the other hand, do I speak up when necessary — for example, to raise ethical issues, technical concerns, potential process improvements, or opportunities to seek new clients or assignments?

✓ When appropriate, do I challenge how things are done in my organisation?

✓ Are other people sufficiently respectful of me?

✓ How brave am I? Am I willing to take appropriate risks in circumstances where, with guardrails in place, it is okay to make mistakes? Am I willing to fail from time to time in order to learn and grow? Is such a mindset acceptable in my organisation? If not, am I working at the right place?

- **Building your personal brand the old-fashioned way.** Building your personal brand consists of all the daily activities and deliberate actions that build your relationships and reputation, so you are front-of-mind (and on lists and panels) to provide valuable services when existing or potential clients (including people you have yet to meet) have problems that need solving:

  ✓ **Daily activities** are anything you usually do, day-to-day, to serve your clients and assist your colleagues within your organisation. Doing first-rate work, meeting agreed deadlines, building relationships, communicating well, and being a pleasant and cheerful human being will go a very long way to building your personal brand. Not only do such activities not take any extra time, but you are paid to do them.

  ✓ **Deliberate actions** are the types of offline or online activities implicit in the discussion on project management of your personal brand. There are any number of such actions you might undertake, depending on your profession, experience and seniority.

- **Building your personal brand in the digital age.** The three most important tenets of personal branding are just as relevant and important online as they are in the real world:

  ✓ Personal branding is based in authenticity—what's true, genuine and real.

  ✓ Personal branding is about differentiation—standing out from others in your field.

  ✓ Personal branding means delivering exceptional value, which makes you relevant and compelling to the people who are making decisions about you.

- **Online presence.** The usefulness of an online presence will vary enormously depending on your profession, job, organisation and circumstances. There is no one-size-fits-all.
  - ✓ The first two usual places for professionals to build an online presence are their own organisation's website and LinkedIn. Only when you have those two working well is it worth exploring the multitude of other online platforms.
  - ✓ Take your lead from digitally savvy senior professionals in your own and similar organisations. Also look at what your peers are doing.
- **Promote others as well as yourself.** Not only will this help you if you cringe at self-promotion, but research shows that this will actually enhance your standing with other people. Do this online and in the real world.

Chapter 11
What is success?

If you have read the whole of this book and haven't just skipped to this final chapter to find 'the answer', you will know it's been about you, your development and things that have been important in the workplace since before the age of the abacus. Along the way I have provided some ideas to help you answer two questions I first posed in the Introduction:

- How can I become my best possible professional?
- How can I add the most value in the age of artificial intelligence?

But the subtitle of the book foregrounds success so in this final chapter we will ask another fundamental question: what is success? I know, answering this question is right up there with decoding the meaning of life or mastering Australian income tax law. Nonetheless, the subject deserves exploration. Of course, everyone will already have (or should already have) their own answer. At the end of the day, or certainly well before the end of your life, you have to work it out for yourself.

Warren Buffett has long since worked it out in his own life, and when he was 85 he offered this advice to others:

You have lived a successful life if, as you grow older, the people you hope love you, actually do. I have never known anyone who does not feel like a success when they have gotten close to my age and have a lot of people who love them. I know enormously wealthy individuals who have dinners held in their honour, hospital wings named after them, and all that sort of thing, but the truth is that no one thinks much of them. I have to believe that at some point they realize it, and everything gets quite empty after that.[1]

Ask yourself these questions

- Do Buffett's words resonate with me?
- How will I decide, when towards the end of my life I face my own mortality, whether or not I have been successful?

Buffett knows well there is more to a successful life than a stellar career. This chapter, like this book, focuses primarily on success in your working life, however.

Maybe you are satisfied with your current job and you have a clear idea of what success looks like for you, as well as a strategy to achieve your goals. If so, great, go ahead and skip this chapter. If success means making partner in a professional service firm by age 30 and earning serious amounts of money, then good for you. But make sure you have looked after other aspects of your life, so you don't wake up one morning when you are 60 or 65 to realise you are one of those people no one thinks much of.

Relationships

The core of Warren Buffett's advice on relationships is easily adapted to a career setting. In chapter 1 we explored what it means to be a true professional; the first criterion was caring deeply about your clients and, if you work in an organisation, your colleagues. I called this the golden rule of professionalism. From such care will spring good-quality relationships that will sustain you through the highs and lows of a professional life. You will have a relationship rather than a transactional mindset in your dealings with clients and colleagues. In most professional service environments the relentless pressure of the ticking clock is unavoidable. There never seems to be enough time to get work done and to nurture deep relationships with everyone you encounter in your professional life, but don't throw the baby out with the bathwater. Make some choices and allocate time to building relationships with people who share your values, hopes and sense of humour.

If you have any doubt about the importance of relationships, not just at work but in your life generally, you need look no further than the core conclusion of the 80-year Harvard Study of Adult Development[2], which is that the stronger our relationships, the more likely we are to live happy, satisfying and healthy lives.

How will you measure your life?

In a classic *HBR* article[3], Clayton Christensen, a much-loved Professor of Business Administration at Harvard Business School (HBS), recounted how each year, on the last day of class, he would ask his students to produce cogent answers to three questions:

- How can I be sure that I'll be happy in my career?
- How can I be sure that my relationships with my spouse and my family become an enduring source of happiness?
- How can I be sure I'll stay out of jail?

Christensen noted the last question as pertinent as two of the 32 in his class had spent time in jail. As students discussed answers to his questions, Christensen would open his own life to them, as a case study of sorts. 'How will you measure your life' grew out of discussions around six themes with his class of 2010.

1. Create a strategy for your life

Christensen observed that a substantial portion of the 900 students that HBS drew each year from among the world's best had given little thought to the purpose of their lives (see chapter 6). For him, having a clear purpose for his life had been essential, but he had to think long and hard before he understood it.

2. Allocate your resources

Every day you will make decisions about how to allocate your time, energy and other resources. These decisions are what ultimately shape the strategy of your life. If you study why businesses fail, Christensen said, it is often because of a desire for immediate gratification or short-term results. Individuals are prone to making the same mistake in their personal lives. That is, over time, some people end up allocating fewer of their precious resources to the people and things that they once said were the most important. Don't make that mistake. (We looked at planning, the first and most important of the Seven Accelerants, in chapter 9.)

3. Create a culture

Christensen suggested that families, just like companies, have cultures and that they can be built consciously or evolve in a random way.

4. Avoid the 'marginal costs' mistake

Christensen believed we naturally, often unconsciously, employ the marginal-cost doctrine in our lives when we decide between right and wrong: A voice in our head tells us, 'Look, I know that as a general rule most people shouldn't do this. But in this particular extenuating circumstance, just this once, it's okay.' The lesson, he points out, is it's easier to hold on to your principles all of the time than it is to hold on to them 98 per cent of the time. If you decide to give in, just once, this ends up being a slippery slope that you will later regret.

5. Remember the importance of humility

We explored humility as a key element of professionalism in chapter 1 and again in chapter 4. Christensen advised his students to seek out advice not only from smarter people, but from everybody.

6. Choose the right yardstick

Christensen advised his students to be unconcerned with the level of individual success you achieve, but to think about the individuals you have helped to become better people. Finally, think about the indicia by which you would like your life to be judged. Resolve to live every day in accordance with those indicia. That way, in the end your life will be judged a success.

The energising factors of motivation

Another way to gauge your success is to reflect on whether what you are doing in your life at this moment is truly motivating. In chapter 6 we looked at what I call the energising eight factors of motivation: purpose/meaning, autonomy, mastery, relatedness, status, certainty, fairness and feedback. Or maybe you are more motivated by other things. Whatever motivates you, do you feel your current job will allow you to fulfil those needs, if not immediately then down the track? If your answer is regularly 'no', then are you trying to find a new job or career? If not, why not?

The Five Ps of Success

As this book draws to a close, I present for your consideration my Five Ps of Success (figure 11.1). These five interlinked factors, which I've already covered from various angles, will set you up for success.

- **Purpose** is at the centre of the model because it is the first of the energising eight factors of motivation outlined in chapter 6. Having a clear purpose helps you with ...

- **Planning** is the first and most important of the Seven Accelerants, as explored in chapter 9. Your planning will demand ...
- **Persistence** is at the heart of Deliberate Practice, the third Accelerant, which will elevate ...
- **Performance** for a true professional, as discussed in chapter 1, means you will be delivering to your clients at the highest level when you have gained ...
- **Perspective** is the much-prized ability to evaluate situations, issues and problems wisely from multiple points of view rather than simply reacting to them. Together, the Seven Accelerants will broaden your perspective, as will the questions listed in chapter 7 to help boost your transformative learning and adult development.

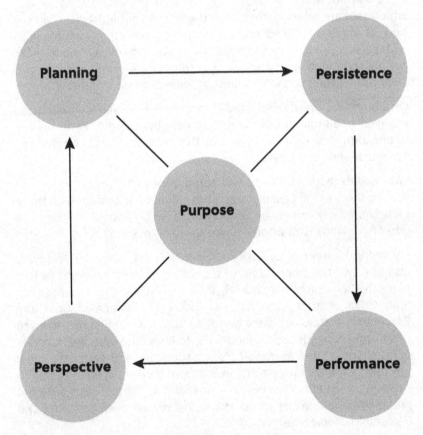

Figure 11.1: The Five Ps of Success

In play

At this stage of my life, I place my thoughts about success into three buckets: each of my two careers and my private life.

As I look back on my first career as a tax adviser, I know I achieved a measure of success. I admit I enjoyed the status that came with my role as managing director of one of Australia's leading tax advisory firms. Humility, sadly, has never been a personal strength of mine. I admit that all my advice about humility is a case of 'do as I say, not as I do or did'.

It took me a few years to develop a significant level of competence, let alone mastery, to operate autonomously, and to develop great relationships with clients and most (not all) of my colleagues and peers. I'm glad I persisted with those efforts, though I have a few regrets about how I handled some things in my first career, most of which concern relationships. With the benefit of hindsight, I can see how at times I focused on transactions rather than relationships with certain people. For example, it was sometimes my role to make people redundant or otherwise end their employment, and I regret I was more legalistic than humane in some of those situations.

On a brighter note, as explained in chapter 6, I derived joy from being involved in all manner of tax reform initiatives and I like to believe I contributed to useful changes in the Australian taxation system. For me, that was success.

With few exceptions, I liked and cared about my clients. As well as serving them to the best of my abilities, I built relationships with those I felt shared my values, hopes and sense of humour. Some became personal friends with whom I have stayed in touch.

My second career is a work in progress, and one I am enjoying immensely. I have been able to tick off my energising eight factors of motivation much more quickly than I could in my first career. I am glad to have graduated with a Master of Science in Coaching Psychology to help equip me for my second act. I am hungry to learn more and I have just enough humility to know this is in the interests of my clients as well as myself. Having spent 34 years getting to know any number of tax lawyers and investment bankers, it is refreshing to be spending quality time building relationships with a quite different group of people in the wonderful world of executive coaching and leadership development.

I have mentioned that in my first career I was not a great role model for self-care, making some poor choices on how I spent my time. Nonetheless I have always treasured my relationships with Catherine, my beautiful wife of almost 40 years, and our two lovely daughters, Elizabeth and Laura. I am lucky enough to have numerous personal friendships, many of them going back more than 50 years to primary school days. As I noted in chapter 6, as a former tax lawyer I probably have more friends than I deserve! I am totally convinced by the Harvard Study of Adult Development's research showing that the stronger our relationships, the more likely we are to live a happy, satisfying and healthy life. To me that is success in the age of AI, or in any age for that matter.

What do you think?

Key takeaways

- **Warren Buffett's definition of success.** You have lived a successful life if, as you grow older, the people you hope love you actually do. I can't beat that!

- **What about you?** Do Buffett's words resonate with you? When, towards the end of your life, you consider your own mortality, how will you decide on your level of 'success'?

- **Relationships.** You will never have enough time to nurture deep relationships with everyone you come across in your professional life, so make some choices, and allocate time and build relationships with people who share your values, hopes and sense of humour.

- **How will you measure your life?** The late Clayton Christensen nailed it with these suggestions:
  - ✓ Create a strategy for your life.
  - ✓ Allocate your resources.
  - ✓ Create a culture.
  - ✓ Avoid the 'marginal costs' mistake.
  - ✓ Remember the importance of humility.
  - ✓ Choose the right yardstick.

- **The energising factors of motivation.** Reflect periodically on whether what you are doing in your life at this moment is truly motivating for you.
  - ✓ In chapter 6 we examined what I call the energising eight factors of motivation: purpose/meaning, autonomy, mastery, relatedness, status, certainty, fairness and feedback. (Maybe you are more highly motivated by other things.)
  - ✓ Whatever motivates you, do you feel your current job can fulfil those needs, if not straight away then down the track?
  - ✓ If your answer is often 'no', then are you trying to find a new job or career? If not, why not?

- **The Five Ps of Success.** These five interlinked factors, which were addressed in earlier parts of the book, will set you up for success:
  - ✓ Purpose
  - ✓ Planning
  - ✓ Persistence
  - ✓ Performance
  - ✓ Perspective.

Conclusion

I began this book by suggesting that professionals today face four interlinked challenges: complexity, increased client demands, remote work and artificial intelligence. Of the four, artificial intelligence seems likely to throw up the most challenges — and the most opportunities — in the years to come. This Playbook to unleash your potential and futureproof your success was designed to assist you in addressing these challenges.

As this book goes to print we are still in the very early days of the Fourth Industrial Revolution, in which 21st-century technology is being embedded in many aspects of our lives. A large part of this revolution centres on the development of artificial intelligence. We don't yet know how powerful or pervasive AI will be in the years to come, and despite alarming predictions, we can't know the extent to which it will accelerate so as to lead to the displacement of human professionals. However, at least three things can be said with some certainty:

- Currently there is still very strong demand for the human beings classed as professionals to provide all manner of valuable services.
- Humans in a range of professions are rapidly figuring out how AI can assist them in providing services to their clients in the most efficient and cost-effective manner.
- Professionals who do not adapt and keep up with the best use of AI within their particular profession (or who fail to attend to challenges of complexity, client demands and remote work) will struggle to remain competitive.

One other thing is certain: you will need to be working in an environment that recognises the opportunities AI can provide. This is true whether you are working in a professional service firm, as an in-house professional or in your own business. You don't want to wake up one day and realise you have been left behind. So keep abreast of AI developments in your profession, and consider jumping ship if your current organisation is not treating AI as seriously as are other players in your sector.

This book has provided you with many ideas, questions, templates and tools to help you build a successful career in the age of AI, and to assist you in answering two essential questions:

- How can I become my best possible professional?
- How can I add the most value in the age of artificial intelligence?

We have seen how one of the best ways to remain relevant as the Fourth Industrial Revolution gathers pace is to ask your clients probing questions about what they value in your services.

There is much more to your career, and your life more broadly, than keeping one step ahead of increasingly smart machines. The Playbook introduces the concept of Five Factors to help you shape your personal and professional life. The first and foundational factor is *self-care*. Remember the aircraft pre-flight safety briefing: first put on your own safety mask and then look out for others; you will be of no use to anyone if you are burnt out.

You will perform at your best and succeed in your career if your work is intrinsically motivating and interesting to you, which is why *motivation* is the second of the Five Factors. Aside from earning reasonable money, we are all motivated by different things, and it is important to think through what motivates you.

Emphasising the value of lifelong learning and development, especially in professional service environments, may sound clichéd, but often an idea becomes a cliché for good reason. *Learning*, the third factor, means consciously and constantly learning new things and trying out new ideas as you become the best professional, and indeed the best person, possible. Think about and take responsibility for your own learning and development, especially if you work remotely, and don't leave your personal growth to the whim of your employer.

Finally, identifying and developing your key skills and *capabilities* (factor 4) and mobilising the *Seven Accelerants* (factor 5) are proven ways to advance a successful career.

● ● ●

I am optimistic about the future for professionals who think about, prepare for and plan their careers and personal development with an eye to a rapidly changing world. Most important, like all humans in the age of AI, professionals will need to understand and adapt to changing circumstances. To survive and thrive in this new world, professionals will need to keep rethinking their roles and skills and the value they bring to their clients and their employers.

No one really knows how developments in AI will impact the market for particular professional jobs — including yours, dear reader — but sooner or later the number of positions for humans in the professional sector seems likely to fall. Your goal is to be in one of those that remain indispensable.

This book has helped equip you for the challenges and opportunities ahead. Whether or not current dire predictions about the impact of AI are realised, the strategies proposed will stand you in good stead.

If I was 24 years old today, I would have no hesitation in choosing a career as a tax adviser. I had a great ride the first time around. Using this volume as my playbook and guide, I would back myself to be the best tax professional I could be while adding great value for my clients, who would be more than willing to pay for services that smart machines could not provide.

If you have enjoyed and derived value from these pages, make sure that when you are a senior professional and this book has long been out of print, you pass it on to the next generation, assuming there are still human beings doing work at least vaguely like that you did when you were younger. The young professionals in your care will be grateful and will respond with enthusiasm and loyalty.

I wish you the very best in learning, changing, growing and having fun as you progress in your career(s) and your successful life.

Acknowledgements

I find it hard to believe, but this book has had a gestation period of almost seven years. There are many people to acknowledge.

My beautiful wife Catherine stoically endured my lengthy explanation of what I hoped to achieve with my book. This occurred during a long flight back from Boston in mid 2018, after I had attended an executive education course at Harvard Business School. Many thanks, Cathy, for your love and support over the journey of this book. Our lovely daughters, Elizabeth and Laura, have also been very supportive and interested throughout the process.

I am very fortunate to know Steven Morris, who is married to Cathy's cousin Elizabeth. Steven, the owner of Lansdowne Publishing, provided me with invaluable expert advice throughout the book's development.

Thank you to my siblings Peter, Tim and Katrina for allowing your brother to prattle on endlessly about some book he took forever to write, and to many others in the wider Frost family who expressed interest in this project, especially my aunt and uncle Margaret and David Winter.

In early 2019 I set up a focus group of professionals to workshop the book and comment on drafts from time to time. Many thanks to focus group members Lucy Adams, Lucy Booth, Alice Deng, Mary Hu, Verina Morwood, Jonathan Ortner and Corinne O'Sullivan.

Also in 2019 I returned to my alma mater, the University of Sydney, to undertake a Master of Science in Coaching Psychology. I am very grateful to the academics and my fellow students in that course. I learned a great deal from all of you, and especially the late great Professor Anthony Grant.

One of the first clients in my second career was awesome in-house corporate legal counsel Claire Martin. Thank you, Claire, for your invaluable input over the years. I enjoyed our discussions on various topics and how to address them in the book, and I greatly appreciate your review and comments on some of the chapters.

I am a member of the excellent Northern Beaches (of Sydney) Coaches group, which meets monthly for earnest discussions on all matters coaching. I have been telling group members about my book since 2020. They have been an important part of my accountability framework for getting the book finished and published. Thank you to present and past members for your encouragement and support: David Armsworth-Maw, Sue Billen, Sue Browne, Justin Clarke, Tess Everingham, Kirsty Grace, Kim Helman, Xandra May, Jacqui Pollock, Therese Rahme, Fran Tiver and Dieter Weinand.

A huge thank you to my friend Professor Michael Adams, who provided detailed and very useful comments on the draft manuscript.

Many other friends listened politely and provided very helpful comments over the book's incubation period. Thank you to Dr Sharmila Betts, Geoff Campbell, Andy Carroll, Craig Costello, Michael Depangher, Viva Hammer, Robert Kenn, Greg Lazarus, Matthew Mailey, Greg McHugh, Susan Paczkowski, Chris Richardson, Craig Stapleton, Ed Stephenson, and Jeremy and Sue Trahair.

Thanks to Sue Billen, I was alerted in late 2023 to Kelly Irving's Expert Author Community (EAC). Being a member of the EAC was a terrific experience and I benefited greatly from following Kelly's advice on how a book of this nature should be structured, as well as from the support and encouragement of other EAC members and Kelly's colleagues, whom I nicknamed the Kelly Gang. Thank you also to the wonderful Lou Johnson from Key People Literary Management, whom I met via the EAC and who helped me greatly improve my book proposal, which was eventually noticed by Wiley.

The team at Wiley have been fantastic to work with over an intense period from initial contact to book launch. Thank you to Renee Aurish, Jem Bates, Leigh McLennon, Lucy Raymond, Chris Shorten and many others. And the biggest thank you goes to Shannon Vargo, a Wiley Vice President and Publisher in New York City, who first identified my book as potentially publishable after I uploaded it, unsolicited, to Wiley's website.

Thank you in advance to my publicist, Scott Eathorne from Quikmark Media, who I am sure will do a first-class job of alerting the world to my book.

Heartfelt thanks to David Gonski AC and Dr George Beaton for their foreword and cover endorsement respectively. Your support is very much appreciated.

Finally, many thanks to all of my clients, colleagues, collaborators and connections in each of my careers. My experiences with so many people, and all that I learned along the way, are what made this book possible. You are too numerous to acknowledge individually, although I will name, with grateful thanks, my key first-career mentors, John Masters, John Brodie and Dr Alicia Fortinberry.

Suggested reading and viewing

In this section I have assembled a wide range of materials, organised by chapter, to help you with your lifelong learning and ongoing professional development. There are books, articles, other publications, video clips and podcasts. They are all excellent and I highly recommend every one of them. The bookcases in my office, now devoid of anything relating to tax law, contain hundreds of books relevant to professionals and personal development. In addition, I have about forty lever arch files full of articles, papers and press clippings. I also use more than my fair share of iCloud space for my compendious electronically stored items. I guess I am a bit of a self-development junkie. Knowing your time is precious and short, I sifted through my bookcases, files, hard drive and other sources to draw together what I regard as the best and most practical learning materials to recommend to other professionals.

Set up your own discussion group

Here is an idea to help make your ongoing professional development more fun, and to assist you in taking control of your progress while introducing elements of commitment, accountability and feedback.

Set up your own professional development discussion group or book club, with like-minded colleagues from your own organisation, and ideally some friends from other organisations, to maximise the diversity of thinking and analysis. The group should not exceed seven people.[1]

Agree to meet regularly, maybe over pizza and good Australian red wine. I suggest about every six weeks or every two months. If you meet too regularly — say, fortnightly or monthly — it may fizzle out too quickly as the demands of your job and family interrupt your best-laid plans. On the other hand, if you meet too infrequently — say, every three months — you may lose momentum and forget what you discussed last time. You might spend a few meetings on the one book or other source if it is of great interest. You could agree to discuss a particular chapter or part thereof at each meeting.

As mentioned in chapter 7, transformative learning means when we are learning new things that involve understanding purposes, values, beliefs and feelings, we really need to engage in discussions with other people to test and debate evidence, arguments, competing interpretations and alternative points of view. Your book club gives you a forum for such discussions.

People learn and develop best in different ways. Some like to read books like this one and those I have recommended and to watch motivational videos; and some don't. That you have got this far in this book suggests you are someone who likes to read books as part of your development. If you try to set up a group, don't be disheartened if you get some knock-backs. Eventually you will find other like-minded professionals, perhaps in other organisations, who share your passion for reading books like these and discussing them with other people to help themselves and others to learn and grow. You may end up effectively coaching and mentoring each other.

Here is a suggested framework for you and your group to help structure your discussions:

1. Agree in advance on which book/chapters, articles, video clip(s) and so on will be discussed at the next meeting. Of course, start with this book! But don't be limited to this book and the materials listed. No doubt group members will have all manner of suggestions.

2. At the meeting, go around the group and share key insights and what really resonated for each person. What are your practical takeaways from what you have read or seen and discussed in the group? Also, what didn't make sense for you? Make sure everyone gets a turn.

3. Discuss the questions listed towards the end of chapter 7, which are designed to challenge your thinking and assumptions. Ask these questions out loud during your meetings.

4. Discuss and share issues you would like to raise with your boss(es), possibly as points for inclusion in your work-based personal development plans.

5. Are there suggestions you could make to your boss, or others at your organisation, based on the things you have read and discussed in your meetings? How could you help improve the work processes of your organisation?

6. After the meeting, reflect on whether and how to revise your Prime Capabilities and Enablers, and your associated action plans for personal development.

If your group is up and running, I would love to join you in a meeting at a convenient time if I happen to be in your city and country. Sydney is easiest. Drop me an email at tony@frostleadership.com.au and I'll see what I can do.

Universal resources

Before listing items by chapter, here are some resources of general appeal and interest to many professionals across a range of topics, including but not limited to those discussed in this book.

Scott Galloway. I would like to give a quick plug for Professor Scott Galloway, Professor of Marketing at NYU's Stern School of Business. As we saw in the 'In play' section in chapter 6, Professor Galloway is not especially enamoured with tax lawyers. Nonetheless I am a huge fan of him. Check out his website (www.profgalloway.com) and all manner of other places on the internet where he pops up. There are plenty of great things for your group to read, watch, listen to and discuss that cut across many aspects and themes in this book.

Adam Grant. As TED says, 'Organizational psychologist Adam Grant takes you inside the minds of some of the world's most unusual professionals to explore the science of making work not suck' ('WorkLife with Adam Grant: A TED original podcast'). What's not to like?

Seth Godin. Godin is an entrepreneur, best-selling author and speaker, with all manner of blogs, podcasts and other resources of interest to professionals collected at: https://www.sethgodin.com and https://seths.blog.

Chapter 1. Are you a true professional?

Maister, DH (2000). *True Professionalism*, Simon & Schuster.

Maister, DH, Green, CH, and Galford, RM (2000). *The Trusted Adviser*, The Free Press.

Susskind, R, and Susskind, D (2022). *The Future of the Professions*, updated edition, Oxford University Press.

Brown, Brené (2010). 'The Power of Vulnerability', TED talk.

Chapter 2. The robots are coming, sort of

Susskind, R, and Susskind, D (2022). *The Future of the Professions*, updated edition, Oxford University Press.

Shrier, DL (2024). *Basic AI*, Robinson.

Netflix (2024). *What Can AI Do for Us/to Us*, episode 1 in 'What's Next? The Future' with Bill Gates.

Walsh, T (2018). *2062: The World that AI Made*, La Trobe University Press.

Walsh, T (2022). *Machines Behaving Badly: The Morality of AI*, Black Inc.

Daugherty, P, and Wilson, HJ (2024). *Human + Machine: Reimaging Work in the Age of AI*, updated edition, Harvard Business Review Press.

McGeorge, D (2023). *The ChatGPT Revolution, How to Simplify Your Work and Life Admin with AI*, Wiley.

Grill, A (2024). *Digitally Curious: Your Guide to Navigating the Future of AI and All Things Tech*, Wiley.

Shadbolt, N, and Hampson, R (2018). *The Digital Ape: how to live (in peace) with smart machines*, Scribe.

Zytnik, M (2024). *Internal Communication in the Age of Artificial Intelligence*, Business Expert Press.

Chapter 3. What do (and will) your clients want?

Maraia, MM (2003). *Rainmaking Made Simple: What Every Professional Must Know*, Professional Services Publishing.

Scammell, J (2018). *Service Mindset*, Major Street Publishing.

Scammell, J (2020). *Service Habits*, Major Street Publishing.

McMakin, T, and Fletcher, D (2018). *How Clients Buy: A Practical Guide to Business Development for Consulting and Professional Services*, Wiley.

Chapter 4. What employers want (and should do)

Maister, DH (1997). *Managing the Professional Service Firm*, The Free Press.

Maister, DH (2001). *Practice What You Preach*, The Free Press.

McKenna, PJ, and Maister, DH (2005). *First Among Equals: How to Manage a Group of Professionals*, The Free Press.

Maister, DH (2008). *Strategy and the Fat Smoker*, The Spangle Press.

Empson, L (2019). 'How to Lead Your Fellow Rainmakers', *HBR*.

Empson, L (2017). *Leading Professionals: Power, Politics and Prima Donnas*, Oxford University Press.

Osman, S, Lane, J, and Goldsmith, M (2023). *Becoming Coachable*, 100 Coaches.

Stein, K (2023). *Be Your Own Leadership Coach*, Major Street Publishing.

Clifton, J, and Harter, J (2019). *It's the Manager*, Gallup Press.

Clifton, J, and Harter, J (2021). *Wellbeing at Work*, Gallup Press.

Clifton, J, and Harter, J (2023). *Culture Shock*, Gallup Press.

Bungay Stanier, M (2016). *The Coaching Habit*, Box of Crayons Press.

Lorsch, JW, and Tierney, TJ (2002). *Aligning the Stars: How to Succeed When Professionals Drive Results*, Harvard Business School Press.

Charan, R, Barton, D, and Carey, D (2018). *Talent Wins*, Harvard Business Review Press.

Gardner, H (2017). *Smart Collaboration*, Harvard Business Review Press.

Pfeffer, J (2018). *Dying for a Paycheck*, Harper Business.

Chapter 5. Fit your own oxygen mask first

Edmondson, A (2023). *Right Kind of Wrong: How the Best Teams Use Failure to Succeed*, Penguin.

Calarco, M (2023). *Beating Burnout Finding Balance*, Wiley.

Markway, B, and Ampel, C (2018). *The Self-Confidence Workbook*, Althea Press.

Loer, J, and Schwartz, T (2001). 'The Making of a Corporate Athlete', *HBR*.

Clear, J (2018). *Atomic Habits*, Random House.

Neff, Kristin. 'The Space Between Self-Esteem and Self Compassion', TEDx Centennial Park Women.

Nestor, J (2020). *Breath — The New Science of a Lost Art*, Penguin.

Chapter 6. What gets you out of bed in the morning?

Leipzig, Adam. 'How to know your life purpose in 5 minutes', TED talk.

Frankl, VE (1946). *Man's Search for Meaning*, Beacon Press.

Bolles, RN (2022). *What Color Is Your Parachute?*, Random House.

Newport, C (2012). *So Good They Can't Ignore You*, Grand Central Publishing.

Sinek, S (2009). *Start with Why*, Portfolio Penguin.

Pink, DH (2009). *Drive*, Penguin.

Chapter 7. Lifelong learning, development and curiosity

Argyris, C (1991). 'Teaching Smart People How to Learn', *HBR*.

Kahneman, D (2012). *Thinking, Fast and Slow*, Penguin.

Shrier, DL (2024). *Basic AI*, Robinson.

Dweck, C (2017). *Mindset*, updated edition, Robinson.

Garvey Berger, J (2019). *Unlocking Leadership Mindtraps*, Stanford Briefs.

Berger, JB (2006). 'Key Concepts for Understanding the Work of Robert Kegan'.

Kegan, R (1995). *In Over Our Heads: The mental demands of modern life*, Harvard University Press.

Chapter 8. Prime Capabilities and Enablers: become AI-proof

Beane, M (2024). *The Skill Code: How to Save Human Ability in an Age of Intelligent Machines*, HarperCollins.

Kahneman, D (2012). *Thinking, Fast and Slow*, Penguin.

Webb, PJ (2021). *System 3 Thinking: How to Choose Wisely When Facing Doubt, Dilemma or Disruption*, Publish Central.

Johnson, S (1998). *Who Moved My Cheese?* GP Putnam's Sons.

Godin, S (2023). *The Song of Significance: A New Manifesto for Teams*, Portfolio.

Chapter 9. The Seven Accelerants to supercharge your career

Stone, D, and Heen, S (2014). *Thanks for the Feedback: The Science and Art of Receiving Feedback Well*, Penguin.

Lerner, HG (2013). *Marriage Rules*, Gotham Books.

Maraia, MM (2003). *Rainmaking Made Simple: What Every Professional Must Know*, Professional Services Publishing.

Buffett, W (2015). In *Getting There: A Book of Mentors*, edited by GZ Segal, Abrams.

DeLong, TJ (2011). *Flying Without a Net*, Harvard Business Review Press.

Kets de Vries, MFR (2023). 'How to Get Better at Asking for Help', *HBR*.

Eurich, T (2018). 'What Self-Awareness Really Is (and How to Cultivate It)', *HBR*.

Eurich, T (2017). 'Increase your self-awareness with one simple fix', TED talk.

Wilson, P (2015). *Make Mentoring Work*, Major Street Publishing.

Bain, K (2015). *The Principles of Movement*, Oberon Books.

Pfeffer, J (2022). *7 Rules of Power*, Swift.

Chapter 10. Building your personal brand in the digital age

Peters, T (1997). 'The Brand Called You', *Fast Company 10*, 83–90.

Monarth, H (2022). 'What's the Point of a Personal Brand?', *HBR*.

Pfeffer, J (2022). *7 Rules of Power*, Swift.

Chapter 11. What is success?

Buffett, W (2015). In *Getting There: A Book of Mentors*, edited by GZ Segal, Abrams.

Christensen, CM (2010). 'How Will You Measure Your Life', *HBR*.

Waldinger, R (2016). 'What makes a good life? Lessons from the longest study on happiness', TED talk.

Endnotes

About the author

1. Frost, T, Reilly, J, and Kater, E (2009). *Guide to Taxation of Financial Arrangements*, Thomson Reuters.

Introduction

1. Gates, B (2023). *The Age of AI has begun*, GatesNotes, 21 March.
2. Here is a third good question to ask yourself regularly: *Does my work bring me enough joy and fun?* I tackle this question in an Insight (Joy and Fun at Work) on my website, https://frostleadership.com.au.

Chapter 1

1. Maister, DH (2000). *True Professionalism*, Simon & Schuster.
2. For an excellent analysis of 'the professions', see chapter 1 (The Grand Bargain) in: Susskind, R, and Susskind, D (2022). *The Future of the Professions*, updated edition, Oxford University Press.
3. Standards Australia (2011). *Coaching in Organizations*, SAI Global.
4. The global guru on vulnerability and its value and importance is American academic, researcher and storyteller Dr Brené Brown. Her TED talk 'The Power of Vulnerability' is one of the most-ever-watched TED talks. Dr Brown has written a number of books on vulnerability, leadership and related subjects. She has thoughtfully provided a guide on her website, *Which Book Do I Read First?*
5. The Ethics Centre website: https://ethics.org.au.
6. Tax Practitioners Board, 22 November 2022, PricewaterhouseCoopers.
7. Definition of humility as per *Macquarie Dictionary Online*.

8. Martignetti, T (2024). '3 Ways Humility Can Undermine Your Leadership', *HBR*.

9. Field, HM (2017). *Aggressive Tax Planning & the Ethical Tax Lawyer*, 36 Va. Tax Rev. 261.

10. 36 Va. Tax Rev. 261 (2017) at p. 300.

11. *The role of the ethical leader in an accelerating world*. Address on 9 July 2019 to the AGSM Professional Forum.

12. The reports are accessible at https://financialservices.royalcommission .gov.au.

Chapter 2

1. Often attributed to American baseball player Yogi Berra; however, the sleuths at Quote Investigator conclude that this comical proverb was first expressed in Danish in 1948, author unknown.

2. 'Flying Machines Which Do Not Fly', *New York Times*, 9 October 1903.

3. The expression 'fourth industrial revolution' can be traced to Germany's national strategy in 2009 called the 'Digital Agenda'. Henrik von Scheel was one of the masterminds behind this agenda, which evolved into the Fourth Industrial Revolution and ignited a global wave of themes on digital Industry 4.0.

4. Schwab, K. 'The Fourth Industrial Revolution', *Britannica Online*.

5. Center for AI Safety (2023). *Statement on AI Risk*.

6. Susskind, R, and Susskind, D (2022). *The Future of the Professions*, updated edition, Oxford University Press.

7. Shrier, DL (2024). *Basic AI*, Robinson.

8. Deloitte (2019). *The path to prosperity: Why the future of work is human*, Deloitte Insights report no. 7 in the 'Building the Lucky Country' series.

9. International Monetary Fund (2024). *Gen-AI: Artificial Intelligence and the Future of Work*.

10. ACS (2020). *Technology Impacts on the Australian Workforce*.

11. Telsyte Australian Digital Consumer Study 2023.

12. Fathom (2024). *AI at the Crossroads: Public Sentiment and Policy Solutions*.

13. The other two are: Kahneman, D (2011). *Thinking, Fast and Slow*, Farrar, Straus and Giroux; and Kegan, R (1995). *In over our heads: The mental demands of modern life*, Harvard University Press.

14. Darwin, CR (1876). *The origin of species by means of natural selection, or the preservation of favoured races in the struggle for life*, John Murray, 6th edition. Available and searchable online at http://darwin-online.org.uk.

15. Autor, D (2024). *Applying AI to Rebuild Middle Class Jobs*, NBER Working Paper Series, working paper 32140.

16. Eschner, K (2016). 'The Story of the Real Canary in the Coal Mine', *Smithsonian Magazine*.

17. Chartered Accountants Australia and New Zealand (2020). *Capabilities for Accounting*.

18. Bowles, M, Ghosh, S, and Thomas, L (2020). 'Future proofing accounting professionals: Ensuring graduate employability and future readiness', *Journal of Teaching and Learning for Graduate Employability 11*(1).

19. Chartered Accountants Australia and New Zealand (2020). *New capability model to help shape profession of the future*: Capabilities for Accounting.

20. Chartered Accountants Australia and New Zealand (2024). *New guide highlights the power of advanced technologies in audit, and the dangers of over-reliance on them*.

21. Tadros, E (2024). 'Accountants turbocharge growth with AI', *Australian Financial Review*, 19 November.

22. Turing, AM (1950). 'Computing Machinery and Intelligence', *Mind 49*, 433–60.

23. The Turing Test has come in for criticism over the years in that it is more a test of deception than actual intelligence. See, for example, Oremus, A (2022). 'Google's AI passed a famous test — and showed how the test is broken', *Washington Post*, 17 June 2022.

24. IBM. *What is generative AI?*

25. Metz, C (2023). '"The Godfather of A.I." Leaves Google and Warns of Danger Ahead', *New York Times*, 1 May 2023.

26. Pelley, S (2023). '"Godfather of Artificial Intelligence" Geoffrey Hinton on the promise, risks of advanced AI', *60 Minutes, CBS News*.

27. Walsh, T (2018). *2062: The World that AI Made*, La Trobe University Press. In a 2023 Expert Survey on Progress in AI, with 1714 responses, the aggregate forecast time to a 50 per cent chance of 'HLMI' was 2047, where HLMI was defined as 'high-level machine intelligence, when unaided machines can accomplish every task better and more cheaply than human workers'.

28. Walsh, T (2018). *2062: The World that AI Made*, La Trobe University Press.

29. Eggleston, M (2019). 'Job fears over growth of AI are exaggerated', *Australian Financial Review*, 19 June.

30. Koetsier, J (2025). 'OpenAI CEO Sam Altman: "We Know How To Build AGI"', *Forbes*.

31. Walsh, T (2022). *Machines Behaving Badly: The Morality of AI*, Black Inc.

32. Department of Industry, Science and Resources, Australian Government (2024). *Mandatory guardrails for safe and responsible AI: have your say.*

33. National Artificial Intelligence Centre (2024). *The AI Impact Navigator.*

34. van Leeuwen, H (2023). 'Chief scientist urges swift action on ChatGPT', *Australian Financial Review*, 31 January.

35. Google (2024). 'What are AI hallucinations?'

36. CSIRO (2023). Australia's AI ecosystem momentum report.

37. Bick, A, Blandin, A, and Deming, DJ (2024). *The Rapid Adoption of Generative AI*, National Bureau of Economic Research Working Paper 32966.

38. EY (2024). *The EY 2024 Work Reimagined Survey.*

39. Telsyte Australian Digital Consumer Study 2023.

40. Bridgeman, A, Weeks, R, and Liu, D (2024). 'Aligning our assessments to the age of generative AI', the University of Sydney, 26 November.

41. White, D (2024). 'Uni students allowed to use AI', *The Sydney Morning Herald*, 27 November.

42. Felten, E, Raj, M, and Seamans, R (2023). 'How will Language Modelers like ChatGPT Affect Occupations and Industries?' SSRN.

43. Deloitte Access Economics (2023). *Generation AI: Ready or not, here we come!*

44. Roose, K (2023). 'A Conversation With Bing's Chatbot Left Me Deeply Unsettled', *New York Times*, 16 February.

45. Kang, C (2023). 'OpenAI's Sam Altman Urges A.I. Regulation in Senate Hearing', *New York Times*, 16 May.

46. Orduña, N (2023). 'What Young Professionals Need to Know About Generative AI', *HBR*.

47. Allen & Overy (2023). A&O announces exclusive launch partnership with Harvey.

48. PwC Global (2023). PwC announces strategic alliance with Harvey, positioning PwC's Legal Business Solutions at the forefront of legal generative AI.

49. Harvey (2023). *Sequoia and OpenAI Back Harvey to Redefine Professional Services, Starting with Legal*: https://www.harvey.ai/blog.

50. van Leeuwen, H (2024). 'MinterEllison: AI will "liberate" grad lawyers', *Australian Financial Review*, 17 May.

51. EY (2024). 'CFOs and tax leaders optimistic about transformative power of GenAI amid rising cost and regulatory challenges, survey finds.'

52. Gray, PD (2023). 'Artificial intelligence: efficient, effective and essential applications for everyone', *LSJ Online*.

53. Collins, M (2023). 'Why lawyers must engage with the dark side of AI', *Australian Financial Review*, 19 May.

54. Shanahan, M (2024). 'Human v AI on trial: lawyer wins the argument as bot stumbles', *Australian Financial Review*, 18 October.

55. Thomson Reuters Institute (2023). *ChatGPT & Generative AI within Law Firms*.

56. Meisenbacher, S, Machner, N, Vladika, J, and Matthes, F (2024). *Legal AI Use Case Radar 2024 Report*, Technical University of Munich, July.

57. PwC (2023). *PwC US makes $1 billion investment to expand and scale AI capabilities*, 26 April.

58. KPMG. *KPMG Ignite: Accelerating, automating and augmenting business decisions through artificial intelligence*.

59. Thomson Reuters and Momentum Intelligence (2020). *Tech and the Law 2020 Report*.

60. Brook, C, Gherhes, C, and Vorley, T (2020). 'Artificial intelligence in the legal sector: pressures and challenges of transformation', *Cambridge Journal of Regions, Economy, and Society 13*(1), 135–52.

61. Reynolds, M (2023). 'How ChatGPT and other AI platforms could dramatically reshape the legal industry', *ABA Journal*, 1 June.

62. Lakhani, KR (2023). 'AI Won't Replace Humans — But Humans with AI Will Replace Humans Without AI', *HBR*.

63. Galloway, S (2023). 'Office Hours, No Mercy/No Malice'.

64. Cartland Law. http://cartlandlaw.com.

Chapter 3

1. Quote Investigator has a very interesting account of the origin of this phrase.
2. Quote Investigator also has a very interesting account of the origin of this phrase.
3. Beaton, G (2024). LinkedIn. See also The Beaton Team (2024), 'The warning signs that you're losing clients' trust — and how to win it back'.
4. Former US president Barack Obama was interviewed by LinkedIn editor in chief Daniel Roth in June 2023.
5. If you think you have unreasonable clients, listen to the hilarious 'I'm Billing Time', by the Bar Grill Singers, based on Cyndi Lauper's song 'Time After Time'.
6. Swift, T (2022). Lyric from the song 'Anti-Hero', on the album *Midnights*.
7. There are any number of ways to design and conduct client surveys. PSFs either create their own, which are often over-engineered, or use surveys created by consultants who specialise in this area. A widely used and respected survey tool is the simple and elegant Net Promoter Score (NPS) framework developed originally by Frederick Reichheld and Bain & Company. This article gives a good overview of NPS: Reichheld, F (2003). 'The One Number You Need to Grow', *HBR*.
8. Gates, B (1999). *Business @ The Speed of Thought*, Grand Central Publishing.
9. Client Choice Awards: https://clientchoiceawards.net.
10. Horn, DM, and Meislik, I (2018). 'How to Ride the Coming Tidal Wave of Technology and Competition', *Probate & Property* *32*(6), 1–8.
11. Westpac Banking Corporation (2024). *How AI is Changing Client Relationships*.

Chapter 4

1. Productivity is a pretty big deal in the professional services arena, but to do the subject justice is beyond the scope of this book. If this is a topic that you want to focus on, here are two great articles filled with practical ideas to help you on your quest: Pozen, RC, and Downey, K (2019). 'What Makes Some People More Productive Than Others', *HBR*; and Imber, A (2020). 'What Super Productive People Do Differently', *HBR*.

2. Although this vitally important concept is mentioned a number of times in this book, it is beyond the scope of this work to discuss psychological safety in any depth. A great place to start an exploration is any *HBR* article on the topic by the guru on the subject, Harvard Business School professor Dr Amy Edmondson or, for a deeper dive, her 2019 book *The Fearless Organization* (Wiley). See also *Xueyang* Qi *and Yu* Wen (2021). *Research on the Relationship between Psychological Safety and Individual Job Burnout*, SHS Web of Conferences 96, 02004.

3. For example, see Lena, M, Neumeier, L, Brook, L, Ditchburn, G, and Sckopke, P (2017). 'Delivering your daily dose of well-being to the workplace: a randomized controlled trial of an online well-being programme for employees', *European Journal of Work and Organizational Psychology 26*(4), 555–73.

4. Fleming, WJ (2024). 'Employee well-being outcomes from individual-level mental health interventions: Cross-sectional evidence from the United Kingdom', *Industrial Relations Journal 55*, 162–82.

5. Reitz, M, and Chaskalson, M (2020). 'Why Your Team Should Practice Collective Mindfulness', *HBR*. Mindfulness at a team rather than just at an individual level is a relatively recent area of study in the peer-reviewed literature, having been introduced in this paper: Yu, L, and Zellmer-Bruhn, M (2018). 'Introducing team mindfulness and considering its safeguard role against conflict transformation and social undermining', *Academy of Management Journal 61*, 324–47.

6. Gallup (2023). *State of the Global Workplace Report*.

7. Gallup (2022). *State of the Global Workplace Report*.

8. Gallup. *What Is Employee Engagement and How Do You Improve It?*

9. Harter, J (2024). *The New Challenge of Engaging Younger Workers*, Gallup.

10. Gallup, *How to Prevent Employee Burnout*.

11. Zenger, J, and Folkman, J (2023). '7 Ways to Make Employees Feel Respected, According to Research', *HBR*.

12. Culture Amp. *The 4 fundamentals of successful performance management*.

13. Gallup and Workhuman (2023). *Empowering Workplace Culture Through Recognition*.

14. Kim, S, Shields, J, and Chheti, A (2021). 'Performance Management in Australian Organisations: Current Practices and Future Plans, A Report on the State of Play', a joint study by AHRI and the University of Sydney Business School.

15. These three forms of feedback and their short descriptions are taken from Stone, D, and Heen, S (2014). *Thanks for the Feedback: The Science and Art of Receiving Feedback Well*, Penguin, p. 18.

16. Yes, I know, many qualified coaches will have rolled their eyes at that short description of coaching. There is, of course, no agreed definition of the term. The International Coaching Federation offers this definition: '... partnering with clients in a thought-provoking and creative process that inspires them to maximize their personal and professional potential. The process of coaching often unlocks previously untapped sources of imagination, productivity and leadership.'

17. Good, practical guidance on showing 'appreciation' in the workplace can be found in Littlefield, C (2023). 'Simple Ways to Show Appreciation at Work', *HBR*; and Zenger, J, and Folkman, J (2022). 'Do You Tell Your Employees You Appreciate Them?', *HBR*.

18. For example, the late and well-regarded clinical psychologist, author and teacher Marshall Rosenberg regarded 'appreciation' as a vital means of communication, but 'praise' and compliments as 'life-alienating' forms of communication that are best avoided. See Rosenberg, MB (2015). *Nonviolent Communication: A Language of Life*, 3rd edition, PuddleDancer Press.

19. Murray, B, and Fortinberry, A (2016). *Leading the Future: The Human Science of Law Firm Strategy and Leadership*, p. 126.

20. Gallup and Workhuman (2023). *Empowering Workplace Culture Through Recognition*.

21. Gallup and Workhuman (2023). *From Praise to Profits: The Business Case for Recognition at Work*.

22. Clifton, J, and Harter, J (2019). *It's the Manager*, Gallup Press.

23. Garvin, DA (2013). 'How Google Sold Its Engineers on Management', *HBR*. See also, Bryant, A (2011) 'Google's Quest to Build a Better Boss', *New York Times*. 12 March.

24. Drummond, M (2021). 'Cook', *Australian Financial Review Platinum 70 Magazine*.

25. Grant, AM (2017). 'The third "generation" of workplace coaching: creating a culture of quality conversations', *Coaching: An International Journal of Theory, Research and Practice 10*(1).

26. The paper is available on the ResearchGate website.

27. For a good analysis of the pros and cons of annual performance reviews, see Woehr, DJ, and Roch, SG (2016). 'Of Babies and Bathwater: Don't Throw the Measure Out With the Application', *Industrial and Organizational Psychology* 9(2).

28. Clifton, J, and Harter, J (2019). *It's the Manager,* Gallup Press, p. 81.

29. Bungay Stanier, M (2016). *The Coaching Habit,* Box of Crayons Press.

30. Stein, K (2023). *Be Your Own Leadership Coach*, Major Street Publishing.

31. Kellogg, KC, and Hadley, CN (2023). 'How AI Can Help Stressed-Out Managers Be Better Coaches', *HBR*.

32. Wilson, P (2015). *Make Mentoring Work*, 2nd edition, Major Street Publishing.

33. Zada, M, Khan, J, Saeed, I, Zada, S, and Yong Jun, Z (2023). 'Curiosity may have killed the cat, but it has the power to improve employee creativity', *Current Psychology 11*, 1–5.

34. Aaker, J, and Bagdonas, N (2021). 'How to Be Funny at Work', *HBR*.

35. Herrando, C, and Constantinides, E (2021). 'Emotional Contagion: A Brief Overview and Future Directions', *Frontiers in Psychology,* 16 July.

36. *HBR* and the EY Beacon Institute (2015). *The Business Case for Purpose.*

37. Sinek, S (2009). *Start with Why*, Portfolio Penguin.

38. Drummond, M (2021). 'Cook', *Australian Financial Review Platinum 70 Magazine.*

39. PwC (2021). *Leading with Trust, Transparency and Purpose.*

40. Scales, D, and Biderman-Gross, F (2020). *How to Lead a Values-Based Professional Services Firm*, Wiley.

41. Friedman, S (2024). 'Your Career Doesn't Need to Have a Purpose', *HBR*, 23 April.

42. With over 30 million sold, Dale Carnegie's 1936 book *How to Win Friends and Influence People* is one of the all-time bestsellers. It has become fashionable, especially in academic psychologist circles, to look down on this book. Although it can seem a little one-dimensional and insufficiently nuanced from a current perspective, the book is full of great advice, much of which (okay, not all), together with other comments by Carnegie, have been subsequently validated by evidenced-based research. In his book, Carnegie says, 'People work for money, but go the extra mile for recognition, praise and rewards.'

43. Stone, DN, Deci, EL, and Ryan, RM (2009). 'Beyond talk: creating autonomous motivation through self-determination theory', *Journal of General Management 34*(3).

Chapter 5

1. Parker, M (2016). '13 of Audrey Hepburn's Most Inspiring Quotes', *Time*, 4 May.

2. Footwear company ASICS engaged renowned researcher Dr Brendon Stubbs from Kings College London to oversee a 'Desk Break experiment' in 2024. It was found that '... when office workers added just 15 minutes of movement into their working day, their mental state improved by 22.5% with participants' overall State of Mind scores increasing from 62/100 to 76/100. The experiment showed that taking a daily Desk Break for just one week lowered stress levels by 14.7%, boosted productivity by 33.2% and improved focus by 28.6%. Participants reported feeling 33.3% more relaxed and 28.6% more calm and resilient. 79.2% of participants said they would be more loyal to their employers if offered regular movement breaks': ASICS public service announcement warns the world about workplace mental health threat.

3. On improving self-esteem and self-confidence, I highly recommend this excellent book, which I use with my clients: Markway, B, and Ampel, C (2018). *The Self-Confidence Workbook*, Althea Press.

4. On impostor syndrome, I highly recommend Episode 189 of the Psychologists Off the Clock podcast series: *Imposter Syndrome with Jill and Debbie*, featuring clinical psychologists Jill Stoddard and Debbie Sorensen. The home page for that podcast links to other excellent resources on impostor syndrome. Another excellent resource, including a very readable account of the development of the 'impostor *phenomenon*', which came to be relabelled 'impostor *syndrome*': Jamison, L (2023). 'Why Everyone Feels Like They're Faking It', *The New Yorker*.

5. Edmondson, A (2023). *Right Kind of Wrong: How the Best Teams Use Failure to Succeed*, Penguin.

6. Clark, P (2023). 'Just Say No If Working While Female', *Financial Times*, 15 July.

7. Grenny, J (2019). 'How to Say "No" at Work Without Making Enemies', *HBR*.

8. Calarco, M (2023). *Beating Burnout Finding Balance*, Wiley.

9. Westring, AF (2021). 'There's No "Right" Way to Do Self-Care', *HBR*.

10. Beyond Blue website's self-care page.

11. Loehr, J, and Schwartz, T (2001). 'The Making of a Corporate Athlete', *HBR*.

12. Happily, you can (legally) access a number of *HBR* articles from their website each month without becoming a paying subscriber like me.

13. Abraham Maslow's famous theory of motivation, the idea that human needs exist in a hierarchy that people strive to satisfy progressively, is usually presented diagrammatically as a pyramid. However, Maslow himself never in fact used a pyramid to express his theory: Bridgman, T, Cummings, S, and Ballard, J (2019). 'Who Built Maslow's Pyramid? A History of the Creation of Management Studies' Most Famous Symbol and Its Implications for Management Education', *Academy of Management Learning & Education 18*(1), 81–98.

14. On habits, my favourite resource and the one I recommend to my clients is: Clear, J (2018). *Atomic Habits*, Random House.

15. Meditation and mindfulness are large topics beyond the scope of this book. A good place to start is the online version of this short article, with embedded links to further articles and research results: Schootstra, E, Deichmann, D, and Dolgova, E (2017). 'Can 10 Minutes of Meditation Make You More Creative?', *HBR*.

16. 'Rafael Nadal Showcases His Bizarre Pre-Match Rituals at the 2022 US Open': https://www.distractify.com/p/rafael-nadal-rituals.

17. Sauer, M (2023). 'Bill Gates says Warren Buffett taught him to value free time: Filling 'every minute of your schedule' doesn't make you more serious', CNBC Online, 9 July.

18. Kim, T, Sezer, O, Schroeder, J, Risen, J, Gino, F, and Norton, MI (2021). 'Work group rituals enhance the meaning of work', *Organizational Behavior and Human Decision Processes 165*, 197–212.

19. 'Good sleepers have lower risk of heart disease and stroke', *Science News*, 26 August 2022.

20. Hill, VM, Rebar, AL, Ferguson, SA, Shriane, AE, and Vincent, GE (2022). 'Go to bed! A systematic review and meta-analysis of bedtime procrastination correlates and sleep outcomes', *Sleep Medicine Reviews 66* (2022).

21. Ibid.

22. Krizan, Z, and Hisler, G (2019). 'Sleepy anger: Restricted sleep amplifies angry feelings', *Journal of Experimental Psychology: General 148*(7), 1239–50.

23. Patten, S (2022). 'What You Really Need: More Sleep', *Australian Financial Review*, 19 August.

24. Foster, R (2022). *Life Time: The New Science of the Body Clock, and How It Can Revolutionize Your Sleep and Health*, Penguin.

25. Jackson, A (2023). 'Elon Musk says he's upped his sleep to 6 hours per night — and that his old routine hurt his brain', CNBC Online, 18 May.

26. Neff, K (2003). 'Self-Compassion: An Alternative Conceptualization of a Healthy Attitude Toward Oneself', *Self and Identity* 2, 85–101.

27. Ibid.

28. 'The Space Between Self-Esteem and Self Compassion: Kristin Neff at TEDx Centennial Park Women.'

29. Neff, K. (2015). *Self-Compassion: The Proven Power of Being Kind to Yourself*, William Morrow.

30. Self-compassion, Dr Kristin Neff: https://self-compassion.org.

31. 'The Space Between Self-Esteem and Self Compassion: Kristin Neff at TEDx Centennial Park Women.'

32. There are now various websites devoted to self-compassion for lawyers, although I haven't yet found one specifically for tax lawyers. This one is great: https://www.selfcompassionforlawyers.com.

33. Henderson, JD. 'Self-Care Is Not the Solution for Burnout'.

34. Go to Google Scholar and type in 'resilience burnout' and you will be rewarded with endless peer-reviewed articles exploring the linkages between these concepts. Overwhelmingly the research has been done with doctors, nurses and other health professionals.

35. Tsai, J, Sandra, B, and Morissette, S (2022). 'Introduction to the Special Issue: Resilience and Perseverance for Human Flourishing', *Psychological Trauma: Theory, Research, Practice, and Policy 14*, S1–S3.

36. Flynn, PJ, Bliese, PD, Korsgaard, MA, and Cannon, C (2021). 'Tracking the Process of Resilience: How Emotional Stability and Experience Influence Exhaustion and Commitment Trajectories', *Group & Organization Management 46*(4), 1–45.

37. Zhang, A, Zhou, L, Meng, Y, et al. (2024). 'Association between psychological resilience and all-cause mortality in the Health and Retirement Study', *BMJ Mental Health 27*, 1–6.

38. Working with Resilience: https://workingwithresilience.com.au.

39. McEwen, K (2022). 'Building Resilience at Work: A Practical Framework for Leaders', *Journal of Leadership Studies 16*(2), 42–9.

40. Bond, S, and Shapiro, G (2014). *Tough At the Top: New Rules of Resilience for Women's Leadership Success*, Shapiro Consulting.

41. Pfeffer, J (2022). *7 Rules of Power*, Swift.

42. Empson, L (2019). 'How to Lead Your Fellow Rainmakers', *HBR*. If you like that taster, then go for the main course: Empson, L (2017). *Leading Professionals: Power, Politics and Prima Donnas*, Oxford University Press.

43. Nestor, J (2020). *Breath — The New Science of a Lost Art*, Penguin.

44. Dr Weil has produced a number of online video clips in which he demonstrates this technique. Google 'Dr Andrew Weil breathing'.

Chapter 6

1. Gallup (2023). *State of the Global Workplace Report*.

2. Rosso, BD, Dekas, KH, and Wrzesniewski, A (2010). 'On the meaning of work: A theoretical integration and review', *Research in Organizational Behaviour 30*, 91–127.

3. Wrzesniewski, A, McCauley, C, Rozin, P, and Schwartz, B (1997). 'Jobs, Careers, and Callings: People's Relations to Their Work', *Journal of Research in Personality 31*, 21–3.

4. Sanchez, L (2022). '100-year-old Brazilian breaks record after 84 years at same company', Guinness World Records.

5. Adam Leipzig. 'How to know your life purpose in 5 minutes', TED talk.

6. Another excellent resource on creating an elevator pitch is Gallo, C (2018).' 'The Art of the Elevator Pitch', *HBR*.

7. Craig, N, and Snook, S (2014). 'From Purpose to Impact', *HBR*.

8. Frankl, VE (1946). *Man's Search for Meaning*, Beacon Press.

9. Kang, Y, et al. (2021). 'Purpose in Life, Loneliness, and Protective Health Behaviors During the COVID-19 Pandemic', *Gerontologist 61*(6), 878–87.

10. Jobs, S (2005). Commencement Address at Stanford University.

11. Newport, C (2012). *So Good They Can't Ignore You*, Grand Central Publishing.

12. Cable, D (2020). 'What You Should Follow Instead of Your Passion', *HBR*.

13. Moss, J (2019). 'When Passion Leads to Burnout', *HBR*.

14. Scott Galloway on 'follow your passion', YouTube.

15. Bolles, RN (2022). *What Color Is Your Parachute?*, Random House.

16. Pink, DH (2009). *Drive*, Penguin.

17. Ibid., at p. 134 of the Cannongate Books 2018 edition.

18. Quote Investigator explains the origin of this phrase, its translation into English, and its profound effect on Viktor Frankl, who cites Nietzsche in his famous book *Man's Search for Meaning*.

19. The creators of SDT are Edward Deci and Richard Ryan. Although Deci had been researching human motivation since the early 1970s, his collaboration with Ryan from the late 1970s led eventually to the formulation of SDT. Either together, individually, or with other collaborators, they have published extensively on SDT. For an academic but very readable, 11-page summary of SDT, see Ryan, RM, and Deci, EL (2000). 'Self-Determination Theory and the Facilitation of Intrinsic Motivation, Social Development, and Well-Being', *American Psychologist 55*(1), 68–78. Better still, check out the wealth of material on the website for the Center for Self-Determination Theory, set up by Deci and Ryan: https://selfdeterminationtheory.org. Daniel Pink gives a great introduction to the development and significance of SDT in his best-selling book: Pink, DH (2009), *Drive*, Penguin.

20. The descriptions of autonomy, competence and relatedness are based on Ryan, RM, and Deci, EL (2020). 'Intrinsic and extrinsic motivation from a self-determination theory perspective: Definitions, theory, practices and future directions', *Contemporary Educational Psychology*, 101860; and Stone, DN, Deci, EL, and Ryan, RM (2009). 'Beyond talk: creating autonomous motivation through self-determination theory', *Journal of General Management 34*(3).

21. University of Rochester Medical Center website: 'Our Approach – Self Determination Theory'.

22. Rock, D (2008). 'SCARF: a brain-based model for collaborating with and influencing others', *NeuroLeadership Journal*, 1.

23. 'Two Monkeys Were Paid Unequally': excerpt from Frans de Waal's hilarious TED talk.

24. A delightful article on success and motivation published 30 years ago in *The Atlantic* argued that 'the motivation industry, being a weed rather than a cultivated plant, doesn't have strict boundaries' (Lemann, N (1994) 'Is There a Science of Success?', *The Atlantic*). In the ensuing decades, there has been a global explosion of all manner of theories, models and thinking on human motivation, with wildly different components, evidence bases and reliability.

25. Bandura, A (2012). 'Cultivate Self-efficacy for Personal and Organizational Effectiveness', chapter 10 in *Handbook of Principles*

of Organizational Behavior: Indispensable Knowledge for Evidence-Based Management, 2nd edition, Wiley.

26. Murray, B, and Fortinberry, A (2019). *The Human Science of Strategy: What works and what doesn't*, Ark Group.

27. Power sometimes features in motivation theories and models. For example, in 1961, Professor David McClelland of Harvard University published *The Achieving Society*, setting out his model of human motivation. McClelland stated that three dominant needs — for achievement, for power and for affiliation — underpin human motivation. https://psychology.fas.harvard.edu/people/ david-mcclelland. His motivation model has largely fallen out of favour in recent decades with the rise of self-determination theory, which has some parallels to McClelland's approach.

28. David, S, Clutterbuck, D, and Megginson, D (eds) (2013). *Beyond Goals: Effective Strategies for Coaching and Mentoring*, Gower Publishing. Despite its title, this book is a treasure trove of goal-related research, tips and resources.

29. Doran, GT (1981). 'There's a S.M.A.R.T way to write management's goals and objectives', *Management Review 70*(11), 35–6. Yes, I know, there is a lot more to goals than making them SMART. A classic article on the ins and outs of goals is this one, by the father of goal theory, Edwin Locke: Locke, EA (1996). 'Motivation through conscious goal setting', *Applied & Preventive Psychology 5*, 117–24.

30. Kennedy's address to the Joint Session of Congress, May 1961.

31. For a fascinating account of the Apollo program generally, and the impact of President Kennedy's death in particular, see Logsdon, JM (2011). 'John F. Kennedy's Space Legacy and Its Lessons for Today', *Issues in Science and Technology XXVIII*(3). Logsdon writes, 'With Kennedy's death ... Apollo became a memorial to the fallen young president, and any possibility of changing it into a cooperative U.S.-Soviet effort disappeared. The country remained committed to the goal set for it by Kennedy.'

32. Barty, A (2023). *Goal setting for success*, LinkedIn.

33. American Psychological Association (2023). *Want to achieve your goals? Get angry.*

34. If you want to know more about Dr Alter's ideas, this four-minute video clip on YouTube is a good place to start (before delving into his books): 'Goal Setting Is a Hamster Wheel. Learn to Set Systems Instead'. For me, however, 'setting systems' seems very similar to identifying SMART actions to achieve SMART goals.

35. This explanation of UpSideDown coaching is based on notes kindly provided by Nickolas Yu at an excellent workshop of his attended by the author.

36. Scott Galloway on 'follow your passion', YouTube.

37. The problem, in a nutshell, was a question of timing. When exactly should the profit or loss from a derivative financial instrument be recognised for tax purposes? Yes, I know, this sounds like a first world problem. However, the sums involved were huge and the tax law was giving crazy results as to the allocation of the overall gain or loss to particular years of income. Suffice to say, I was very happy to have spent 19 years helping to fix the problem, although it would have been far better if it had been achieved more quickly.

38. The length of time between Kennedy's moon-shot speech to the US Congress on 25 May 1961 and the lunar landing of Apollo 11's Eagle lander module on 20 July 1969 was eight years and not quite two months.

39. Quote Investigator, 'The Hardest Thing in the World to Understand Is Income Taxes'.

Chapter 7

1. World Economic Forum, *The Future of Jobs Report 2023*.

2. Lee, S. *Lifelong learning as a path to happiness*? DVV International.

3. IHME-CHAIN Collaborators (2024). 'Effects of education on adult mortality: a global systematic review and meta-analysis', *The Lancet Public Health*, 23 January.

4. A word on jargon in the world of learning. Pedagogy, strictly, is the teaching of children or dependent personalities. Andragogy is the facilitation of learning for adults, who are self-directed learners. Heutagogy is the management of learning for self-managed learners: University of Illinois Springfield, *Pedagogy, Andragogy, & Heutagogy*.

5. Mezirow, J (1978). 'Perspective Transformation', *Adult Education Quarterly 28*, 100–10.

6. Mezirow, J (1997). 'Transformative Learning: Theory to Practice', *New Directions for Adult and Continuing Education 74*, 5–12.

7. Carey, B (2014). *How We Learn*, Pan.

8. 70:20:10 Institute website: https://702010institute.com/702010-model/.

9. Harding, R (2022). 'Debate: The 70:20:10 "rule" in learning and development — the mistake of listening to sirens and how to safely navigate around them', *Public Money & Management 42*(1), 6–7.

10. Shrier, DL (2024). *Basic AI*, Robinson.

11. Ibid., p. 80.

12. Witt, A, Toyokawa, W, Lala, KN, Gaissmaier, W, and Wu, CM (2024). 'Humans flexibly integrate social information despite interindividual differences in reward', *Proceedings of the National Academy of Sciences 121*(39).

13. Wu, C (2024). '"With a grain of salt": How humans learn from others', *Science Daily*. Charley Wu leads the Human and Machine Cognition Lab at the University of Tübingen, Germany.

14. Ransbotham, S, Kiron, D, Khodabandeh, S, Chu, M, and Zhukhov, L (2024). 'Learning to Manage Uncertainty, with AI', *Sloan Management Review*.

15. Dweck, CS (2016). 'What Having a "Growth Mindset" Actually Means', *HBR*. If you are still curious, the next place to go is Dweck, CS (2017). *Mindset*, updated edition, Robinson.

16. Burgoyne, AP, Hambrick, DZ, and Macnamara, BN (2020). 'How firm are the foundations of mind-set theory? The claims appear stronger than the evidence', *Psychological Science 31*(3), 258–67.

17. Yeager, DS, and Dweck, CS (2020). 'What can be learned from growth mindset controversies?', *American Psychologist 75*(9), 1269–84.

18. Oregon State University, 'Growth Mindset: What it is, and how to cultivate one': https://success.oregonstate.edu/learning/growth-mindset.

19. Kross, E (2021). *Chatter: The Voice in Our Head and How to Harness It*, Vermilion.

20. Kegan, R (1994). *In Over Our Heads*, Harvard University Press.

21. Ibid., p. 5.

22. Berger, JB (2006). 'Key Concepts for Understanding the Work of Robert Kegan'.

23. Kegan, R (1994). *In Over Our Heads*, Harvard University Press, p. 32.

24. Berger, JB (2006). 'Key Concepts for Understanding the Work of Robert Kegan'.

25. I love this question, which I have borrowed from Garvey Berger, J (2019). *Unlocking Leadership Mindtraps*, Stanford Briefs, p. 52.

26. Tseng, AA (2022). 'Scientific evidence of health benefits by practicing mantra meditation: Narrative review', *International Journal of Yoga 15*, 89–95.

Chapter 8

1. Chartered Accountants Australia and New Zealand (2020). *New capability model to help shape profession of the future*, Capabilities for Accounting. An updated version was released in November 2024.

2. Parlamis, J, and Monnot, MJ (2019). 'Getting to the CORE: Putting an End to the Term "Soft Skills"', *Journal of Management Inquiry 28*(2).

3. Here are just two of many such attempts: Heckman, JJ, and Kautz, T (2012). 'Hard evidence on soft skills', *Labour Economics, 19*(4), 451–64; and Dixon, J, Cody, B, Chad, A, and Konrad, L (2010). 'The Importance of Soft Skills', *Corporate Finance Review, New York 14*(6), 35–8.

4. Here are just five such *HBR* articles, all of which are worthy of review as you ponder your Prime Capabilities and Enablers: Gustein, AJ, and Sviokla, J (2018). '7 Skills That Aren't About to Be Automated', *HBR*; Kosslyn, SM (2019). 'Are You Developing Skills That Won't Be Automated?', *HBR*; Lewis, A (2021). '5 Key Human Skills to Thrive in the Future Digital Workplace', *HBR*; Tan, J (2022). 'Don't Just Focus on Your Technical Skills. Focus On Your People Skills', *HBR*; Sadun, R, Fuller, J, Hansen, S, and Neal, PJ (2022). 'The C-Suite Skills That Matter Most', *HBR*. However, 'soft skills' are still sometimes mentioned — for example, Lyons, M (2023). '5 Essential Soft Skills to Develop in Any Job', *HBR*.

5. Godin, S (2023). *The Song of Significance: A New Manifesto for Teams*, Portfolio.

6. Lewis, A (2021). '5 Key Human Skills to Thrive in the Future Digital Workplace', *HBR*; Kosslyn, SM (2019). 'Are You Developing Skills That Won't Be Automated?', *HBR*; Gustein, AJ, and Sviokla, J (2018). '7 Skills That Aren't About to Be Automated', *HBR*; Marr, B (2022). 'The Top 10 Most In-Demand Skills for the Next 10 Years, *Forbes*; Lyons, M (2023). '5 Essential Soft Skills to Develop in Any Job', *HBR*; Chamorro-Premuzic, T (2023). '5 Ways to Future-Proof Your Career in the Age of AI', *HBR*; Chamorro-Premuzic, T, and Akhtar, R (2023). '3 Human Super Talents AI Will Not Replace', *HBR*; 'These are the 5 most useful skills for the jobs of the future', World Economic Forum post on LinkedIn (2024), based on WEF's *The Future of Jobs Report 2023*.

7. For a more detailed and updated analysis from time to time, visit the OECD's website to read progress on its ambitious multi-year project: *Artificial Intelligence and the Future of Skills*.

8. Evans, D, Mason, C, Chen, H, and Reeson, A (2024). 'Accelerated demand for interpersonal skills in the Australian post-pandemic labour market', *Nature Human Behaviour* 8, January, 32–42.

9. Shrier, DL (2024). *Basic AI*, Robinson.

10. Black, E (2024). 'Office workers are losing social skills', *Australian Financial Review*, 4 October.

11. Sauer, M (2024). 'Millionaire founder: This is the No. 1 skill young people need to thrive in the AI era — it's not coding', CNBC *Make It*.

12. Hammond, H (2024). 'Are AI robots the future of planning for retirement?', *The Sydney Morning Herald*, 16 November.

13. Australian Securities & Investments Commission (2024). *Beware the gap: Governance arrangements in the face of AI innovation*: http://asic.gov.au.

14. Pelly, M (2024). 'Top-earning lawyer charges $50,000 a day', *Australian Financial Review*, 28 June.

Chapter 9

1. McNevin, M (2023). 'How to Develop a 5-Year Career Plan', *HBR*.

2. 'We Don't Build Bridges from Instinct: An Interview with Dr. Robert Hogan' (2018).

3. Osman, S, Lane, J, and Goldsmith, M (2023). *Becoming Coachable*, 100 Coaches.

4. Stone, D, and Heen, S (2014). *Thanks for the Feedback: The Science and Art of Receiving Feedback Well*, Penguin.

5. Ibid., p. 18.

6. Yoon, J, Blunden, H, Kristal, A, and Whillans, A (2019). 'Why Asking for Advice Is More Effective Than Asking for Feedback', *HBR*.

7. Lerner, HG (2013). *Marriage Rules*, Gotham Books.

8. Anders Ericsson, K, Prietula, MJ, and Cokely, ET (2007). 'The Making of an Expert', *HBR*.

9. Gawande, A (2017). 'Want to get great at something? Get a coach', TED talk.

10. Mavrova Heinrich, DR (2019). 'Cultivating Grit in Law Students: Grit, Deliberate Practice, and the First-Year Law School Curriculum', *Capital University Law Review 47*(2), 341–78.

11. Grant, A (2023). *Hidden Potential: The Science of Achieving Greater Things*, WH Allen.

12. Edmondson, A (2023). *Right Kind of Wrong: The Science of Failing Well*, Penguin.

13. Wilson, P (2015). *Make Mentoring Work*, Major Street Publishing.

14. Andersen, E (2014). '5 Qualities to Look for in a Mentor, *Forbes*.

15. Goleman, D (1996). *Emotional Intelligence, Why it can matter more than IQ*, Bloomsbury.

16. Salovey, P, and Mayer, JD (1990). 'Emotional Intelligence', *Imagination, Cognition and Personality 9*(3), 185–211.

17. For example: Mattingly, V, and Kraiger K (2019). 'Can emotional intelligence be trained? A meta-analytical investigation', *Human Resource Management Review 29*, 140–55; and Hodzic, S, Scharfen, J, Ripoll, P, Holling, H, and Zenasni, F (2018). 'How Efficient Are Emotional Intelligence Trainings: A Meta-Analysis', *Emotion Review 10(2)*, 138–48.

18. Walraven, E (2019). *Wild Leadership*, Reed New Holland.

19. Laumer, IB, Winkler, SL, Rossano, F, and Cartmill, EA (2024). 'Spontaneous playful teasing in four great ape species', *Proc. R. Soc. B* 291: 20232345.

20. Locke, EA (2005). 'Why emotional intelligence is an invalid concept', *Journal of Organizational Behavio*r 26(4), 425–31. This paper has been widely cited, given psychologist Edwin Locke's status as a leading proponent of goal-setting theory.

21. The Genos Emotional Intelligence Model of Workplace Behaviour.

22. For a summary of the research and tips on how to improve your self-awareness, see Eurich, T (2018). 'What Self-Awareness Really Is (and How to Cultivate It)', *HBR*. For a deeper dive, this book is excellent: Eurich, T (2017). *Insight*, Crown Publishing Group.

23. As Dr Eurich makes clear in her *HBR* article and in her book, there are right and wrong ways to go about self-reflection, to avoid unhelpful types of introspection and rumination.

24. Pirsoul, T, Parmentier, M, Sovet, L, and Nils, F (2023). 'Emotional intelligence and career-related outcomes: A meta-analysis'. *Human Resource Management Review*.

25. Runde, J (2016). 'Why Young Bankers, Lawyers, and Consultants Need Emotional Intelligence', *HBR*. Another great quick read along similar lines is Beck, M, and Libert, B (2017). The Rise of AI Makes Emotional Intelligence More Important', *HBR*.

26. For an excellent analysis of how the meaning of 'executive presence' has changed in recent years, see Hewlett, AH (2024). 'The New Rules of Executive Presence', *HBR*.

27. This is the definition of executive presence used by BTS/Bates Communication Inc.

28. The Sweden-based BTS Group acquired Bates Communication in January 2021. As this book went to print, the executive presence model was still known as Bates ExPI.

29. BTS/Bates, *Executive Presence: A Model of Highly Effective Leadership*, white paper.

30. CoachSource, *Executive Coaching Industry Research, Full Report*.

31. Human Capital Institute and the TRACOM Group (2020). *Executive Presence: Desired but Ill-defined*.

32. Buffett, W (2015). In *Getting There: A Book of Mentors*, edited by GZ Segal, Abrams.

33. Ibid.

34. Bain, K (2015). *The Principles of Movement*, Oberon Books.

35. Ibid., p. 90.

Chapter 10

1. Peters, T (1997). 'The Brand Called You', *Fast Company 10*, 83–90.

2. Monarth, H (2022). 'What's the Point of a Personal Brand?', *HBR*.

3. Trang, NM, McKenna, B, Cai, W, and Morrison, AM (2023). 'I do not want to be perfect: investigating generation Z students' personal brands on social media for job seeking', *Information Technology & People*.

4. Clark, D, and Nieto-Rodriguez, A (2022). 'Approach Your Personal Brand Like a Project Manager', *HBR*. Here is another excellent article along similar lines: Avery, J, and Greenwald, R (2023). 'A New Approach to Building Your Personal Brand', *HBR*.

5. Arruda, W (2021). 'How Personal Branding Went Digital And What It Means For Your Career', *Forbes*.

6. VanEpps, EM, Hart, E, and Schweitzer, M (2023). 'How to Self-Promote — Without Sounding Self-Centered', *HBR*.

Chapter 11

1. Buffett, W (2015). In *Getting There: A Book of Mentors*, edited by GZ Segal.

2. Robert Waldinger has given one of the most watched TED talks of all time on the Harvard Study of Adult Development: 'What makes a good life? Lessons from the longest study on happiness'. Of course,

there is a book on this study as well: Waldinger, R, and Schulz, M (2023). *The Good Life*, Rider.

3. Christensen, CM (2010). 'How Will You Measure Your Life', *HBR*.

Suggest reading and viewing

1. O'Keeffe, A (2011). *Hardwired Humans*, Roundtable Press, has an excellent discussion on the usefulness of a group of seven people in various environments.

Index